WRITING

VOICE

WRITING

VOICE

The Complete Guide to
Creating a Presence on the
Page & Engaging Readers

WD
WRITER'S DIGEST
BOOKS

WritersDigest.com
Cincinnati, Ohio

For more resources for writers, visit www.writersdigest.com.

21 20 19 18 17   5 4 3 2 1

Distributed in Canada by Fraser Direct
100 Armstrong Avenue
Georgetown, Ontario, Canada L7G 5S4
Tel: (905) 877-4411

Distributed in the U.K. and Europe by F+W Media International
Pynes Hill Court, Pynes Hill, Rydon Lane, Exeter, EX2 5AZ, United Kingdom
Tel: (+44) 1392-797680, Fax: (+44) 1626-323319
E-mail: postmaster@davidandcharles.co.uk

Library of Congress Cataloging-in-Publication Data

ISBN-13: 978-1-4403-4912-6

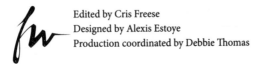

Edited by Cris Freese
Designed by Alexis Estoye
Production coordinated by Debbie Thomas

TABLE OF CONTENTS

PART III: THE MECHANICS OF VOICE

PART IV: FICTION-SPECIFIC VOICE

PART V: NONFICTION-SPECIFIC VOICE

FOREWORD

BY REED FARREL COLEMAN

If it works, it works.

I've been called the ultimate pantser by my colleagues. *Pantser?* A pantser is a writer who works without a net: no outline, no story arc, no series arc, no character bios. Just an idea. Many authors work this way. Stephen King, for example. Others, like James Patterson, don't. But as a former adjunct instructor of English at Hofstra University and as a founding member of Mystery Writers of America University, I have never suggested that my process is the right and only path to success. My philosophy, in terms of process and style, has always been that if something works, it works. It seems self-evident, I know. The trick is that you don't know if something works until you try it out, and that's the rub: getting the opportunity to find your way.

When, in 1987, I sat down to write a novel, I had never written a long-form piece of fiction in my life, though several of my college professors might disagree. Many would claim that my term papers were largely works of fiction. That said, I struggled mightily for two and a half years to produce the manuscript for what would be my first published novel. As an inexperienced writer of fiction, one of my most difficult hurdles—and there were many—was finding my authorial voice. I've often said that I used my first three novels to teach myself the bare minimum of craft.

The publishing landscape today is a very different one than existed back in the late 1980s. It is always evolving, and today the rate of its evolution is alarming. These days, writers setting out to work on their first books—fiction, memoir, nonfiction—don't often have the luxury of a three-book contract to learn their craft, to discover their unique voice, and to get it right. Even those writers talented and fortunate enough to place their manuscripts with publishing houses, large or small, are not usually afforded more than one or two books to get it right and to sell in sufficient numbers to justify another contract.

Thirty years and twenty-four series and stand-alone novels later, I have the benefit of perspective. What I see is that if I were starting out today, I would do things differently. Keep in mind that writing is an art, but publishing is a business, and there is an ever-changing and blurry line where they intersect. Given the realities of the current marketplace, I wouldn't dare risk trial and error as a means of developing my voice or getting published. In today's atmosphere, I would take advantage of books on the market designed to save me from making many of the errors I made early on. That's why I wholeheartedly endorse and recommend *Writing Voice: The Complete Guide to Creating a Presence on the Page and Engaging Readers.*

I have had the good fortune of serving as executive vice president of Mystery Writers of America. While I served in that capacity, the great Janet Evanovich was our president. I remember listening to Janet give sage advice to other writers and one thing she said has stuck with me ever since. I'm paraphrasing here, but, essentially, she said an author's voice mattered above all else. That presence on the page and a unique, recognizable voice was absolutely crucial.

With that in mind, I would point to four essays in particular, contained within the covers of this book: Adair Lara's excellent piece on finding your voice for memoir, Gabriela Pereria's section on how the authorial voice can work on several levels, Paula Munier's contribution dealing with specific voices for specific genres, and James Scott Bell's revealing and informative analysis of the tension and balance between voice and style. These people not only know what they are talking about, but they also present it in a way that will enable you to absorb and adapt it for your own writing.

Like I said, if it works, it works. And, if you want it to work, give yourself every advantage you can. Learn from those who have been here before you and have made the errors so you won't have to.

REED FARREL COLEMAN, called a hard-boiled poet by NPR's Maureen Corrigan, is the *New York Times* best-selling author of Robert B. Parker's Jesse Stone series. He is also the author of his own Gus Murphy series for Putnam. He has published twenty-four series and stand-alone novels, several short stories, poems, and essays. Reed is a three-time recipient of the Shamus Award for Best PI Novel of the Year and a three-time Edgar Award nominee in three different categories. He has also won the Macavity, Audie, Barry, and Anthony awards. He is a former Executive Vice President of Mystery Writers of America, a founding member of MWA University, and a former adjunct English instructor at Hofstra University. He lives with his family on Long Island.

INTRODUCTION

A writer's voice is unique; his voice is his own. A voice isn't developed over night, but is crafted painstakingly over the course of years, or maybe an entire career. A voice stands out in a crowd, and is the reason we can recognize one writer from another. And some will argue that without a strong voice, you're going nowhere as an author. It's the basis of good writing.

Yet, voice has always felt, inherently, like one of those things that cannot be taught. Like creativity, a writer either has that unique talent or not.

That's where this book comes in. *Writing Voice* is meant to be a comprehensive guide for developing a voice for your prose—whether you're crafting a novel, a short story, a memoir, or an article for a specfiic publication. It's a guide that will shatter the notion that voice cannot be taught.

Every chapter brings a unique angle to voice, compiling the very best advice and instruction from top writers, editors, agents, and other professionals in the industry. Whether you're just getting started with writing, or have been toiling for years, you'll find something to develop your craft in this book.

LIFT YOUR VOICE

Each part of this book will show you the importance of crafting a strong, unique voice for your writing, while offering techniques and perspective on the best way to stand out. Using these tips from the experts, you'll learn exactly what voice is—right down to the gritty details—and how to create your own.

- Part I introduces voice, providing an explanation of what it is, and setting a foundation for you to begin exploring the unique style of your writing.
- Part II shows you how to create your voice, covering the perspective of an agent on the importance of the subject, and detailing the styles and voices of famous writers.
- Part III details the nuances of voice, including the differences between voice and style, developing a tone, and the importance of word choice in your writing.
- Part IV delves into the specifics of voice in fiction, such as crafting a perfect point of view, matching your voice to your genre, and creating a unique narration style.
- Part V helps you with your nonfiction voice, focusing on ways to give your subject depth, making your voice personal, and developing a style for memoir.

Each of these sections is packed with information and advice for developing the voice you *need* as a writer.

There's something in this book for everyone. The seasoned writer might find a new way to refresh her voice and open the door to new readers. The beginning writer can understand exactly what it takes to craft compelling prose that keeps the reader turning pages. Start with page one and work your way through each chapter, or pick a topic to assist you in your current work, right now—whatever method you choose, this book will give you a complete picture of the importance of voice.

Let the experts in *Writing Voice* show you the way. They've been where you are. When you're finished, you'll understand that your voice was something you've indeed had all along—you just needed some help in bringing it out.

PART I

WHAT IS VOICE?

CHAPTER 1

WRITING FOR READERS

BY BARBARA BAIG

Voice, of course, has a strong connection with your imaginary reader.

—JOAN AIKEN

When you practice writing to, rather than for, readers, you will inevitably begin to develop your own individual voice on the page. And the more confidence you have in this voice, the easier it becomes to develop a piece of writing—knowing you have a voice you feel comfortable with enables you to discover more things to say. Voice is also an essential characteristic of all good writing, so let's examine it more closely.

Imagine that you are talking face-to-face with someone, gesturing with your hands, making eye contact and breaking it, emphasizing a word or phrase by putting more energy into it. Now imagine that your hands have been taken away, then your eyes, your face, your whole body. What is left to get across your meaning to the person you are talking to? Only your voice.

This imaginary scenario is your real situation when you write: For your voice on the page is the bridge—the only one you have—that carries meaning from your mind into the mind of another person, your reader. And it's only your writing voice that can move that person in the way you intend.

It's easy to recognize voice when we hear someone speak, but what is voice in writing? Most simply, voice on the page is the sound of a person speaking which, as we read, we can hear with our "inner ear." Every good writer has his or her own distinctive voice (or, sometimes, voices); we can often identify a particular writer just by the sound of her voice on the page.

One's writing voice is not necessarily the same as one's speaking voice: Whether we are writing a novel or a magazine article, it's unlikely that the voice we use will sound exactly like the way we speak. Nonetheless, there is something that is uniquely "us" in those words on the page. This matter of finding one's own voice is something that beginning writers often struggle with. Why is that?

THE TYRANNY OF VOICELESS WRITING

We live in an era when voiceless writing predominates. In the academy, in corporations, in governmental bureaucracies, keeping the sound of a live human being *out* of one's writing is the required norm. Just listen to this example:

> The ontological relativity advocated here is inseparable from an enunciative relativity. Knowledge of a Universe (in an astrophysical or axiological sense) is only possible through the mediation of autopoietic machines.

And to this one:

> Our complex, metastatic, viral systems, condemned to the exponential dimension alone... to eccentricity and indefinite fractal scissiparity, can no longer come to an end.

Such prose ignores the fundamental truth about the act of writing: It is a way for one human being to communicate with others. But many of us have no choice about writing like this: Our jobs or our schoolwork demand it. After year upon year of writing such voiceless prose, it's no wonder that many people feel they have no writing voice of their own. Even worse, when we must write for people who intimidate us, such as a particular professor or boss, we can feel that our own writing voice has been silenced forever.

HOW TO RECOVER YOUR VOICE

If you feel that you have lost your voice on the page—or never found it in the first place—don't despair. There are ways you can find or recover it. And it's actually much easier and safer to find your own voice in writing than in life, as long as you do it through practice writing. In life, once words are said, they are out there. But you can say anything you want to on paper, and no one will ever hear those words unless you choose to show them. That privacy gives you the freedom to be bold, to experiment, to play with different voices. If you don't like the sound of one voice, you can try another; you can let your voice change and develop over time. And it has been my experience that, in strengthening one's writing voice, one also can strengthen one's speaking voice.

These days many teachers of creative writing seem to believe that to find an individual voice on the page, a beginning writer must excavate his or her most personal (preferably traumatic) experiences and share them with readers. I don't agree: You can discover your voice in much less painful ways, and your writing voice does not *have* to be a confessional one. Consider the following approaches for discovering and training your voice.

1. Get Comfortable with Private Writing

Some beginners (or those who have been wounded as writers) may find that to discover a natural writing voice they must, for a while, engage only in private writing. Such a writer may need to hear and feel comfortable with his writing voice for a while before attempting to use it in writing to others. If this is the case for you, then by all means, take all the time you need. There is no rush. You can find your writing voice, over time, by simply practicing. While you are finding the subjects you want to write about and discovering things to say about them, you will also be practicing using your voice on the page. And when you have things to say that you really want to share with others—*I want to tell you this! Listen to the cool things I've discovered!*—then you can practice using your voice to share them.

2. Develop Confidence in Your Powers

Taking the time you need to develop your powers will give you confidence that you have things to say. Beginning or inexperienced writers often sound insecure on the page, like people who don't believe they have anything to say worth hearing: *er ... Excuse me ... I just thought that maybe ... um, perhaps ... oh well, never mind ...* Experienced writers, by contrast, are often (on the page) like people who have a lot of confidence in themselves: *Just listen to what I have to tell you!* The confident writer's voice is powerful and strong. (In writing, as in life, occasionally what sounds like confidence is merely bravado.)

There seems to be a popular assumption these days that the only way to get that kind of power into your voice is to talk about yourself and your own experiences; then your voice will be "authentic," and (therefore) your writing will be good. A writer's voice does have to have power—after all, that voice has to carry meaning from a writer's mind into the minds of readers. But power doesn't necessarily come from authenticity; it comes from *authority*. A writer's voice needs to sound, not authentic, but *authoritative*: It needs to have a sound in it that indicates that the writer knows what she is talking about. And how do we get that sound into our writing voice? By getting to know our subjects as well as possible, and by being clear in what we have to say about them. Strengthen your writer's powers; collect and develop your material—these activities will bring the quality of authority to your writing voice.

When you have that authoritative quality in your writing voice, readers will trust you, because they will feel that you know what you are talking about. Even if you are writing fiction, readers still need to feel that you know your material—the world and the characters you have invented.

3. Practice Writing to Readers

Since it can take some time to break lifelong habits of voiceless writing, it helps to do a lot of practice in reestablishing the natural relationship between writer and reader, as described in the previous chapters. Whether you share your words with live human beings or not, practicing writing *to* someone will naturally bring to your words the energy and aliveness of voice.

You can also have a good time playing around with using different voices on the page. Think about how we change voices in real life depending on whom we're talking to. If you are explaining to your five-year-old why he can't have more candy, you will probably use a different voice from the one you use to make a presentation to a client at work. The same thing can happen in writing. The voice a writer uses on the page is not always the same: It depends on what he's saying, on who his readers are, and on the effect he wants his words to have. A writer who wants primarily to make her readers laugh will use a different voice than if she is trying to inform them or make them think seriously about a subject. You can experiment with different voices by asking yourself these questions with a piece that you are working on: Who is speaking? To whom? For what purpose? Often a piece of writing won't come together until the author has found the right voice for it. Experiment with various purposes: Write to persuade readers to do something; write to inform; write to entertain. If you're feeling brave, read your practice writing to other people and find out whether you've achieved your intended effect.

PRACTICE: PLAYING WITH VOICE

Pick a subject and collect some material. Then choose a specific reader or group of readers, real or imagined. Write to a five-year-old or to someone who's ninety-five. Write to mothers or to people who hate children. Write to people who know lots about your subject or to people who know nothing. Now write to your chosen audience in a voice that feels appropriate. Now keep the same subject, and write about it to a different audience. What happens to your voice?

---

4. Be Considerate Toward Readers

There's a quality that all readers appreciate in a writer's voice. That quality is what I think of as considerateness: The writer remembers that the reader is not inside her head, and she takes the time to guide him carefully through what she is saying so he won't get lost or confused. When we read writing like this, we relax, recognizing that we won't have to work unnecessarily hard to understand it. If you remember that it's your job to make your writing clear and understandable to your readers, your voice on the page will have this quality of kindness.

5. Listen to Your Writing

To develop your voice, you also need to learn how to listen to your own writing: Reading one's words aloud is an essential writing practice. Many beginning writers find this difficult. But even though you may cringe at first when you hear your words (the way people often do when listening to the playback of their own recorded voices), persevere. Don't judge your voice, just listen to it: What do you notice? See if you can detach a little from the words you wrote and really hear what your voice is saying. Are you making sense? Is there a quality to this voice that you like? See whether you can find the specific words or sentences that have that quality; then try to write other things using that voice. Learn from yourself. Trust your writer's intuition.

Some people find it helpful to read their words into a tape recorder and then listen to the recording—or to have someone else read them aloud. However you do it, though, make hearing your writing out loud one of your regular practices. Doing this does more than let you hear your voice; it helps you hear the content of your writing as if you were a reader—which makes it much easier to revise.

6. Read for Voice

You can also learn about voice from the writers you love. Read their words aloud and listen to each writer's voice. What characteristics does it have that you like? Do some experimenting and try to imitate that voice. Then try the same practice with another favorite writer.

Most of all, it is a writer's choice of words and her particular way of putting those words together that creates her distinctive voice on the page.

HOW TO READ ALOUD FOR ANALYSIS

• Relax. If you tend to criticize your writing as you read it, try to let go of those critical voices in your mind. You are not going to judge your writing; you're just going to listen to it.

• As you read, slow down. Naturally, since this is your own writing, you're already familiar with the content of your piece, so it's easy to speed up as you read. But when you slow down, you can hear what you have said.

• Try not to focus on the words. Simply notice what you are saying, how your voice is getting across your content. Let yourself notice, for example, whether the content is exactly what you intended or whether there are places where you have left things out. Perhaps, too, you have repeated things that don't need to be repeated; perhaps there are other places where you need to repeat something: a gesture, a theme, a detail.

• If you like, imagine that you are someone else who is listening to your piece. Notice how this person responds to what you are saying with your voice.

....

BARBARA BAIG's innovative approach to teaching writing is based on the proven principles of expertise training. Author of Writer's Digest books *How to Be a Writer* and *Spellbinding Sentences*, Barbara teaches in the MFA Program in Creative Writing at Lesley University and offers free writing lessons at www.wherewriterslearn.com.

Writing for Readers   13

CHAPTER 2

TAPPING YOUR UNIQUE VOICE

BY JUDY BODMER

> "Mrs. Joe was a very clean housekeeper, but had an exquisite art of making her cleanliness more uncomfortable and unacceptable than dirt itself."
> —Charles Dickens, *Great Expectations*

> "In the late summer of that year we lived in a house in a village that looked across the river and the plain to the mountains."
> —Ernest Hemingway, *A Farewell to Arms*

> "When I'd first started coming to the church, I couldn't even stand up for half the songs because I'd be so sick from cocaine and alcohol that my head would be spinning, but these people were so confused that they'd thought I was a child of God."
> —Ann Lamott, *Operating Instructions*

Pick up a book by Dickens, Hemingway, or Lamott and, without glancing at the cover, you know immediately whose work you're reading. Why? Because these authors each have a unique writing voice. They have a style that's all their own, a way of putting their thoughts on paper, a way of creating places and characters that are distinctive. Editors are hungry for authors who've learned how to do this.

The good news is that you already have a unique voice. It just needs to be honed and developed. In my years of teaching creative writing at a local college and now editing for several publishing houses, I've discovered that some authors instinctively tap into this innate way of writing. Others of us stumble around, making many mistakes before we discover the voice within. If you're one of those, here are six tips to help you.

DON'T TRY TO COPY FAMOUS AUTHORS

Beverly Cleary made me laugh out loud, and I wanted to be funny, just like her. I spent the first five years of my writing career trying to write humorous children's books and short stories. They were quickly rejected. It wasn't until I realized I needed to write out of my heart that I found my voice.

The first time I tried this, I wrote a short story about a girl who captures a pigeon and puts it in a cage. Instead of writing from my head, I went to a deep place within me and drew out strong emotions and placed them on paper for everyone to read. It was scary because it was so personal. But it was worth the risk. "A Cage of Love" was the first short story I sold.

DISREGARD HOW YOU THINK AN AUTHOR SHOULD SOUND

Many of my students are humorous, charming people, but when they hand in their assignments, they're serious and boring. They've traded in their personalities in a misguided attempt to sound "writerly." I tell them to forget everything they've ever been taught and to let their words flow as they'd speak them. When they do, it transforms their manuscripts. And as they read their revised work in class, they can sense the positive response from the other students. This revelation changes their writing style forever.

HONE YOUR UNIQUE WAY OF LOOKING AT THE WORLD

When I look at a mountain prairie, golden in the summer sun, I can smell the ripening wheat and sense the anticipation of the farmers as they prepare for the harvest. You may look at the same prairie and see something quite different—breezes gently tossing the heads of grain may remind you of the ocean. This is good. We all must use what we've experienced and what we know to make the world come alive for our readers. I can research and describe a battle scene, but I can't bring Hemingway's unique perspective on war to my writing. On the other hand, another writer couldn't express my personal viewpoint on showing a pig at the county fair.

PLAY WITH WORDS

The best writers I know are also poets. They use alliteration, similes, and metaphors. Not tired clichés, such as *cool as a cucumber* or *soft as a baby's breath*, but fresh new viewpoints, like *smooth as a new coat of cherry-red polish on manicured nails*. They use specific nouns and verbs (*cabana* versus *house*, *lumbered* versus *walked*) and shy away from adverbs and adjectives.

Poetic writers paint pictures with their words, evoking the five senses—especially the sense of smell, an undisputed emotional trigger. They also employ symbolism, using imagery such as glass doorknobs, yellow ears of corn, or a stuffed lion named Bradley, to stand in for deeper feelings and ideas.

WRITE FAST

When I first began writing, it was hard to get the voices of my English teachers out of my head. I painstakingly chose every word and made sure each sentence was grammatically correct and properly punctuated before moving on to the next sentence. The result was writing that felt stilted and jerky.

When I learned to write fast, those voices went away. Admittedly, writing fast was difficult when I wrote with pen and paper or on my portable Royal. Thank goodness for the computer—now I can get the words down on paper as fast they come out of my brain. And that means the writing is closer to being me. The words aren't perfect, but that's fine. I can go back and make everything perfect later. But fast-and-furious writing is one way I capture my voice and the voices of my characters.

PRACTICE, PRACTICE, PRACTICE

Finding your voice comes with practice. Write whenever you can—on the couch, while you wait in the dentist's office, at a coffee shop, on a park bench.

When you first find your voice, you'll know it. It'll be like singing a perfect note. It will resonate in your ear and in your heart as being true. The rewards will be many, including a sense of being truly yourself and a delighted audience.

....

JUDY BODMER is the author of two nonfiction books, *When Love Dies* and *What's in the Bible for Mothers*. She taught creative writing at Lake Washington Technical College for eight years, is a frequent speaker at writing conferences in the Pacific Northwest, and does freelance copyediting for Revell/Baker Books and other small publishing houses.

CHAPTER 3

AWAKEN YOUR AUTHENTICITY

BY JORDAN ROSENFELD

A man sees in the world what he carries in his heart.

—JOHANN WOLFGANG VON GOETHE, FROM *FAUST*

To begin this chapter I draw upon the whimsical wisdom of Dr. Seuss, who wrote in his authentic, unparalleled, memorable voice, "Today you are You, that is truer than true. There is no one alive who is Youer than You."

Authenticity is a key part of your writing voice and your impact on readers. The irony about authenticity is that often you are the last person to figure out what is authentic about yourself. Similarly you may not yet know what your voice is—part of the journey is learning to determine that—but I guarantee that others could identify the "you-ness" of you if asked. I always take it as a compliment when someone hears a song or reads a quote or a book and says, "This made me think of you," or buys me a gift that is so magnificently perfect for me. This tells me that I possess unique qualities that others can identify.

As a writer, you will (and must) learn to distinguish an authentic voice. Or you may already be aware of your sensibility and wish to whittle it into new shapes. I want you to think about what that voice is or might be. I guarantee there is a you-ness to your writing. Defining elements distinguish your writing from that of your best friend (or arch enemy), your teachers, best-selling authors you admire, or even me. And beneath that, there are elements that are remarkably, indelibly, magnificently you, which no other writer on the planet possesses, because these elements only came into being with the rise of your mind. It's easy to believe that someone else has a more interesting voice, a better way of telling a story, a more compelling handle on language, or even just better material to work with, but the fact is, how and what other people write has very little bearing on your writing. What's your voice? What are your themes? How do sentences sing to you? What kinds of characters do you carve out of the ether of creativity and shape on the page?

If you have any doubt, let me remind you:

Your voice is worthy of being read

- even if you struggle to find it.
- even when it's so soft you aren't sure you can hear it.
- even when it seems to shift and change before your eyes.
- even if you think nobody is listening.

FIND YOUR VOICE

If, however, you still aren't sure of the composition of your voice, the following are some tips for finding it.

In seeking your voice, look to your obsessions and desires: that which haunts you and keeps you up at night. Think of the books you like, the shows you watch, the music that evokes deep emotion within you. The way words stick in your inner ear and the rhythms of your prose combine and manifest in your voice. As do the dialects you're familiar with and the kinds of conversations you are drawn to eavesdrop upon. Voice is an amalgam of your tastes, your interests, your terrors, and your deepest desires.

You may have also heard voice described as "style." Just as you have a style in the way you clothe yourself and arrange your home, you style your words, and, more important, your thoughts, in very specific ways. But the deepest contribution to your voice is your personal themes.

Mine Your Personal Themes

Writers are incredibly impressionable creatures. That is, we take in, hold, absorb, and then mutate the experiences that happen to and around us—and then put them on the page. By pulling from the roots of your formative years as well as from the events of last week, you can find recurring characters, settings, tones, and moods if you learn to see them. You already hold inside you all the words, characters, and settings you need to write thousands of pages.

But don't take my word for it; consider this quote from Albert Camus, from the introduction to his *Lyrical and Critical Essays*: "Every artist is undoubtedly pursuing his truth. If he is a great artist, each work brings him nearer to it, or at least, swings still closer toward this center, this buried sun where everything must one day burn."

Camus was a man of metaphor, of course, but what he means is that you already have a "buried sun"—a treasure chest, really—of language, love, life experience, themes, and more either waiting to be excavated and revealed or molded into shape. It doesn't mean everything you write must be about you or that you must follow to the letter the famous writer's axiom "Write what you know." To write what you know means to write what compels and fascinates you. For example, when I attended my masters in writing program at Bennington College, my professors—all of them published authors—helped me see that I continually repeated certain themes in my work. In fact, Alice Mattison suggested that I could call my collection of stories *Bad Mothers and Absent Fathers*.

To this day, though I write about all kinds of subjects that compel me (everything from healing to dark family secrets), at the root of all my fiction are themes of dysfunctional parenting and parenthood. This is not to say that I actually had a bad mother and an absent father—I could have gleaned these themes just as easily from the copious afterschool specials I watched, which usually featured children from broken homes, and the novels about orphans that I loved reading. People who claim to be able to heal and people who have had psychic experiences (neither of which have happened to me) also fascinate me, and those themes make their way into my work often. What my mentors helped me see was that by understanding my themes, I could learn to write about them differently, in new ways, with new eyes and better results, and thus consciously mold my voice. (See more in the "Work It" sidebar in this chapter.)

Use Your Experience

Finding your voice also means writing about the areas of your expertise: your job, your hobbies, the topics you have a vested interest in. Some of the best novels have derived from work authors do in their daily lives. Rene Denfeld, who works as a criminal investigator with death row inmates, wrote a powerful novel, *The Enchanted*, that is set in a prison and features characters drawn from the real work she does. Rebecca Lawton's novel *Junction, Utah* draws largely from her work as one of the first female river guides in the Grand Canyon back in the seventies. In your own work, you can draw on your experience as a teacher, a plumber, or a therapist—or whatever occupation you have. Your life informs your work, fleshes it out, gives it taste, color, and full-bodied emotion. If you sit in a room all day, every day, and try to generate material, you may find yourself running a bit dry. Sure, your imagination can come into play, but I believe there is no better material for your writing than what you experience. Therefore, to write what you know also means to "write what you have experience with." And, yes, you can go out and obtain experience in order to write about it. The novelist Jean Hegland once told us in a writing workshop I took that she was training to become certified as a midwife in order to write about it accurately. I know writers who have learned how to ride a unicycle, lived on the streets, learned how to bake, and more just to bring authenticity to their work.

Is there some activity you've always wanted to try, some skill or profession you've always wanted to learn? Do it in service of your writing, and you'll have the best excuse ever: "I'm doing this for my art."

Explore Your Vulnerability

Real, memorable, authentic writing may look different for each person, but it can only exist in the presence of vulnerability. To show your real self and access your true voice, you have to pull down the veil of illusion and write in a way that lays bare your mind, your heart, your secrets, and your longings. This is an act of claiming yourself and saying: This is me, and I won't pretend to be anyone else. Most people I know, myself included, read to find connection, validation, and understanding in the words of others. Donna Tartt says novels are written "by the alone for the alone." Ultimately the best way to reach anyone is to be vulnerable.

But vulnerability comes with anxiety for many. The key is to remember that your vulnerability touches others' vulnerable places and illuminates them. It bears witness for those who can't do so on their own behalf. Think of the times you've read a line, a quote, a whole book even, when you felt seen, heard, and validated by an author you've never met. Thanks to the vulnerability of others, you may find permission inside yourself to be real and open, too.

This past year I've been reading a lot of personal essays published in such journals as *The Rumpus*, *The Manifest-Station*, and *Full Grown People*. The bravery and beauty of people sharing their stories has given me permission to do the same, to write about difficult subjects in a way that I have found healing as well as inspiring. This new permission to be vulnerable is now infusing itself into all aspects of my writing—I'm weaving more personal emotion into my fiction and telling the truth more plainly.

I like to remember what social scientist and author Brenè Brown says: "Vulnerability is the birthplace of innovation, creativity, and change."

Write Like Yourself (and Avoid Comparison)

If you're like most writers I know, you've probably experienced a feeling similar to this: After reading X Author's work, I never want to write again!

At one point or another, most of us suffer from envy, desiring to write like other talented writers. And it's understandable—the literary landscape is rich with a symphony of voices and resonant with talent.

One of my best friends, Amy, wrote poetry in college about one of her favorite topics: the natural world. She told a teacher: "I want to write a poem about leaves, but that's been done so many times."

The teacher wisely said, "But every poem about leaves is different. Write *your* poem about leaves."

Another friend of mine, Nanea, who writes powerful essays, confessed, "I always feel my life is so vanilla that I don't have anything interesting to say." And then she proceeded to send me an essay about the absurdity of death and the resilience of the human spirit in which "vanilla" never even made an appearance.

This is all to say that you are not always the best person to judge your uniqueness (especially if you're feeling low or insecure). But you are the only one who can make a difference in the quality of your writing. Only you can seek and capture and hone that which makes your writing special.

When you doubt your voice, speak to yourself the way you would a best friend struggling to value herself. Says Anne Lamott, "I doubt that you would read a close friend's early efforts and, in his or her presence, roll your eyes and snicker. I doubt that you would pantomime sticking your finger down your throat. I think you might say something along the lines of, 'Good for you. We can work out some of the problems later, but for now, full steam ahead!'" You wouldn't be mean to your friend if she asked you to assess her work, and you also wouldn't encourage her to stop or abandon meaningful pursuits. When you hear the voices saying you aren't good enough and you don't have anything to say, talk them down. Remind them that you are the only one who can write the way you do. Your voice is worthy. Your voice is unique.

Discover Your Personal Lexicon

Recently I was surprised to discover, from responses to a series of Facebook status updates I made, that I often use words with meanings not everyone knows, like *quotidian*, *gravid*, *somnolent*, and *plangent*. I don't use them because they sound important or fancy; I use them because they are an inherent part of my lexicon—the vocabulary of a person, language, or branch of knowledge—and they made their way into common usage in my speech and writing. Plus, I like the way they sound. As an only child, my primary form of entertainment was reading, which has carried over into my adulthood. (Reading widely is a wonderful way to stretch your vocabulary, by the way.) I soon came to realize that these words were part of my written voice, that they emerge regularly (and sometimes need to be pared back from excess usage), and that even when I try to curb them they show up. They're just a part of my lexicon.

You, too, have a lexicon, whether you know it or not. Some writers' voices are colored by their geography. Southern writers often have a noticeable voice that's drawn as much from the literal sound of the Southern accent as from the rich physical geography and powerful history; writers who speak multiple languages often bring their first language over into the other languages they know. Writers who grew up among highly intellectual people may write differently from writers who grew up among those who never graduated high school. And trying to force yourself into another person's voice is not only nearly impossible—unless you're an expert mimic—it's tantamount to tossing away your own style and individuality. Better to learn to become aware of and familiar with the language you use. If you feel you'd like to stretch your vocabulary, there are easy ways to do this, but instead I recommend getting to know yours as though it's a language you're learning for the first time.

Steer Clear of Conformity

"What are you willing to risk as a writer to go for your goals, to drum up your dreams?" This is a question only you can answer and one that may take some meditation time. But inside the answer is a map that will lead you toward authenticity if you let it. Once you know what you're willing to risk, you will be more inclined to make choices that align with what feels right for you. This writer's code is the foundation of your authenticity. Once it's in place, you have a plan you can stick with, even when faced with the desire or demand to conform.

So now you're stumbling, running, or waltzing toward the discovery of your voice. Someone wants you to write something "a little more like this." Or perhaps he's asking, "Could you just change the theme of it?"

Can you? Will you?

You can. You might. But does it resound with the code you made for yourself? Do you really want others to dictate what you say and how you say it? I venture you're better off writing like you.

It's natural to look for support, encouragement, and help when things get hard; in fact, I recommend forming a creative support team. But being your own ally means that:

- you trust yourself.
- you determine your own value.
- you advocate on your own behalf.
- you make your own writing practice.
- you decide what goals to pursue.
- you choose what feels right for you.

Being your own ally means that you stop looking outside yourself for validation and affirmation, and find it, generate it even, inside yourself first. I know that may sound a little easier said than done.

WORK IT

1. When you meet with resistance in your writing or feel uncertain about whether you're writing something true to you, ask, *How am I being vulnerable here? What is another way I can express this authenticity where I may either be heard or gain the skills or connections I need?*
2. Comb through your less-formal writing, the writing no one will see— journals, letters, notes for stories—and highlight phrases that stand out and words you use often. Become familiar with your own lexicon and learn to polish and be proud of it.
3. Now go through your more formal work: the stories, novels, and essays written with the idea of publication or feedback. Notice recurring themes, happenings, and characters. Do you return often to favorite settings? What scenarios, moods, and tones show up over and over? Make a list and watch your unique voice emerge.

MOVE IT

We all have different bodies that move in different ways and are comfortable with different kinds of exercise. What we all have in common is a need to take breaks from extended periods of sitting and writing. Whether you love slow stretching or hard cardio, pick from one of the following exercises for your five-minute stretch break. A quick Google or YouTube search will show you how to do any of the following. If you have health issues, please be careful and cautious, or consult your doctor.

- **LOW INTENSITY:** Gentle neck and head stretches. First tilt your head to the right, toward your shoulder, and use your right hand to pull your head just a little further to the right. Do not stretch to the point of pain. Repeat on the left side. Next, interlace your fingers, and if you can do so without pain, reach your arms behind your head, palms facing the back of your head, against the base of your skull. Press your head back toward your hands, while your hands resist the pressure slightly. You can also tilt your head toward your chest and then alternate the move and look up at the ceiling.
- **MEDIUM INTENSITY:** Downward dog yoga pose. If you've ever seen a dog stretching, you'll know how this pose got its nickname. With palms on the floor, butt in the air, and feet flat on the ground, make sort of a triangle of your body, pressing into your palms and soles, and stretching your spine upward. Hold the pose for as long as is comfortable, then push forward into child's pose (folded forward like a baby taking a nap). You can repeat the stretch a couple of times.
- **HIGH INTENSITY:** In one-minute intervals, do one of the following exercises two to three times, with ten seconds of rest between each one: jumping jacks, burpees, or mountain climbers.

JORDAN ROSENFELD is the author of eight books, most recently *Writing the Intimate Character* (Writer's Digest Books). Her work has been published in *The Atlantic*, *GOOD magazine*, *mental_floss*, *The New York Times*, *Pacific Standard*, *Publishers Weekly*, *Salon*, *The San Francisco Chronicle*, *The Washington Post*, *Writer's Digest*, *The Writer*, and many more publications.

CHAPTER 4

A SINGULAR VOICE

BY DONALD MAASS

Do you have style?

Some authors have a plain prose style. That is said often of John Grisham, James Patterson, and Nicholas Sparks. Other writers are known almost entirely for their way with words. Reviewers swoon over their "lapidary" prose (look it up) and their "closely observed" take on their subjects, which I sometimes think is code for *not much happens.* Prose stylists can sell well also, which, for me, implies that fiction's punch and appeal is achieved in part by writing with force.

Now by that, I do not mean just words as bullets; I mean that impact can be felt from the many ways in which the author's outlook comes across. Having something to say—a theme—is important, but just as powerful can be how you say it, or how your characters do. Let's look at ways in which voice can shout out.

GIVING CHARACTERS VOICE

Most characters I meet are ordinary Joes and Janes. (Well, in romance novels, they might be named Cyan and Blake.) It isn't that all characters must be outrageous. That would be exhausting; more to the point, it isn't right for most stories. On the other hand, why do characters have to be uninteresting?

Any character can stand out without being a ridiculous caricature. It may only be a matter of digging inside to find what makes them different and distinct from you and me. It can be as simple as giving them their own unique take on things.

Criminals definitely look at things in a different way. Elmore Leonard, since *52 Pickup*, has brought us inside the world of crooks, killers, and con men, mostly in Detroit. In *Killshot*, he spins the story of real estate agent Carmen Colson and her ironworker husband, Wayne, who accidentally happen upon an extortion scheme run by two killers and enter the Federal Witness Protection Program, only to find that it isn't a safe place to hide.

Leonard opens *Killshot* in the point of view of one of the bad guys, a half-Ojibway, half-French Canadian hit man named Armand "Blackbird" Degas. Blackbird gets a phone call in his Toronto fleabag hotel offering him a hit. He haggles for a better price, musing about the way punks talk to each other:

> The phone rang. He listened to several rings before picking up the receiver, wanting it to be a sign. He liked signs. The Blackbird said, "Yes?" and a voice he recognized asked would he like to go to Detroit. See a man at a hotel Friday morning. It would take him maybe two minutes.
>
> In the moment the voice on the phone said "De-troi-it" the Blackbird thought of his grandmother, who lived near there, and began to see himself and his brothers with her when they were young boys and thought, *This could be a sign.* The voice on the phone said, "What do you say, Chief?"
>
> "How much?"
>
> "Out of town, I'll go fifteen."
>
> The Blackbird lay in his bed staring at the ceiling, the cracks making highways and rivers. The stains were lakes, big ones.
>
> "I can't hear you, Chief."
>
> "I thinking you're low."
>
> "All right, gimmie a number."
>
> "I like twenty thousand."
>
> "You're drunk. I'll call you back."
>
> "I'm thinking this guy staying at a hotel, he's from here, no?"
>
> "What difference is it where he's from?"
>
> "You mean what difference is it to me. I think it's somebody you don't want to look in the face."
>
> The voice on the phone said, "Hey, Chief? Fuck you. I'll get somebody else."

> The guy was a punk, he had to talk like that. It was okay. The Blackbird knew what this guy and his people thought of him. Half-breed tough guy one time from Montreal, maybe a little crazy, they gave the dirty jobs to. If you took the jobs, you took the way they spoke to you. You spoke back if you could get away with it, if they needed you. It wasn't social, it was business.

That could pretty much be Leonard's own philosophy of voice. Punks. They have to talk like that. It's business. Leonard's business is to get it down the way it sounds, unadorned, fragmentary, all muscle, subtle in the way two fingers poking hard against your chest is subtle. Street shit.

What's the lingo of the lawyers in your courtroom thriller? Do the cowboys in your romance talk like real ranch hands, or do they sound more like English literature majors? Everyone's got a style of talking. You use words that I wouldn't, and vice versa. (Hey, I'm from New York, fuckin' get over it.)

Characters' outlook can be as distinctive as their way of talking. Their opinions speak for the story and, in a way, for the author. Why, then, are many fiction writers reluctant to let their characters speak up? Often when I have finished reading a manuscript, I cannot tell you much of anything about what the protagonist believes, loathes, or even finds ridiculous.

Nick Hornby, in novels such as *About a Boy*, has established himself as a wry and witty observer of British shortcomings and discontent. In *How to be Good*, he introduces Dr. Katie Carr, who is married to a malcontent, David, who trumpets himself in his newspaper column as "The Angriest Man in Holloway." Fed up, Katie has an affair with an unexpected consequence: David has a deep and sudden religious conversion and decides to give up his anger in favor of being good.

Being good, it turns out, is massively inconvenient and irritating. Be careful what you wish for. At any rate, David's new focus causes Katie to examine many aspects of her life and question what it really means to be good. At one point, she reflects on the pervasive English delight in cynicism:

I got sick of hearing why everybody was useless, and ghastly, and talent-less, and awful, and how they didn't deserve anything good that had happened to them, and they completely deserved anything bad that had happened to them, but this evening I long for the old David—I miss him like one might miss a scar, or a wooden leg, something disfiguring but characteristic. You knew where you were with the old David. And I never felt any embarrassment, ever. Weary despair, sure, the occasional nasty taste in the mouth, certainly, flashes of irritation almost constantly, but never any embarrassment. I had become comfortable with his cynicism, and in any case, we're all cynical now, although it's only this evening that I recognize this properly. Cynicism is our shared common language, the Esperanto that actually caught on, and though I'm not fluent in it—I like too many things, and I am not envious of enough people—I know enough to get by. And in any case it is not possible to avoid cynicism and the sneer completely. Any conversation about, say, the London mayoral contest, or Demi Moore, or Posh and Becks and Brooklyn, and you are obliged to be sour, simply to prove that you are a fully functioning and reflective cosmopolitan person.

Katie is a woman of definite opinions, capable of missing her husband's sourness. She is one who reflects on the inner life of her countrymen and women. Or is she? Come to think of it, the passage above actually was written by Nick Hornby. Hmm.

What kind of opinions do your characters have? How do they express them? You can develop the way they talk, or their outlook and opinions, or both. In doing so, you will be developing not just characters more interesting to read about, but a voice of your own that speaks with force and authority.

DETAILS AND DELIVERY

Some novelists imagine it is best to have a narrator as neutral as a TV news anchor—a universal American into whom all readers can project themselves. I wonder. Even the most ordinary people have a life that's unique. The details that make it so are a secret source of what we call "voice."

Jonathan Letham broke into the mainstream with his memorable novel *Motherless Brooklyn*, in which Lionel Essrog, an orphan with

Tourette's syndrome, recalls his Brooklyn childhood and in particular his relationship with neighborhood tough guy and fixer Frank Minna. As adults, Minna and his minions become a *de facto* detective agency and limo service, until Minna is killed and Lionel himself must turn detective. One Christmas, Minna brings Lionel to his mother's apartment:

> Carlotta Minna was an Old Stove. That was the Brooklyn term for it, according to Minna. She was a cook who worked in her own apartment, making plates of sautéed squid and stuffed peppers and jars of tripe soup that were purchased at her door by a constant parade of buyers, mostly neighborhood women with too much housework or single men, young and elderly, bocce players who'd take her plates to the park with them, racing bettors who'd eat her food standing up outside the OTB, barbers and butchers and contractors who'd sit on crates in the backs of their shops and wolf her cutlets, folding them with their fingers like waffles. How her prices and schedules were conveyed I never understood— perhaps telepathically. She truly worked on an old stove, too, a tiny enamel four-burner crusted with ancient sauces and on which three or four pots invariably bubbled. The oven of this Herculean appliance was never cool; the whole kitchen glowed with heat like a kiln. Mrs. Minna herself seemed to have been baked, her whole face dark and furrowed like the edges of an overdone calzone. We never arrived without nudging aside some buyers from her door, nor without packing off with plateloads of food, though how she could spare it was a mystery, since she never seemed to make more than she needed, never wasted a scrap.

Bocce, OTB, sautéed squid, and a mother with a face baked like a calzone ... this can't be anywhere but Brooklyn. What creates the narrator's unique voice is not his grammar or outlook, but the details he chooses to convey. Elsewhere in the story, Lionel's Tourette's gives him a different perspective than normal, but for the moment, his unique voice is made up of nothing but the particulars of Brooklyn in 1979.

Sometimes it is not the details but a manner of expression that creates a sense of voice. In a departure from earlier novels such as *Reservation Road*, in *The Commoner* John Burnham Schwartz turned to the cloistered and crushingly formal world of Japan's Chrysanthemum Throne. In 1959 a young woman, a commoner called Haruko, is asked by the Crown Prince to be his consort. Although she was well raised, the gulf between Haruko's life and that of the court causes her father anxiety, which he expresses to the Prince's representative:

> There is in the Imperial Palace—how shall I put this—the old guard. The nobility. You yourself are such a worthy man. It is my understanding that such people make up nearly all of that world, and certainly all of the positions of relevance. Now, I'm the first to admit that I don't know much about any of this. I am a simple businessman—which I suppose is precisely my point. If I myself, out in the world fifty years, don't know anything about the ways and customs of imperial life, then how could Haruko? She would be utterly lost, humiliated. More than that, and I mean this sincerely, Doctor, she would be a humiliation to the Crown Prince and the entire Imperial Family. She would be a humiliation to Japan. And yet here you are—honorably, respectfully, on behalf of His Highness—asking us to agree to give her up for a role which we sincerely believe her to be unfit. A problem that, of course, has little to say about the other kind of loss being asked of us, one that you yourself, as you say, would feel only too painfully. To lose a daughter to another household is comprehensible; to lose her to another world defeats the mind, to say nothing of the heart. And, once she had committed herself, it is for life. She will never be able to leave that world. She will be sealed in forever.

The cultural authenticity here comes from the father's extreme self-effacement. Also consider, if you would, although I may be pushing too hard, I know, the number of commas, of parenthetical phrases, and the high and noble language in this passage, which so exquisitely—to a point of painfulness—expresses a father's anguish; and, perhaps, his duty, which of course is to refuse the high honor on the basis of his family's low position, as is expected of him.

In other words, a character's voice—and by extension, your own voice—can arrive through syntax as well as through the details you deploy in what he or she says, does, observes, and experiences.

DIFFERENT WAYS OF RELATING A STORY

There are many ways to tell a story, many points of view from which to look. What sort of storyteller are you? Are you a benevolent observer, reporting what happens to your characters with objective neutrality? Or are you an active participant: pulling strings, stacking the deck, letting your readers know how you feel, and calling attention to your themes?

There is nothing wrong with any particular choices. What bugs me is that many writers do not seem to have made a choice in the first place. Most manuscripts wander along in the way that it first occurred to their authors to write them. They do not confront me, insist that I listen, or seek to surprise me with a different way of seeing. They feel flat.

Choices of first versus third person, or present tense versus past tense, are fundamental to how a novel will read. There's no right way, just the way that works best and feels best to you.

There are so many ways to relate what happens, and so many perspectives to bring. Why not take advantage of some of those options?

Mohsin Hamid's *The Reluctant Fundamentalist* employs a striking perspective. The narrator of this post-9/11 novel is Changez, a young Pakistani who is thoroughly Americanized, a Princeton graduate, a highly paid employee of a New York valuation firm, a social success with a rich and beautiful girlfriend. Then the towers fall. Changez's reaction is the opposite of most: He sympathizes with the attackers.

What makes Hamid's novel even more unusual is that Changez relates his story in one long monologue delivered to an American stranger (an operative?), whom he approaches in a café in Lahore:

> Excuse me, sir, may I be of assistance? Ah, I see I have alarmed you. Do not be frightened by my beard: I am a lover of America. I noticed that you were looking for something; more than looking, in fact you seemed to be on a mission, and since I am both a native of this city and a speaker of your language, I thought I might offer you my services.
>
> How did I know you were American? No, not by the color of your skin; we have a range of complexions in this country, and yours occurs often among the people of our northwest frontier. Nor was it your dress that gave you away; a European tourist could as easily have purchased in Des Moines your suit, with its single vent, and your button-down shirt. True, you hair, short-cropped, and your expansive chest—the chest, I would say, of a man who bench-presses regularly, and maxes out well above two-twenty-five—are typical of a certain type of American; but then again, sportsmen and soldiers of all nationalities tend to look alike. Instead, it

> was your bearing that allowed me to identify you, and I do not mean that as an insult, for I see your face has hardened, but merely as an observation. Come, tell me, what were you looking for?

This direct-to-the-reader address gives Hamid's novel an immediacy and intimacy that a simple first-person point of view would not accomplish. It is urgently important to Changez that the man to whom he is speaking *understands* him.

Is your focal character someone sort of like you? That's not a bad way to go. It certainly makes the writing easier. It can also give heroes and heroines a numbing familiarity. Why? I'm not sure, but as I've noted before, a great many protagonists do not come alive as distinctive people.

That's a shame, because paradoxically, heroes and heroines can be the most winning when they are the most different. In his novel *The Curious Incident of the Dog in the Night-Time*, Mark Haddon chose as his narrator Christopher Boone, a boy who is autistic. Christopher has a savant quality. He relaxes by doing math problems, but because he cannot understand other people's cues or use intuition, he fits the world and the way it works into formulae and physical laws.

When he is falsely accused of killing a neighbor's poodle, Christopher undertakes to learn who actually did the deed:

> This is a murder mystery novel.
>
> Siobhan [a social worker at his school] said that I should write something I would want to read myself. Mostly I read books about science and maths. I do not like proper novels. In proper novels people say things like, "I am veined with iron, with silver and with streaks of common mud. I cannot contract into the firm fist which those clench who do not depend on stimulus." What does this mean? I do not know. Nor does Father. Nor does Siobhan or Mr. Jeavons. I have asked them.
>
> Siobhan has long blond hair and wears glasses which are made of green plastic. And Mr. Jeavons smells of soap and wears brown shoes that have approximately 60 tiny circular holes in each of them.
>
> But I do like murder mystery novels. So I am writing a murder mystery novel.

You would think that seeing the world from the perspective of an autistic savant would be exhausting, but instead it is exhilarating. Granted,

Haddon gives us a structure, a mystery, onto which to hold and through which to filter Christopher's unfiltered narration. As solid as that strategy is, it's not a gimmick. Christopher is more than accessible: He is alive, and so is Haddon's novel, in ways that it would not have been had he chosen a safer way to write it.

When thinking about voice, it is easy to focus on words, as if painting pretty pictures, capturing moments, and building metaphors is all that there is to it. I'm not opposed to any of that. But the more I read, the more I feel that skillful use of words and an author's ability to get down a fleeting illusion of reality can cover up a novel's core emptiness.

Not all beautifully written novels have a voice, or much of one. Potboiler plots may be exciting but also may have little flavor. It is when the words on the page demand that readers take notice that they begin to hear the author's voice. It isn't words alone that do that, I find, but rather the outlook, opinions, details, delivery, and original perspectives that an author brings to his or her tale.

Above all, a singular voice is not a lucky accident; it comes from a storyteller's commitment not just to tell a great story, but to tell it in a way that is wholly his or her own.

DONALD MAASS heads the Donald Maass Literary Agency in New York City, which represents more than 150 novelists and sells more than 150 novels every year to publishers in American and overseas. He is a past president of the Association of Authors' Representatives, Inc., and is the author of several Writer's Digest books, including *Writing the Breakout Novel, The Fire in Fiction, The Breakout Novelist, Writing 21st Century Fiction,* and *The Emotional Craft of Fiction.*

CHAPTER 5
ALL ABOUT THAT VOICE

BY ADAIR LARA

I was at a writing conference when an agent on a panel about narrative nonfiction grew exasperated and yelled to the crowd of aspiring writers: "Voice! Voice! Anything else you can fix!"

She meant that when you're writing narrative nonfiction—whether it's an essay, a memoir, or another type of true story with an arc—the success of the story being told is completely dependent upon the person telling it. You have to nail the storytelling voice from the beginning because it governs everything you do next—in choosing what to show us, interpreting events for us, informing us, entertaining us and gluing everything together.

Voice is the personality behind the writing. Even when writing a first-person account, your voice should be shaped for each particular story. And conversely, even when the author keeps himself entirely off the page, his voice is still there. It's in the attitude he has toward his subject—grave, amused, scientific, intimate. It's in his word choice—"in October," or "under an October sky." It's even in the details he notices— Mary Roach in *Packing for Mars*, for instance, can't resist asking the astronauts about their diapers.

For a book to succeed, the reader has to relate to the voice. Nothing else matters if she doesn't. The book will be lying across the room, unread, or sitting in a desk drawer, unpublished. A relatable voice is confident, intelligent, vulnerable, personable, authentic, and trustworthy. You want to follow this person around. You want to be her friend.

The content—the story you're telling, the one you want to amaze people with, change their lives with? That comes second. Say you fall out of a prop plane in the Andes and are captured by a lost tribe, only to survive, go online, and find it happened to six other people, all of whom have written books and already have agents.

With a great voice, though, you can write about something that's been written about before and sell it anyway.

Paula Balzer, the agent who received a manuscript called *Candy Girl* from a former stripper named Diablo Cody, said: "I wasn't interested based on the subject matter alone. Stripping had been covered before (no pun intended), and I didn't think the author was likely to add much to an already crowded market. But then there was the voice. After just one paragraph, I was, a) completely convinced that stripping was the solution to all of her problems, b) laughing uncontrollably, and c) definitely interested in being along for the entire ride, or at least 250-plus pages."

The trick is to get it right from the beginning. You can't go back and fix the voice later. It's not the paint on the wall, it's the wall itself.

TO SET THE MOOD, START WITH THE FIRST SENTENCE

I'm over at my bookshelves, leafing through first pages.

Jenny Lawson's memoir, *Let's Pretend This Never Happened*, begins: "This book is totally true, except for the parts that aren't." There's a confident voice.

Eats, Shoots & Leaves by Lynne Truss, a bestseller about punctuation, opens with: "Either this will ring bells for you, or it won't." We could be sharing a glass of wine while mulling the uses of the semicolon.

My well-worn copy of Bill Bryson's book about going to Europe, *Neither Here nor There*, opens with: "In winter Hammerfest is a thirty-hour ride by bus from Oslo, though why anyone would want to go there in winter is a question worth considering."

First he gives us a fact. A fact doesn't have voice. Anybody can state that same fact in the same way. But this is not a guidebook. The fun is in the reading, and, I suspect, in the writing. Bryson has a point of view about this Hammerfest place.

Bryson is funny, but a good voice doesn't have to be funny. No one ever accused Joan Didion of having a sense of humor. Here she is in her essay collection *The White Album*, ruminating on the California pipelines: "Some of us who live in arid parts of the world think about water with a reverence others might find excessive. The water I will draw tomorrow from my tap in Malibu is today crossing the Mojave Desert from the Colorado River, and I like to think about exactly where that water is."

All of these writers are in a mood, aren't they? Who even thinks about where the water in the tap comes from, let alone exactly where it is in its journey? This is not the authorial voice droning on. It's a person.

How did they arrive at those voices? They started with their own personalities, whether personable and chatty, or reserved. Then they picked up tricks from other writers. Cynthia Ozick kept a copy of E.M. Forster's *A Passage to India* on her desk. Junot Díaz was blown away by Cormac McCarthy. Pull apart the narrative nonfiction books you particularly love. As you read, you'll recognize yourself in them, your sensibility, your slant on things. Ask yourself what makes them work. Use them as models.

TO MAKE IT NATURAL, MAKE IT FAST

Dewey, a student in one of my workshops, has been trying to write a book, part memoir and part guide for parents of kids with learning abilities, for ten years. She's written dozens of drafts. Each time she'd read a section aloud in class, it was a struggle to concentrate on the reading, though the room was quiet. Dewey didn't see that her passion for the subject, her desire to get a message out to other parents, made her voice on the page sound academic.

Those of us in the workshop knew Dewey had a voice. She'd once sent us all a memorable e-mail explaining, "My husband and I have just returned from depositing our 24-year-old dyslexic daughter in her sight unseen, overpriced apartment in London for her four-month internship with a 'social club' startup." That was Dewey off the cuff. That was a voice that held our attention. And that was the voice that we coaxed her to bring to her book.

I make my students write fast by e-mailing them prompts (tailored for their individual writing projects) to be completed in one fifteen-minute writing session. I'm always astonished at how much flows from that—unscripted, unselfconscious sentences set down fast. It's impossible not to succeed at prompts. You're freed from worrying about craft—where this will fit in the book or how to construct a scene—and your natural voice emerges.

When you're seriously at work writing your serious book, you can get caught up in all that you have to say. That can freeze voice in its tracks. It might be coming out a little stiff and self-conscious.

So don't work seriously on your serious book. Play around. Experiment. Loosen up. And the best way I know of to do that is to write fast.

TO GET IT FINISHED, PUT YOURSELF ON DEADLINE

In Ray Bradbury's *Zen and the Art of Writing*, he tells of how he wrote *Fahrenheit 451*. He'd been unable to get any writing done at home because he had young children who wouldn't stop screaming. So he went to the library to write. The library had typewriters that you could use for thirty minutes when you put in a dime. Ray was struggling with money at the time, so he didn't have many dimes. He'd pop in the coin and then type frantically for 30 minutes. In between, he'd walk around the library, planning his next session. The rest, as they say, is history.

Know how Tom Wolfe got started? He'd been assigned a story about a hot rod and custom car show in California for *Esquire* when he found himself blocked. He knew how magazine pieces were written, but his wasn't coming out right, no matter how many times he crumpled up the page and started over.

He gave up and called his editor, Byron Dobell, who said, "Well, okay, just type up your notes and send them over."

So Wolfe started typing at about 8 P.M. in the form of a memo that began, "Dear Byron." He started with the first time he saw the custom cars. Freed of any need to write the piece properly, he typed like a madman. All night. At 6:15 he took the forty-nine-page memo over to *Esquire*.

At 4 P.M. Dobell called to say he was taking off the "Dear Byron" and running the rest in the magazine. That became "The Kandy-Kolored Tangerine-Flake Streamlined Baby," a benchmark in narrative nonfiction.

TO GET IT RIGHT, MAKE YOUR READER THE BOSS

Voice is the most obvious thing in the world, but it's hard to see it objectively in something you wrote yourself. You see there's a problem—the writing is flat or something. But it doesn't occur to you that that problem is your own voice. We look at our pages and see what we intended to write—the content—but not how it sounds.

Speaking for myself, every moribund writing project stacked on the shelves of my office petered to a halt because the voice was wrong. Did I realize it at the time? I did not. Instead I'd decide something else was wrong. I'd take it apart and put it together again, change it from the first to the third person, beef up the role of one character and eliminate another, rewrite the sentences until each one was a jewel, cover the dining table with notes and outlines, and then bombard friends with yet another version of the first fifty pages.

Those friends sometimes said a little timid something about the voice, something I could easily overlook. While readers nicely point out the images they like, or the interesting fact about cow dipping, no one wants to criticize the voice on the page, because it's yours—and you're standing right there.

Push them to tell you what they don't like. "I didn't want to hear the history of the F-16 on the first page." "The narrator sounds kind of whiny." "My mind wandered on the second page. What happened to the cow?"

My student Ann hitchhiked through the Middle East with her sister Boo in the early 1960s, before anybody else even thought of going there, and is writing about it. I wasn't afraid to challenge her to stop saying "we." Nothing ever happens to a "we" on the page. Her sister would likely tell her own version of that story. This one belongs to Ann.

The truth is, the voice can drift even when the sentences are lovely, and even when your choice of "cerulean" to describe the sky is so fetching that it takes the reader a couple of pages to realize that he's been wondering how long it's been since he got his tires rotated.

Zero in on anything you might skip over while reading a section aloud to somebody, or anyplace where an honest reader tells you her interest waned. This often comes down to backstory—the stuff you think we need to know before you can tell us what happened. Usually, we can do without it. Just plunge in—you'll know when you need a flashback, because there is something that can only be explained that way. Sometimes I think that backstory is a rest stop for the writing. It's tiring to keep driving a story forward—it takes energy, imagination, grit. How much more pleasant to pull into the equivalent of the rest stops that dot the highways, stop the car, and write about something you already know well and feel comfortable yammering on about?

Also, this may seem counterintuitive when it comes to voice, but cut out all the talking. That delicious blank page might seem just the place to air some views you have that are pertinent to the topic at hand. You know you're doing it because the writing just got easier. You're in the flow, saying it like it is!

Writing does not usually flow. Done right, it's hard work. Back when I had a newspaper column, I'd sometimes hit a passage where I just knew I was nailing it, saying something so eloquent, so important … and after some experience, I knew enough to just stop. I wasn't writing, I was just talking on the page.

Cut anything that smacks of an agenda, or anything boring. You can't fix boring. You want to talk about losing the winery in an acrimonious family lawsuit. The reader doesn't want to read that. He wants the funny story of how you became a wine consultant on a cruise ship afterward.

This will be your constant process: Cross out nonvoice; keep the lively bits. Fill in the holes with voice.

Without voice there is no reader, except perhaps your most dedicated and selfless friends.

Make the reader the boss. The reader *is* the boss. He likes the person talking to him to have some unexpected insight or some authority to hold forth on whatever the topic is. He wants to be entertained or moved. He wants to have his curiosity aroused, not driven off by information overload. And he wants to read writing that flatters his intelligence: subtext, indirection, irony, subtlety.

WHY SO SERIOUS?

We tend to be serious about ourselves and about our chosen subjects. But it's hard to find a voice that way. Here are two exercises to help you look at the main character in your story—whether that's you or another real-life figure—in a less reverential way.

1. Write a sloppy and funny synopsis—a few pages will do—in which you make as much fun of your narrator's beliefs and actions in the course of the story as you can. Here's part of my student Jason McMonagle's memoir-in-progress:

   I had just been dumped by my partner; he was perfect—handsome, charismatic, spiritual. He did, however, lack one small detail that became too hard to ignore; he did not find me at all attractive. When this point became obvious, the climactic breaking of my heart occurred. So naturally, I thought for just a moment, it would be in my best interest to begin drinking again.

2. Write a one-page portrait of the main character as her worst enemy would describe her. Not sure where to begin? Try one of these:

   • *I know what Mary's about. The thing about Mary that nobody else knows is ...*
   • *He was embarrassed about the smallest things. For instance ...*
   • *She is so ridiculous. Let me give you an example.*

ADAIR LARA (adairlara.com) is a writer, teacher, and former editor in San Francisco. She is the author of *Naked, Drunk and Writing*. Her book of voice lessons in writing, *Make Your Memoir Suck Less*, will be released soon, from Ten Speed Press.

PART II

CREATING A VOICE

CHAPTER 6

FINDING YOUR VOICE

BY LARRY BROOKS

By far the most common entry-level mistake in the writing game, the thing that can get a perfectly good story rejected by an editor on the first page, is *overwriting*: a writing voice that is laden with energy and adjectives, that tries too hard, that is self-conscious in a way that detracts from the story, that is obviously the work of a writer trying to poeticize a story that doesn't stand a chance.

Bad writing voice is like wearing a clown suit to the Oscars. Chances are you won't make it past the lobby.

Of course, one writer's clown suit is another's tuxedo. Which is to say, you may believe your eloquence is palatable and beautiful, and you may feel the need to stuff all this fat into your sentences because you don't feel they're muscular enough as is. It's always an opinion—yours and the editor's, and finally the reader's—but it's a critical one.

The mailrooms of the big publishing houses are full of these manuscripts created by writers who try to trick up their sentences, who reach for contrived eloquence, who attempt to liberate their inner poet, who overtly imitate someone famous who writes that way (J.D. Salinger has inspired more rejected manuscripts than any writer in history), and generally stinking up the place with strings of words that detract instead of enhance.

Overwriting will get your work rejected faster than a ridiculous *deus ex machina* in the final act.

That's not to say *stylistic* writing, a voice full of attitude and personality, is a bad thing. Hell, I'm doing precisely that right here. But it's how I write, and it's seasoned with several decades worth of professional experience (including the scars to prove it) in fine-tuning. Shooting for a level of personality in your narrative is always a risk.

To mitigate that risk, carve this into your forehead: *Less is more.* Just don't minimize your writing voice to the point where it sounds like copy from a metropolitan telephone directory. Somewhere between a love letter scripted by a drunken, suicidal poet and the world's driest technical copy awaits a level of style that suits you. And, just as important, it will suit your story or manuscript.

Your journey as a writer, as a storyteller, is to find it.

IT'S CALLED WRITING *VOICE*

The essence of your writing voice is significant for your writing career. Which means you have to get it right before you can turn pro. That word—*pro*—is critical here, because while it may be simplistic or positively John Updike-like, it absolutely, unequivocally, needs to be *professional.*

Where that bar resides is, once again, an opinion. One thing, however, is always true about this—the further you move in either direction from a safe and clean middle ground, the higher the risk your work will be perceived as less than professional.

Writing voice, in my humble opinion, gets too much airtime at writers conferences filled with people who are actually in need of mentoring on their storytelling. It remains a staple of academia—high school in particular—but it's actually the least challenging of other writing obstacles you'll face when it comes to publishing your work.

You don't have to write like J.D. Salinger or John Updike to get published. Pick up any random published book from a shelf at the mall and you'll see this to be true. While there is a huge variance in style among those authors, they all have one thing in common: They've met the bar of professionalism. Which in today's commercial market means clean, crisp, efficient writing that doesn't stink up the place with too much *effort.*

Think of writing voice as you might regard a singer's voice. Not everybody making records sounds like Josh Groban or Maria Callas. Some of them sound like they woke up from inadequate anesthesia during an appendectomy. Any singer, though, can mess up a song with too much melodic gymnastics. Think Adam Lambert trying to trick up the national anthem. Great voice, but the crowd at Wrigley Field wouldn't approve.

THE AROMATIC BENCHMARK OF VOICE

Writing voice is like air: If you can smell it, something is cooking, and it may not be appetizing to everyone. In fact, something may be rotten. The scent of a Chihuahua slowly roasting on a spit over an open flame may play well in the North Hamgyong Province of Korea, but it turns stomachs in rural Massachusetts. And yet, in both corners of the planet, everybody loves a clean, fresh breeze totally void of scent.

Less is more. The more personality and humor and edge you are looking for, the truer this is.

Attempting to imbue your writing with noticeable narrative style is always risky, because you're hoping and assuming that whoever is reading your work will be attracted to that particular style. The safest bet—one placed by a bevy of best-selling writers that includes Dan Brown and John Grisham, Stephenie Meyer and James Patterson, and a whole bunch of other authors who are too often and unfairly accused of *not being all that good* because their writing bears no stylistic scent— is to write cleanly and crisply. To write *simply*. Sort of like that breath of fresh air, the hallmark of which is that it doesn't smell like anything at all. It's just, well, pleasant. It flows. It goes down easy.

At the very least, it's *professional*.

The personality and voice of your writing should be natural, not something contrived. It can take years to find your natural writing voice, and when you do you'll never fear the color purple—as in, purple prose—again. Because only when you are writing naturally, without forcing it and without abusing adjectives (in *Elmore Leonard's 10 Rules of Writing*, he advises writers to remove every single adjective from their manuscripts) will the scent of your narrative be as subtle and functional as it needs to be to attract a buyer.

Consider the novelist Colin Harrison. Harrison has been called the "poet laureate" of American thriller writers, but not because of what that tag implies. You'd think someone with that on his nametag would be positively Shakespearean with his words. But eloquence isn't your goal as storyteller—*essence*, as conveyed through tonality and attitude, *is*. And nobody does that better than Colin Harrison.

Here's the first paragraph of Harrison's novel *Manhattan Nocturne*:

> I sell mayhem, scandal, murder, and doom. Oh, Jesus I do, I sell tragedy, vengeance, chaos, and fate. I sell the sufferings of the poor and the vanities of the rich. Children falling from windows, subway trains afire, rapists fleeing into the dark. I sell anger and redemption. I sell the muscled heroism of firemen and the wheezing greed of mob bosses. The stench of garbage, the rattle of gold. I sell black to white, white to black. To Democrats and Republicans and Libertarians and Muslims and transvestites and squatters on the Lower East Side. I sold John Gotti and O. J. Simpson and the bombers of the World Trade Center, and I'll sell whoever else comes along next. I sell falsehood and what passes for truth and every gradation in between. I sell the newborn and the dead. I sell the wretched, magnificent city of New York back to its people. I sell newspapers.

There are only four adjectives here. Two each in two separate sentences. That's it. And yet, this paragraph screams attitude and personality. It is a soaring, melodic example of writing voice, one that is completely in keeping with the dark city detective thriller that it is, only written by a master linguist. Use this as a model of writing voice that's way out there from the boring, vanilla middle of the stylistic continuum, and allow it to inspire your musings at that level.

Just don't imitate the guy. Or anyone, for that matter. Editors can smell a rip-off a mile away.

Less is more. Even when you're shooting for more. Just keep trying things, checking in with how it works, and listening to the feedback. Allow your writing voice to evolve, unforced but certainly subject to the highest standards you can bring to it.

Many of us become writers in the first place because we have been told for years that we have *a way with words*. That can actually be a curse in this game. Just make sure that the words don't have a way with you and your career.

Novels—and especially screenplays—don't sell because of writing voice. But they do get *rejected* because of writing voice. What sells are great stories, told well. *Well*, in this context, being a balanced mastery of all your writing skills, including a writing voice that smells like money.

THE VOICE OF DIALOGUE

If you write fiction, by definition you write dialogue. Which means that dialogue, for better or worse, is part of your writing voice, and will be judged as such by an agent or editor long before it stands a chance of reaching the reading public.

For some writers this comes very naturally, and for others—even those who don't struggle in the slightest with their narrative prose—their dialogue sounds like it came from the script of a bad third-grade play.

Writing great dialogue is very much like narrative prose—it cannot be taught. But a *sense* of it can be *evolved*, and for that to happen you need to develop an *ear* for it.

If you have the ear, you can write it down in your stories.

Dialogue as Reality

The overwhelming fault in dialogue from many newer writers is dialogue that doesn't sound genuine. It's just not how real people in the real world talk.

You have to begin by throwing all that you know about grammar and the physics of a respectable sentence out the window. Because people just don't talk that way to each other. Never have, never will.

Some people speak via certain shorthand. They don't say half of what they mean, yet they are perfectly understood. Others speak indirectly, and still others imbue their communications with agenda and unspoken subtext.

Dialogue is also specific to variables such as age, culture, geography, relationships, and agenda. When Mike Rich, a very white guy from a very upscale part of town, wrote the screenplay for *Finding Forrester*, his spot-on street dialogue was attacked by some as having been brushed up by someone else, someone who had lived the life of his inner-city protagonist. But Rich did what all writers need to do—he jumped into the contextual heads of his cast and allowed them to speak as they really would, not as a white guy who has never seen a crack pipe might think they would. This took work, which Rich legitimately claims with pride. The actors and the director get less credit than the screenwriter relative to the keen ear employed in the dialogue, which made the scenes ring true.

Let's look at two examples of the same moment, a contrived slice of dialogue created for this purpose. One is how a newer writer might do it, the other how it might actually sound. This reflects the writer's own point of view and awareness—nobody *chooses* to write dialogue that is off the mark—and thus defines the challenge at hand. You can't settle for *you* in your character dialogue, you have to get outside yourself and make it *real*.

Two old friends who haven't seen each other since graduation run into each other at halftime of an NBA game.

> "Hey! Holy cow, man, how are you?"
> "I'm fine, you?"
> "Yeah. You look ... successful."
> "Doing okay. How about you?"
> "Can't complain. How long has it been ... like, a year?"
> "Three. Are you married?"
> "Engaged. You?"
> "Divorced. Hey, that's how it goes sometimes."

Yeah, that pretty much sucks, I know. But that's what lands on too many desks of too many editors. Not because the writers are bad, but because they don't bring an ear to the dialogue. They can't seem to imbue characters with a realistic ambiance and edge.

This would play better:

> "Dude! 'Sup, man?"
> "God, you look ... what are you, like, running the show over there?"
> "Can't complain, livin' the dream."
> "You look like Donald Trump's son or somethin'."
> "Better hair."

"Hear that. What's it been, like, a year?"

"Ya think? Try three. LeBron was still learning his crossover. You married yet?"

"Nope. Still chillin'."

"Dude."

"I know. You? Don't see a ring or a tan line."

"Divorced. Thank God for prenups, the bitch."

"Dude. Sorry to hear."

"Don't be. My new girlfriend looks like Trump's daughter ... it's all good."

Writing dialogue with *street cred* isn't the point. Rather, make sure your dialogue adds to the reading experience by transporting the reader into the moment, and via nuance and subtext, into the agendas and lives of the characters involved.

The best way to develop an ear is to listen. Not just to real life—which is the mother lode of all dialogue—but to snappy, rich dialogue from every book you read and movie you see.

Avoid *on-the-nose* dialogue when you can—something your conservative aunt might say on her first trip out of Iowa, ever—that doesn't add any color or personality whatsoever. (Unless, of course, that's really how your character talks in the story.) Dialogue is a great—and inherent—opportunity for characterization, and like many of the creative choices you face, to not seize it is to choose mediocrity.

And while your narrative voice can be pleasantly mediocre in context to a killer story, your dialogue should never warrant that same description.

....

LARRY BROOKS is the best-selling author of five psychological thrillers, in addition to his work as a freelance writer and writing instructor. He is the author of *Story Engineering*, *Story Physics*, and *Story Fix*, and the creator of storyfix.com, one of the leading instructional writing sites on the Internet. His most recent novel is *The Seventh Thunder*.

Writing Voice

CHAPTER 7

CREATING YOUR OWN VOICE

BY DON FRY

The oldest surviving inscription in Attic Greek, from about 720 B.C.E., circles the shoulder of a small wine pitcher. It says, "Whoso now of all the dancers most playfully sports [wins me]."[1] The little pot is the prize in a dancing contest. It speaks to the contestants through the voice of its inscription. And that's the basic metaphor of all writing: the text speaks to the reader.

Readers experience the illusion of a person speaking to them through the page or from the screen. They assign personality to that illusion, which is called "the *persona.*" This *persona* is not the author but an artifact created by the author. You could think of the *persona* or voice as a mask between the author and the reader, similar to the metaphorical masks people use when they talk with other people.

What is voice? Voice is a collection of devices used consistently to create the illusion of a person speaking through the text. Writers create their voices by repeating the same devices over and over, such as sentence complexity and length, level of language, and sophistication of reference. Voice differs from tone, the emotional cast. The same voice can sound elated or sad, even in the same text. Some people equate voice with style, although the latter usually refers to larger issues, such as "epic style."

The following examples will give a sense of the range of voices these devices can create for you. Read each example aloud to hear what I'm

1 Kellen Robb. *Literary and Paideia in Ancient Greece.* (Oxford: Oxford University Press, 1994). 24. Dipylon Oinochoe, National Museum, Athens.

describing. Here's the first paragraph of my friend Roy Peter Clark's *Writing Tools* (a terrific book, by the way):

> Americans do not write for many reasons. One big reason is the writer's struggle. Too many writers talk and act as if writing were slow torture, a form of procreation without arousal and romance—all dilation and contraction, grunting and pushing. As New York sports writer Red Smith once observed, "Writing is easy. All you do is sit down at a typewriter and open a vein." The agony in Madison Square Garden.[2]

What devices make this paragraph sound like Roy? He varies his sentence lengths, including some quite long ones ("Too many ... pushing."). He uses everyday language mixed with higher levels of diction ("procreation"), and strong nouns and verbs. He has few adverbs (*once* observed"). He uses images of sex ("arousal and romance") and birth ("dilation and contraction") and sports (Red Smith) and New York. Roy simply can't write without coupling procreation and sports. And he puts a religious pun ("agony ... Garden") in the final, emphatic position. Everything Roy writes will sound like that. Roy sounds like Roy, and that's what voice means.

JULIA CHILD

Here's one of America's favorite voices, Julia Child, writing about peeling hard-boiled eggs:

> The perfect hard-boiled egg is one that is perfectly unblemished when peeled; its white is tender, its yolk is nicely centered and just set, and no dark line surrounds it. Excess heat toughens the egg, and excess heat also causes that dark line between yolk and white ...
>
> Because of the egg's commercial importance, scientists at the University of Georgia undertook a study involving over 800 of them and concluded that the best way of shrinking the egg body from the shell, to make for easy peeling, was to plunge the just-boiled eggs into iced water for one minute, meanwhile bringing the cooking water back to the boil, then to plunge the eggs into boiling water for ten seconds, and

---

2 Roy Peter Clark. *Writing Tools: 50 Essential Strategies for Every New Writer.* (New York: Little, Brown), 2006). 3.

right after that to peel them. The iced water shrinks egg from shell and the subsequent short boil expands shell from egg.

I tried out the Georgia method, found it good, and described it in my monthly column for *McCall's* magazine, thereby receiving even more new suggestions, including one from a testy 74-year-old asking if the U. of Georgia had nothing better to do! They should ask their grandmothers, said she who has been boiling eggs since she was a little girl: she boils them 12 to 15 minutes, plunges them into cold water, and has never had the slightest bit of trouble peeling them.[3]

Sounds like Julia, doesn't it, but why? (Remember that I'm talking about her writing voice, not how she spoke on television.) First, notice the very long but clear sentences, the repetition of key words and phrases, the simple language, the lists of actions in order, and eccentric punctuation. Julia simplifies the science ("that dark line"), cites recent food research, and then invokes the wisdom of grandmothers. This authoritative voice convinces you that you're listening to a real person who's a real expert. She assures you by her confident tone that she knows what she's talking about, and you can do it, too. Just the sort of person you want to eat *Charlotte Malakoff aux Fraises* with. *Bon Appétit.*

THOMAS JEFFERSON

Now study the voice of the most important sentence in American history, the beginning of *The Declaration of Independence* (in Jefferson's original spelling):

> We hold these truths to be self-evident: that all men are created equal; that they are endowed by their creator with certain inalienable rights; that among these are life, liberty, & the pursuit of happiness; that to secure these rights, governments are instituted among men, deriving their just powers from the consent of the governed; that whenever any form of government becomes destructive of these ends, it is the right of the people to alter or abolish it, & to institute new government, laying it's foundation on such principles, & organizing it's powers in such form, as to them shall seem most likely to effect their safety & happiness.[4]

---

3 "HB Eggs. An unusual and successful way to boil and peel them." *Julia Child, Julia Child & Company.* (New York: Knopf, 1978). 34-35.
4 Merrill D. Peterson, ed. *Thomas Jefferson Writings.* Library of America. (New York: Literary Classics of the United States, 1984). 19.

Walter Isaacson describes Thomas Jefferson's prose as "graced with rolling cadences and mellifluous phrases."[5] (*Mellifluous* from Latin *mel* 'honey' + *fluus* 'flowing.') Jefferson writes long, but reads short. He uses long, parallel clauses, with repeated openings ("that ..."). His language mixes simple words ("all men are created equal") with elevated diction ("endowed," "inalienable," "instituted"). He lists our rights ("life, liberty, & the pursuit of happiness") and then tells us what we have to do to keep them, moving from abstraction to action. His absolutely assured tone leaves no room for argument ("We hold these truths to be self-evident ..."). He doesn't give you time to decide if you want to be part of that initial "We"; he just pulls you along with his driving prose until you reach the end, and you think, "Yes, of course, 'safety & happiness.' Sign me up." You can't write that sentence, nobody else could, but you can sound like it, and that's what voice does.

JANE AUSTEN

Here's another familiar voice offering self-evident truth, Jane Austen:

> It is a truth universally acknowledged, that a single man in possession of a good fortune, must be in want of a wife.
> However little known the feelings or views of such a man may be on his first entering a neighbourhood, this truth is so well fixed in the minds of the surrounding families, that he is considered as the rightful property of some one or other of their daughters.[6]

This voice also depends on long, complex sentences that deliver their key words at the end ("wife," "daughters"). It's aphoristic, wry, and edgy. Austen uses linking verbs ("is") rather than action verbs, giving a conversational feel, and she uses simple language interspersed with abstractions ("truth" twice). And the point of view is always rural, domestic, and female. Like Jefferson's, you can't argue against this voice's assurance.

---

5 Walter Isaacson. *Benjamin Franklin An American Life.* (New York: Simon & Schuster, 2003). 311.
6 *Pride and Prejudice* (1813). R.W. Chapman, ed. *The Novels of Jane Austen.* (Oxford: Oxford University Press, 1932). 2, 3.

ERNEST HEMINGWAY

Take a look at one of fiction's most recognizable voices, Ernest Hemingway:

> In the morning it was raining. A fog had come over the mountains from the sea. You could not see the tops of the mountains. The plateau was dull and gloomy, and the shapes of the trees and the houses were changed. I walked out beyond the town to look at the weather. The bad weather was coming over the mountains from the sea.[7]

Every clause has essentially the same rhythm and structure: subject, verb, then more in the right branch. Hemingway keeps showing the reader aspects of the same things from different viewpoints. He uses the simplest language with lots of repeated images and words. Every word counts, and you can't remove even one without causing damage. You might characterize this voice as somewhat flat, restrained, and weary, but absolutely under control.

GAIL COLLINS

Columnist Gail Collins has a witty voice that delivers devastating judgments deftly:

> "Sometimes you misunderestimated me," Bush told the Washington press corps. This is not the first time our president has worried about misunderestimation, so it's fair to regard this not as a slip of the tongue, but as something the president of the United States thinks is a word. The rhetoric is the one part of the administration we're surely going to miss. We are about to enter a world in which our commander in chief speaks in full sentences, and I do not know what we're going to do to divert ourselves on slow days.[8]

Collins has a sharp ear for other people's language, which she treats as a key to their character. She plays with their wording ("misunderestimated") in her own long sentences and simple, everyday language. In

---

7 *The Sun Also Rises* (1926), ch. 16. Charles Poore, ed. *The Hemingway Reader.* (New York: Scribner's, 1953). 224.
8 "He's Leaving, Really." *The New York Times* (1-15-2009). A27

a piece about Bush's silly lingo, she elevates president-elect Obama to "commander in chief." Her wit is wry, and a little weary ("divert ourselves"). Her voice speaks in the context of the other voices on the op-ed page, which tend toward high seriousness and abstractions. She sounds like the ordinary person amid the titans. It takes great effort, skill, and attention for Gail Collins to sound effortless and consistently funny.

E.B. WHITE

Every writer should own a copy of Strunk and White's *Elements of Style*. Here is White's voice, describing Strunk's teaching style and its effect.

> "Omit needless words!" cries the author on page 23, and into that imperative Will Strunk really put his heart and soul. In the days when I was sitting in his class, he omitted so many needless words, and omitted them so forcibly and with such eagerness and obvious relish, that he often seemed in the position of having shortchanged himself—a man left with nothing more to say yet with time to fill, a radio prophet who had outdistanced the clock. Will Strunk got out of this predicament by a simple trick: he uttered every sentence three times. When he delivered his oration on brevity to the class, he leaned forward over his desk, grasped his coat lapels in his hands, and, in a husky, conspiratorial voice, said, "Rule Seventeen. Omit needless words! Omit needless words! Omit needless words!"
>
> He was a memorable man, friendly and funny. Under the remembered sting of his kindly lash, I have been trying to omit needless words since 1919, and although there are still many words that cry for omission and the huge task will never be accomplished, it is exciting to me to re-read the masterly Strunkian elaboration of this noble theme. It goes: [now quoting Strunk]
>
> *Vigorous writing is concise. A sentence should contain no unnecessary words, a paragraph no unnecessary sentences, for the same reason that a drawing should have no unnecessary lines and a machine no unnecessary parts. This requires not that the writer make all his sentences short, or that he avoid all detail and treat his subjects only in outline, but that every word tell.*[9]

I would describe White's *persona* as bemused, wry and witty, richly observant, playful, and authoritative. White mixes levels of diction

---

9 *The Elements of Style*. 3rd ed. (New York: Macmillan, 1979). xii-xlv.

(high and medium) and formality, swooping from one to another, clause by clause. He piles phrases and clauses on top of one another, making long sentences that take a while to land, alternating with medium lengths. He repeats key phrases; this passage is about repetition, after all. He exaggerates as he describes actions sharply, uses no contractions, and invents words ("Strunkian"). He makes fun of himself with his mock-serious high tone. His voice resembles Gail Collins, but with more complex and playful sentences.

White ends by quoting a paragraph of Strunk, so go ahead and analyze his voice too, which White calls "Sergeant Strunk snapping orders to his platoon." Strunk's forceful tone drives the reader to his conclusion at the emphatic end of the third sentence, five plain words ("but that every word tell.") He uses simple, everyday, masculine diction, with lots of repetition ("no unnecessary" four times). The middle sentence has four parallel clauses, saying the same thing with different references. You have no doubt what Strunk means, so you just salute.

NATALIE ANGIER

Natalie Angier has an appealing voice that explains the most abstruse concepts of modern science, here the orbits of the inner planets:

> Location is everything, and it was ours during the birth of the solar system that granted us our annum. Earth sails around its orbit of more than half a billion miles at 66,600 miles per hour because of its distance relative to the gravitational master, the sun. Venus, by contrast, is 26 million miles closer to the sun than we are, which means that (a) its orbit is shorter than ours; (b) the comparatively greater gravitational pull of the sun prompts Venus to dash through each lap at a heightened pace (78,400 miles per hour); and (c) a year there lasts only 226 Earth days, another unpleasant thought for book writers with contracts to fulfill. And let's not dwell on that solar toady of a planet named after the Roman god with feathers on his shoes, where a "year" lasts less than three months.[10]

---

10 Natalie Angier. *The Canon*. (Boston and New York: Houghton Mifflin, 2008). 73.

I would describe this *persona* as chatty and witty, wry and learned, sophisticated, conversational and friendly, extremely clear, and therefore authoritative. Now look at the devices that compose that voice.

<[LEFT BRANCH] SUBJECT + VERB [RIGHT BRANCH]>

Her clear explanation flows from long but simple sentences: start with subject and verb, open to the right, put things end to end. The third, long sentence ("Venus ... fulfill.") has one main simple clause, which leads to a list consisting of three simple clauses. She uses ordinary language throughout, with only three technical terms: "solar," "gravitational," and "orbit," each appearing twice. She plays with language in the first sentence, using Latin *annum* for "year," but doesn't explain it. In the last sentence, she calls Mercury "a planet named after the Roman god with feathers on his shoes," again with no explanation. Her allusions assume that you share her classical background.

Angier drops comic asides, such as "another unpleasant thought for book writers with contracts to fulfill," implying her literate and professional audience. She mixes active, passive, and linking verbs for conversational feel, with graphic action verbs. She moves readers along rapidly through complex materials by putting witty bits at the ends of paragraphs.

ABRAHAM LINCOLN

Abraham Lincoln had a powerful and distinctive voice, best heard in his Gettysburg Address:

> Four score and seven years ago our fathers brought forth, upon this continent, a new nation, conceived in Liberty, and dedicated to the proposition that all men are created equal.
>
> Now we are engaged in a great civil war, testing whether that nation, or any nation so conceived, and so dedicated, can long endure. We are met here on a great battlefield of that war. We have come to dedicate a portion of it as a final resting place for those who here gave their lives that that nation might live. It is altogether fitting and proper that we should do this.

But in a larger sense we can not dedicate—we can not consecrate—we can not hallow this ground. The brave men, living and dead, who struggled, here, have consecrated it far above our poor power to add or detract. The world will little note, nor long remember, what we say here, but can never forget what they did here.

It is for us, the living, rather to be dedicated here to the unfinished work which they have, thus far, so nobly carried on. It is rather for us to be here dedicated to the great task remaining before us—that from these honored dead we take increased devotion to that cause for which they here gave the last full measure of devotion—that we here highly resolve that these dead shall not have died in vain; that this nation shall have a new birth of freedom; and that this government of the people, by the people, for the people, shall not perish from the Earth.[11]

Ten sentences, 272 words of luminous prose. What devices make this voice distinctive?

Lincoln begins with archaic language and phrasing, not "in 1776" or "87 years ago," but "four score and seven years ago." "Brought forth, upon this continent" has the sweep and ring of the King James Bible. He ends his first paragraph by quoting Thomas Jefferson and *The Declaration of Independence*: "all men are created equal," echoed in the closing: "this government of the people, by the people, for the people, shall not perish from the earth."

Lincoln uses simple diction throughout, with some middle level: "conceive," "dedicate" five times, "devotion," "resolve," "perish." He repeats simple words: "here" nine times, "we" ten, "us" four, "nation" five, and "dedicate" five, creating a sense of unity. His powerful verbs picture actions.

Mostly he writes sentences that branch to the right, with a few short insertions, creating a flowing rhythm and great clarity. His sentences turn on parallel phrasing:

"any nation so conceived, and so dedicated"

"we are engaged ... We are met ... We have come ..."

"we can not dedicate—we can not consecrate—we can not hallow this ground."

---

11 http://avalon.law.yale.edu/19th_century/gettyb.asp

"It is for us ... It is rather for us ..."

"what we say here, ... what they did here."

"government of the people, by the people, for the people."

Most of his sentences are roughly the same length, until he gets to the last one, eighty-four words long, almost a third of the whole address. The entire speech is heavily punctuated except the last sentence. The shorter sentences build up a rolling rhythm, and that last, long sentence delivers his message in powerful, memorable form.

Lincoln mixes imagery of birth and death with references to land and ground and fields, appropriate for a funeral oration.

Forgetting for a moment what you know about Lincoln, what personality emerges from these devices? I would call it strong and determined, simple and sincere, patriotic, clear, and absolutely compelling. As with Jefferson, readers want to follow anyone who talks and writes like that.

FRANK MCCOURT

Now you'll analyze Frank McCourt's voice and see how he creates it. In this passage from *Angela's Ashes*, Frank and his brother Malachy take their infant brother Alphie for a stroll in his baby carriage:

> We play games with Alphie and the pram. I stand at the top of Barrack Hill and Malachy is at the bottom. When I give the pram a push down the hill Malachy is supposed to stop it but he's looking at a pal on roller skates and it speeds by him across the street and through the doors of Leniston's pub where men are having a peaceful pint and not expecting a pram with a dirty-faced child saying Goo goo goo goo. The barman shouts this is a disgrace, there must be a law against this class of behavior, babies roaring through the door in bockety prams, he'll call the guards on us, and Alphie waves at him and smiles and he says, all right, all right, the child can have a sweet and a lemonade, the brothers can have lemonade too, that raggedy pair, and God above, 'tis a hard world, the minute you think you're getting ahead a pram comes crashing through the door and you're dishing out sweets and lemonade right and left, the two of ye take that child and go home to yeer mother.[12]

---

12 Frank McCourt. *Angela's Ashes*. (New York: Simon & Schuster, 1999). 249-250.

Writing Voice

How would you describe the vivid personality speaking here? He's remembering something that happened decades earlier, and impersonating himself then. He comes off as a bemused outlaw, an almost-innocent criminal, knowingly committing a reckless, silly, dangerous, potentially tragic act. He shows no sense of remorse, then or now, and thoroughly enjoys the retelling. He's enthusiastic in the boyish act. Neither child apologizes to the barman, yet McCourt is clearly sympathetic with the bartender's rant. And this speaker has a good ear for common speech. He's a clear storyteller.

What devices produce this personality, this voice?

McCourt sets up the scene and the action with firm geography and expectations about what each character will do, then shoves the pram downhill. The sense of pell-mell action results from a lack of punctuation for the rest of the sentence, and the contrast of chaos and normality. The speeding pram interrupts the men drinking "a peaceful pint," and halts with the baby saying "Goo goo goo goo."

The second half of the paragraph is all one sentence of the barman's reaction, again speeded along with sparse punctuation. His speech alternates direct and indirect quoting without quotation marks. He speaks a little bit of dialect and slang: "bockety," "ye," "yeer." The whole paragraph races along with strong action verbs, lots of repetition, and mostly short, ordinary words. McCourt tells the anecdote entirely in the present tense, giving it immediacy; you, the reader, are right there.

Now go back and read the selection aloud. Don't you agree that this is an attractive voice, a storyteller you want to listen to, even as he tells you the most appalling things?

GARRISON KEILLOR

Here's a familiar voice that most people listen to rather than read. Actually, Garrison Keillor's radio and writing voices are close, because he normally writes for reading aloud. This selection comes from a whimsical survey of six state fairs. He expands the third item in a list of "Ten Chief Joys of the State Fair":

Of the ten joys, the one that we Midwesterners are loath to cop to is number three, the mingling and jostling, a pleasure that Google and Facebook can't provide. American life tends more and more to put you in front of a computer screen in a cubicle, then into a car and head you toward home in the suburbs, where you drive directly into the garage and step into your kitchen without brushing elbows with anybody. People seem to want this, as opposed to urban tumult and squalor. But we have needs we can't admit, and one is to be in a scrum of thinly clad corpulence milling in brilliant sun in front of the deep-fried-ice-cream stand and feel the brush of wings, hip bumps, hands touching your arm ("Oh, excuse me!"), the heat of humanity with its many smells (citrus deodorant, sweat and musk, bouquet of beer, hair oil, stale cigar, methane), the solid, big-rump bodies of Brueghel peasants all around you like dogs in a pack, and you—yes, elegant you of the refined taste and the commitment to the arts—are one of these dogs. All your life you dreamed of attaining swanhood or equinity, but your fellow dogs know better. They sniff you and turn away, satisfied.[13]

How would you characterize the *persona* speaking here? (Forget that you've heard and seen him; just consider his prose.) You would probably judge it as wry and comic, ironic, edgy, hip, suburban, comfortable and uncomfortable, and vigorous, as well as homely and sophisticated at the same time. A voice filled with contradictions.

What devices create this familiar voice? First, you notice the long, sprawling sentences. Despite their length, they're clear because Keillor gives you the subject and verb early, and keeps expanding to the right. His parenthetical insertions fall at places that don't impede the flow. These sentences would be even easier to follow on radio, with his voice punctuating, although he wrote this piece for *National Geographic*. The effect is a rich, compelling, clear explainer.

Most people think of state fairs as rural, but the worldview here is suburban, with the sensibility between the farm and city. The first-person plural pronoun "We," beginning with "We midwesterners," actually refers to all Americans.

13 "Top Ten State Fair Joys." *National Geographic* (7-2009). 64-81; http://ngm.nationalgeographic. com/2009/07/state-fairs/keillor-text. Copyright 2009, Garrison Keillor, National Geographic Scoiety. Used with permission.

Writing Voice

Keillor propels the reader with strong verbs and rolling sentences. He uses mostly simple words, mixed with more sophisticated vocabulary: "tumult and squalor," "scrum," "corpulence," "bouquet of beer," "commitment." He even makes up words: "swanhood" and "equinity."

He tosses off a reference from the fine arts ("solid, big-rump bodies of Brueghel peasants") without explicating it. He presents all the imagery of the state fair without explanation; he assumes you know what he's talking about and probably have experienced it. Even if you haven't, he puts you there.

Garrison Keillor, this very American voice says, is our representative, our point of view, immersed in a situation that characterizes us.

BARACK OBAMA

Now analyze candidate Barack Obama's voice in his 2008 victory speech after winning the Iowa caucuses. It begins like this:

> Thank you, Iowa.
>
> You know, they said this day would never come.
>
> They said our sights were set too high. They said this country was too divided, too disillusioned to ever come together around a common purpose.
>
> But on this January night, at this defining moment in history, you have done what the cynics said we couldn't do.
>
> You have done what the state of New Hampshire can do in five days. You have done what America can do in this new year, 2008.
>
> In lines that stretched around schools and churches, in small towns and in big cities, you came together as Democrats, Republicans and independents, to stand up and say that we are one nation. We are one people. And our time for change has come.
>
> You said the time has come to move beyond the bitterness and pettiness and anger that's consumed Washington.
>
> To end the political strategy that's been all about division, and instead make it about addition. To build a coalition for change that stretches through red states and blue states.
>
> Because that's how we'll win in November, and that's how we'll finally meet the challenges that we face as a nation.[14]

---

14 http://www.nytimes.com/2008/01/03/us/politics/03obama-transcript.html.

Obama starts conversationally, "You know ...," and keeps his language simple and direct. His driving rhythm results mostly from repetition of short phrases:

> "They said ... They said ... what the cynics said ... You said ..."
>
> "too divided, too disillusioned ..."
>
> "said we couldn't do ... You have done ... You have done ..."
>
> "... can do in five days ... can do in this new year, 2008."
>
> "to move beyond the bitterness ... To end the political strategy ..."
>
> "To build a coalition ..."

He revs up some sentences with opening phrases that delay the subject:

> "But on this January night, at this defining moment in history ..."
>
> "In lines that stretched around schools and churches, in small towns and in big cities ..."

The whole passage turns on imagery of time and space, from lines stretching to the whole nation. He uses contrasting pronouns: "they" versus "you" and "we." His tone is absolutely assured, without qualifiers.

Most of his sentences are either long or medium length, except for two: "We are one people. And our time for change has come." And those two sentences, emphatic by their short punchiness, are the heart of his message in this speech. Barack Obama sounds like Lincoln and Martin Luther King Jr.

DAVID BROOKS

David Brooks has a firm voice, as in this excerpt from his book, *The Social Animal*:

> If the conscious mind is like a general atop a platform, who sees the world from a distance and analyzes things linearly and linguistically, the unconscious mind is like a million little scouts. The scouts career across

the landscape, sending back a constant flow of signals and generating instant responses. They maintain no distance from the environment around them, but are immersed in it. They scurry about, interpenetrating other minds, landscapes, and ideas.

These scouts coat things with emotional significance. They come across an old friend and send back a surge of affection. They descend into a dark cave and send back a surge of fear. Contact with a beautiful landscape produces a feeling of sublime elevation. Contact with a brilliant insight produces delight, while contact with unfairness produces righteous anger. Each perception has its own flavor, texture, and force, and reactions loop around the mind in a stream of sensations, impulses, judgments, and desires.

These signals don't control our lives, but they shape our interpretation of the world and they guide us, like a spiritual GPS, as we chart our courses. If the general thinks in data and speaks in prose, the scouts crystallize with emotion, and their work is best expressed in stories, poetry, music, image, prayer, and myth.[15]

How would we characterize Brooks's *persona*? It's authoritative and strong, learned but unpretentious, moral, and a bit skeptical of the human condition.

What devices create this personality? The passage is stunningly clear, which creates the sense of powerful authority. This guy knows what he's talking about. He takes his time to explain things, rather than jamming heavy concepts into dense, academic prose.

The language is mostly simple, with a mixture of slightly technical words: "linearly," "linguistically," "perception," "interpenetrating," etc., all used in ways that make their meaning clear without explication, setting what sounds like common sense into a philosophical frame, lightly worn.

His sentences are long and straightforward, with a clear subject and verb, nothing inserted between them. He rarely uses contractions, and repeats "we" and "our" and "us" to personalize his applications.

Brooks unifies his argument by repetition. He chains ideas together by repeating and varying a word in one clause in the next:

---

15 David Brooks: *The Social Animal: the Hidden Sources of Love, Character, and Achievement.* (New York: Random House, 2011). xi-xii.

"If the conscious mind is like a general atop a platform, who sees the world from a distance and analyzes things linearly and linguistically, the unconscious mind is like a ..."

He begins related clauses with the same structure:

"The scouts career ..."

"These scouts coat ..."

"... the scouts crystallize ..."

Brooks always injects a wistful note. He has high hopes for the human race, but is skeptical about whether we actually direct our own lives. The clarity of this voice creates authority and power and understanding.

JOAN DIDION

Joan Didion has an influential voice, as in this selection from "Goodbye to All That":

> I am not sure that it is possible for anyone brought up in the East to appreciate entirely what New York, the idea of New York, means to those of us who came out of the West and the South. To an Eastern child, particularly a child who has always had an uncle on Wall Street and who has spent several hundred Saturdays first at F.A.O. Schwarz and being fitted for shoes at Best's and then waiting under the Biltmore clock and dancing to Lester Lanin, New York is just a city, albeit the city, a plausible place for people to live. But to those of us who came from places where no one had heard of Lester Lanin and Grand Central Station was a Saturday radio program, where Wall Street and Fifth Avenue and Madison Avenue were not places at all but abstractions ("Money," and "High Fashion," and "The Hucksters"), New York was no mere city. It was instead an infinitely romantic notion, the mysterious nexus of all love and money and power, the shining and perishable dream itself. To think of "living" there was to reduce the miraculous to the mundane; one does not "live" at Xanadu.[16]

16 http://www.mtholyoke.edu/~zkurmus/html/didion.html.

I would characterize the *persona* speaking here as sophisticated, world weary, sardonic and edgy, intense, knowing, and sad. What devices create this voice?

Her sentences are long and complex, even the short ones. She creates rolling rhythms, mostly with simple words and lengthy clauses, with lots of things inserted into them. She does not use contractions, which lifts the formality slightly. She repeats parallel phrases. Some of her sentences have extended, introductory, dependent clauses. She builds toward powerful images at the ends of sentences: "the shining and perishable dream itself," "one does not 'live' at Xanadu." She uses specific lists of stores and places to build up a sense of plenitude pointing toward abstractions. Readers have a sense that she's thinking in front of them, in her back-and-forth clauses and phrases, all tightly controlled by precise sentences.

WILLIAM FAULKNER

William Faulkner was famous for long, complex sentences, some over a page long. You can't imitate his voice without parody, but you can analyze it for devices. This passage begins his 1950 Nobel Prize acceptance speech:

> I feel that this award was not made to me as a man, but to my work—a life's work in the agony and sweat of the human spirit, not for glory and least of all for profit, but to create out of the materials of the human spirit something which did not exist before. So this award is only mine in trust. It will not be difficult to find a dedication for the money part of it commensurate with the purpose and significance of its origin. But I would like to do the same with the acclaim too, by using this moment as a pinnacle from which I might be listened to by the young men and women already dedicated to the same anguish and travail, among whom is already that one who will some day stand here where I am standing.[17]

Forget what you know about how Faulkner looked (tiny, elegant) and spoke (deeply Southern), as you ask what kind of personality speaks

---

17 http://nobelprize.org/nobel_prizes/literature/laureates/1949/faulkner-speech.html.

from this paragraph. I would call it tricky and witty, alternately simple and complex, idealistic, humble and aloof, and deeply authoritative. What devices create this *persona*?

First, he uses no qualifiers, but speaks with the absolute assurance of a person who knows who he is and what he is talking about, not that hard to do if you've just won the Nobel Prize. His sentences are either long and simple, or short and simple. The flanking sentences ("I feel ..." and "But I would like ..."), each fifty-six words long, open to the right after the subject and verb, and put new things end to end, not inside something else. He uses fairly simple diction, with only a few longer words: "commensurate," "significance," "pinnacle." He includes slang, "the money part," and some archaic terms: "anguish," "travail," "agony," "acclaim." He mixes ordinary imagery, such as "sweat," with abstractions: "human spirit" and "glory." And he repeats words and phrases and images.

Finally, he's very down to earth about how to win the Nobel Prize: It takes work and suffering and determination. As he achieved this honor, all his novels were out of print.

CREATING ANOTHER VOICE

I keep reinventing myself. My voice is the illusion that my text speaks, and my readers assign it a personality. So when I become a new person, I need a new *persona*, a new voice. My three voices, in my life, so far are professor, writing teacher, and blogger.

My first *persona* had an academic voice, suitable for a brand-new assistant professor of English, a former navy lieutenant, who signed himself "Donald K. Fry." I wanted to write with striking power and clarity, so I turned Strunk and White's *Elements of Style* into a voice. I used all their devices of clarity and avoided anything that sounded conversational, such as the verb "to be." My academic colleagues criticized that first voice as too clear. One sniped, "You don't sound like a professor; people can understand you."

I created a friendlier, less academic voice in 1984, when I changed professions to teaching journalism and renamed myself "Don Fry." I still valued clarity and power, but I also wanted to engage my audiences, to impel them to act on what I wrote about. This new voice kept the formality of Strunk and White, but admitted some conversational devices, such as an occasional "to be" and contractions. I used the second person singular *you* to draw readers into action. My second voice worked. One editor observed, "You could cut yourself on Don Fry's prose." I think that was a compliment.

You're reading my third voice now, drafted by a character named "donfry," who writes a blog. I realized that my first voice sounded like a book because I thought of myself as a book writer. My second voice sounded like someone standing up because that's what I did; I stood up and talked *at* people. My third voice speaks in our brave new world of electronic exchanges, where readers and writers keep switching roles, talking *with* each other, not *at* each other. In my earlier voices, I might have called it "multidirectional." Now I call it fun.

What makes this new, third voice sound the way it does? It still uses all the devices of clarity and power, as well as chatty contractions and sprinkles of the verb "to be." Strunk commanded, "Omit needless words," but now I leave some in. I ended that last sentence with a preposition, perfectly good grammar but informal. I'm also writing about myself, which I rarely did before. As I wrote this chapter, I realized that this third voice allows me to escape my later teachers, Strunk and White, especially "Sergeant Strunk."

I find myself analyzing the prose of respondents to my new style. Whoa, that sentence is in my second voice, not my third. I'll try it again: "I'm watching how friends talk back to my blog." Better.

Most of my writer friends seem to have blogging down pat, writing like bar talk. I'm still experimenting with this new voice and virtual self in front of you, in this book.

CREATING YOUR OWN VOICE

And now I'll show you how to create and recreate your own new voice, as I continue to create mine. There are three ways to build a voice of your own: just let it happen, imitate other writers, and design it from devices.

Most writers create a voice unconsciously. You just write over a period of years, paying no attention to the kind of thinking about *persona* and devices discussed above. Eventually you get a sense of what sounds right to you, how to sound like yourself. You may unconsciously modify that evolved voice by adopting new techniques you learn and like.

This passive method works by default, and it has two drawbacks. Such writers lack the vocabulary and awareness of devices that allows them to discuss their voice with others. They can't describe their voice technically, and find it hard to change. It's difficult to think about something if you don't have the vocabulary for it. Perhaps they object to an editor changing their voice in a piece but aren't equipped to say, "I never begin sentences with dependent clauses." They end up saying, "It doesn't sound right to me." Neither the editor nor the writer knows why. By the end of this section, you'll know why.

Second, you can create your voice by imitation. My son, Jason, started writing seriously at the age of eleven in 1980, the year we bought our first computer, an IBM PC Model 1. With no help from me, he set out to develop his own voice by imitating writers he admired, one per year. The first year, unfortunately for his parents, he imitated the Conan the Barbarian series, all preposterous weapons and overblown language and busty women warriors. But the next year, he took on Arthur C. Clarke. His parodies did sound like the authors he modeled himself on. Later, he settled into his own voice as a columnist and blogger.

So how do you imitate a voice? You choose a writer you want to sound like and read a lot of that person's work, especially on subjects close to what you're likely to write about. It helps to read it aloud. Then you try to imitate that writer's style. Actually, it works better if you parody it, overdo it rather than hit it exactly. Then you keep experimenting until you achieve the voice you want.

Voice is all about sound, and you can use a recorder to test your imitations. Write a piece, and read it into a machine. Then listen to it, paying attention to what sounds the way you want, and what does not, the familiar formula: What works, and what needs work? And then experiment some more. It takes a while.

One drawback: You need a good ear to imitate another writer. You might want to tune your ear by writing fictional dialogue first.

Finally, you can design your own voice from scratch as a collection of devices used consistently, which is the point of this chapter. I've shown you above examples of voices analyzed for personality, *persona*, and devices. Now I'll discuss those devices individually in terms of the effects they create.

Remember that no device creates voice by itself, and all devices interact within a context. For example, the level of diction is relative to the language normally expected in the publication or subject. Think about two magazines: *Foreign Affairs* versus *Seventeen*. All effects lie along a spectrum, from absent to overdone.

Devices That Create Voice

Levels of Diction
Readers perceive first the level of language in a piece: high, medium, or low. Medium would be the normal wording used in everyday speech by educated people, *i.e.*, conversational but moderately correct. You're reading medium-level diction now. You can change the level for different effects:

MIDDLE: You're reading medium-level diction now.

LOW: This's the way folks talk.

HIGH: Readers would experience the diction embodying this document as appropriate to the discourse community of educated, middle-class speech. (Okay, that's a parody.)

This first impression, largely based on diction level, helps readers estimate if they'll understand the piece. If the diction is wrong for the context, readers will grow suspicious of the voice. It "violates decorum." High diction in a low context sounds pompous, and low diction in a high setting sounds cute and condescending.

Breadth of vocabulary also registers here. Most people use the same thousand or so words in their daily speech, and recognize a few thousand more. Using words beyond that range will make the voice seem elevated, sophisticated, and even stuffy. Using "street language" would imply youth, hipness, and lack of seriousness.

Readers don't say to themselves, "Oh, I see this is written in medium-level diction, which fits my education, so I'll understand this." Most of these reader perceptions are unconscious.

Unusual Language: Slang, Dialect, Archaic

SLANG makes prose sound conversational, and lots of hip slang makes it sound young. Slang can shade over into jargon, as any adult can tell you after listening to teenagers discussing the gadgets under their thumbs. Extreme use of professional slang and jargon creates distance between the *persona* and readers. Your doctor says, "You've got a bump on your leg," or "You have an induration on your lower extremity."

DIALECT always creates such a gap, since it is perceived (unfairly) as a mark of someone who does not or cannot speak Standard English. Even a charming dialect, such as an Irish brogue, may elicit snobbery. If you must use dialect, use very little, except for comic purposes. Remember the previous McCourt passage had only three words of dialect in it.

ARCHAIC language has the same effect as a wide and unusual vocabulary, and can lapse into quaintness. Even used in quotations, it makes the voice sound older and odder. Think about words like "wraith," "vainglory," and "happenstance." Take a look at any page in Tolkien's *Lord of the Rings* trilogy.

Formality of Grammar and Usage

Readers don't have to know much, if anything, about grammar or usage to notice formality. Distinctions such as *that* versus *which* or *who* versus *whom* raise the level of formality. Stricter, more formal grammar and usage create a sense of distance and sophistication, which can be welcoming or forbidding, depending on context. You would use *disinterested* formally in *Harper's* and informally (or not at all) in *Parade Magazine*. If you write formally and then use a colloquial verb like *ain't* for effect, it leaps off the screen or page.

Punctuation

Skilled punctuation makes sentences easy to read, and lack of punctuation makes your readers struggle. Easy sentences create authority and trust, and a sense of friendliness. Hard sentences can give a sense of sophistication, unless they become impenetrable. Hard sentences increase distance between *persona* and reader, except in academic writing, where such sentences imply deep thought.

Sentence Clarity

I've discussed sentence clarity at length above, noting that it mostly flows from simplicity: short or no left branch, subject and verb together, open to the right, and nothing inserted inside anything else.

Readers don't share that template, but they experience the simplicity or complexity of sentences. Simple sentences seem conversational. Oddly enough, even long simple sentences can sound like conversation. Complex sentences, regardless of length, prove daunting. They create distance, and suggest learning and sophistication. In extreme form, we associate complex sentences with intelligence. It takes more brainpower to write simply. An editor once advised me, "Easy reading takes hard editing." Nathaniel Hawthorne said, "Easy reading is damn hard writing."

Sentence Length and Varied Length

Readers can see sentence length. A lot of long sentences make the page gray. Big gray pages make most readers want to read something else.

Long sentences make the voice seem tedious, no matter what the complexity. A mixture of sentence lengths creates variety of sound and experience, and moves readers along. A series of sentences about the same length sounds monotonous. But even a negative quality like monotony can be part of voice; remember Hemingway.

Dependent Clauses at the Beginning of Sentences

Such clauses delay the subject and dim the clarity of the sentence. Longer and more complex ones delay it even longer, causing frustration for readers. Lowered clarity lowers authority. I avoid beginning sentences with dependent clauses, not only because I'm a clarity freak, but also because it's part of my voice. Some of these devices help create a *persona* by *not* doing something, such as avoiding contractions.

Insertions

Insertions put one unit (such as this parenthetical aside) inside another unit. They give a sense of a person thinking, unless there are so many that they become confusing, in which case, they make the voice seem wishy-washy. It's a balancing act, like everything else in writing. Insertions, especially those between subject and verb, the two anchors of the sentence, sometimes with insertions inside other insertions, and even going on for half a page, drive readers crazy the way this sentence just drove you crazy. See?

Repetition: Words, Phrases, Imagery

Repetition creates meaning by tying things together. Used clumsily, it links things you didn't intend, and becomes confusing and tedious. The French novelist Stendhal avoided repeating the same word on a page, depriving himself of a powerful device.

Repeating key words and phrases makes them prominent in the readers' memories, unless you repeat them too much, in which case readers notice the repetitions, and they make the voice boring. Repetition puts things in parallel, and invites readers to compare them without saying so.

Repeating meaningful images can spark readers' memory in new contexts. Frank McCourt is the master of this technique, constantly reminding readers of his miserable childhood, Ireland's tragic history, his clotty eyes.

Parallel Structures

Parallels are repetition in form. A series of clauses or sentences with the same shape creates a compelling rhythm, a sense of unity, and authority, unless overdone. Remember Martin Luther King Jr.'s "I have a dream" speech, and especially Winston Churchill's great rallying speech of 4 June 1940:

> We shall go on to the end, we shall fight in France,
> we shall fight on the seas and oceans,
> we shall fight with growing confidence and growing strength in the air,
> we shall defend our Island, whatever the cost may be,
> we shall fight on the beaches,
> we shall fight on the landing grounds,
> we shall fight in the fields and in the streets,
> we shall fight in the hills;
> we shall never surrender.[18]

Variation increases the power of parallels, as you can see in the slight changes in form after each "we shall ..." Parallels have the same compelling quality as chant.

Active, Passive, and Linking Verbs

Active verbs create a sense of power, mostly by being graphic and specific. Passive verbs dilute the voice, and linking verbs ("to be") weaken it. On the other hand, informal American speech uses lots of linking verbs. Using them in prose creates a conversational sound. The active voice used exclusively will sound powerful but formal.

Contractions

Contractions combine two words: *isn't* instead of *is not*. They make prose sound conversational, and the more contractions, the more it sounds like speech, unless the readers notice them. A total avoidance of contractions raises the level of formality.

---

18 http://www.presentationmagazine.com/winston_churchill_speech_fight_them_on_beaches.htm.

Economy of Wording

Again I bring up Strunk's Rule Seventeen: "Omit needless words." Wordy sentences sound more conversational because everyday speech isn't tight or edited. But if you trim sentences skillfully, they flow better, becoming conversational and friendly. On the other hand, extremely tight sentences come off as formal, distancing, and even huffy, like this: "Omit needless words."

I once ended a blog post inviting readers to comment: "Done any experiments with creating a voice?" The following examples add and subtract words to show different effects:

> Have you done any experiments with creating a voice?
>
> What's been your experience trying to create a voice?
>
> Have you tried experiments with your voice?
>
> Ever experiment with voice?

I wouldn't call any of those words "needless," although I could (and would) cut some of them in all three of my voices. I might leave some of them alone if I were trying to sound chummy.

Rhythm and Flow

Rhythms can range from jerky to, as we said of Jefferson, *mellifluous*, which means 'honeyed and flowing.' I'm talking about the sense of movement, how the sounds lead from one to another. Jerky rhythms make the voice seem disorganized, jittery, slightly out of control, even angry. Rolling rhythms create order and unity. Easy flow sounds poetic.

Abstract and Specific

Abstractions make the voice seem elevated, sophisticated, and learned. If you use too great a density of abstractions, the prose becomes remote and tedious. Specific words and images create authority by drawing readers in close. Readers experience an illusion of "being there," and a sense of the *persona* as someone who knows things in detail. For greatest power and authority, use a few abstractions to frame a lot of specifics.

Person and Tense

Journalists avoid the first-person singular *I* because they think it makes them sound un-objective. Overused, *I* sounds egotistical; lightly used, confessional and personal. The first-person plural *we* sounds inclusive. The second-person *you*, singular and plural, addresses readers directly (as I just did), and engages them, unless you use it too often or in a commanding way. Third-person is the norm of prose, with a slight distancing effect.

Most writing involves the past tense, again a comfortable norm. Shifting into the present tense creates a sense of immediacy and presence, but staying in the present becomes mannered and tiresome. Writing in the future tense is difficult to sustain but can be powerful, as in the Churchill masterpiece: "We shall never surrender."

Confidence and Assurance

Speaking of Churchill, a confident tone creates authority because the speaker is sure of what she's saying and also speaks with clarity. Have you ever noticed how scientists seldom sound confident? They're trying to sound scientific, and they put a lot of qualifiers in their sentences. They keep saying they're not sure, concepts are theoretical, the evidence is not totally solid, there might be infinite alternative universes instead of just seventeen, etc. Natalie Angier explains, "By accepting that they can never *know* the truth but can only approximate it, scientists end up edging ever closer to the truth."[19] But that hedging makes them sound uncertain. You can adjust assurance by the number of qualifiers you include, especially early in a piece. Here's a wishy-washy example:

> The Prostate-Specific Antigen test, the subject of increasing controversy, measures, with varying degrees of accuracy, the level of PSA in male blood samples as an indicator, subject to interpretation and laboratory error, of the likelihood of prostate cancer, although infection can warp the results.

---

19 Angier, *Canon.* 38.

Sophistication of Reference and Explanation

References to works outside the text create a sense of breadth and depth. A *persona* explaining the reference will come off as helpful, unless the explanation seems condescending. Nineteenth-century British authors often began explanations with "As every schoolboy knows, ..." Unexplained references imply sophistication and either learning or hipness, depending on the context.

Natalie Angier says, "Obviously my sense of scale has been out of whack and off the map, a puerile version of Saul Steinberg's often imitated Manhattanite's view of the world."[20] She alludes to the iconic magazine cover that hangs as a poster in millions of rooms. Angier assumes you know it, although she hasn't described or explained it. Density of references and their explanation or lack of one can create a relationship with your readers. You can share what you both know, you can bring in new information, or you can puzzle them with things they've never heard of.

Areas of Reference

The references you choose help characterize your *persona*. My friend Bill Blundell only used masculine references; he once said to me, "I went to Houston, and talked to the *guy* in charge there, and *she* told me ..." I apologize that we're now in the realm of stereotypes, but stereotypes shared with readers help create voice. Lots of sports or military references imply maleness, while domestic imagery suggests the female. And so on.

Name-Dropping

Personal names form a large part of reference and can create the illusion that the *persona* actually mixes with the people mentioned. Lots of current names suggest a *persona* who's an insider, and the familiarity of the reference can increase it. Machiavelli would put on his best clothes to read in his study, "and in this graver dress ... enter

---

20 Angier, *Canon*, 72.

the antique courts of the ancients and am welcomed by them."[21] He pictured himself hobnobbing with Cicero and Virgil. My son Jason drops names of singing groups I don't get, and I weave in medieval names he doesn't recognize. Even how you frame names has an effect: "First Lady Michelle Obama" versus "Michelle."

Echoes, Especially Standard Works

Many authors consciously or unconsciously imitate the rhythms, language, and imagery of recognizable texts, especially Shakespeare and the Bible. Melville often sounds like the King James version. (In view of our discussion above of references, notice that I did not spell out *Herman* Melville or the King James version of *what*.) Such echoes give depth and a sense of sophistication.

Imagery

Imagery functions somewhat like references. Certain images and groupings of images become a signature in voice. Roy Clark falls into image clusters of sex and religion and sports, and I tend toward military and aviation metaphors.

Wit and Humor

Humor is funny, while wit is amusing. Humor (or the lack of it) helps establish voice. The sophistication of the humor determines its effect, whether it elevates or deflates prose. Warning: Don't make humor part of your voice unless you're a funny person. I'm not.

Point of View

Point of view is the spot from which the *persona* views the world, mostly determined by references and names. Columnist George Will always speaks from the inside, Woody Allen, from the outside. Point of view can also seem spatial. Some voices see everything from high altitude;

---

21 "Letter to Francesco Vettori," *The Literary Works of Machiavelli*, trans. J.R. Hale. (Oxford: Oxford UP, 1961). 139D.

others, up close. Again it's the abstract versus specific. At a larger level, voices can have a worldview, essentially a stance toward nature and the human race. The higher the worldview, the more remote the voice.

Zest

Some voices show enthusiasm for their subject, and for life in general, and some show the opposite. Cleveland Amory, despite being nutso about cats, was grumpy about almost everything else. Zest engages the reader and suggests youth.

LET'S CREATE A VOICE

First, you describe the personality you want, and then you select the devices to create that *persona*. Your goal for this exercise is to create a breezy travel writer for *Southern Highways*. This *persona* should be clear, conversational but a little formal, witty, and irreverent and should speak to readers as an equal. The devices you need to use include clear, simple sentences of varied length; light explanation and clear references; slightly loose grammar with medium-level diction, slang, and contractions; occasional second-person address; a sprinkle of wry phrasing; and lots of punctuation. Here's a first try:

> The University of Virginia is restoring a national treasure, the Lawn, a World Heritage site, the Rotunda and ten faculty mansions, called "Pavilions." Any American child would recognize Jefferson's signature style: always red brick with white columns and trim. But recent archaeological research suggests that the columns of Pavilion X should be left tan, the natural color of their stucco, and the woodwork repainted the original taupe. I'd sooner colorize the Parthenon.

Not bad, but diction and reference have to come down a little. The sentences sound more like writing than conversation. Here's my second try:

> The University of Virginia in Charlottesville might mess up a national treasure, "The Lawn." It's a World Heritage site, the famous Rotunda and ten "pavilions," or houses where professors live. You'd recognize Jefferson's style: white columns and trim, with red brick. But researchers

studying Pavilion Ten's colors say the columns were originally tan, and the trim was painted taupe. Who could envision that?

Close, but stiff. I'll lighten up the sentences a little more:

> The University of Virginia's messing with a national treasure, "The Lawn." As a school kid, you probably visited the famous Rotunda with its ten "pavilions," or professors' houses. Everybody knows Thomas Jefferson's look: red brick walls with white columns and trim. But now, it turns out that Pavilion Ten had *tan* columns, and the wood was painted *taupe*. Taupe?

And there's your breezy but clear travel-writer voice. I could play with it some more, record it and listen to the results, and keep experimenting until I got it just right.

And that's how voice works. Now you can create your own.

DON FRY, an independent writing coach, works with newspapers and magazines, radio and television stations, and non-profit organizations. He helps writers write better, editors edit better, and managers organize better. He has taught over 10,000 writers to write better and faster without agony.

CHAPTER 8

A VOICE OF YOUR OWN

BY PAULA MUNIER

Your writing voice is the deepest possible reflection of who you are. The job of your voice is not to seduce or flatter or make well-shaped sentences. In your voice, your readers should be able to hear the contents of your mind, your heart, your soul.

—MEG ROSOFF

Voice is who you are as a storyteller: your language, your syntax, and your diction for sure, but, more important, your truth. Finding your voice is as simple—and as difficult—as finding your truth.

Readers recognize that truth when they see it—and they seek it out. Readers, agents, and editors and reviewers among them, are suckers for a strong voice. When readers fall in love with a writer's voice, they will follow it, line after line, page after page, and book after book.

As a reader, I prefer writers with a strong voice; as a writer, I look for voice lessons from writers known for their voices. And as an agent, I search for writers with a distinct voice—because I know that voice alone can sell a story.

Discovering your voice—your true north—may be what makes readers fall in love with you, too. Think of *The Catcher in the Rye* by J.D. Salinger. Millions of readers fell in love with Salinger's voice when they read his classic novel of adolescent male angst, not just because his voice was funny and compelling but because it rang true. (I should note that when I first read the book when I was a young girl, I never finished it. It didn't ring true for me at all. Twenty-five years later, my teenage son had to read the novel for school, which meant that I had to read it again to help him with his book report. This time I read the story all the way through with great pleasure. The voice rang true for me and engaged me thoroughly, because as the mother of an adolescent male, I could finally see the truth in it.)

Tell a story in your own strong and authentic voice, and you may win readers based on the voice alone. Tell a *great* story in your own strong and authentic voice, and you may win the kind of readership these writers have:

> My father's family name being Pirrip, and my Christian name Philip, my infant tongue could make of both names nothing longer or more explicit than Pip. So, I called myself Pip, and came to be called Pip.
>
> —Charles Dickens, *Great Expectations*

> 124 was spiteful. Full of a baby's venom. The women in the house knew it and so did the children.
>
> —Toni Morrison, *Beloved*

> The terror, which would not end for another twenty-eight years—if it ever did—began, so far as I know or can tell, with a boat made from a sheet of newspaper floating down the gutter swollen with rain.
>
> —Stephen King, *It*

> It is a truth universally acknowledged, that a single man in possession of a good fortune, must be in want of a wife.
>
> However little known the feelings or views of such a man may be on his first entering the neighbourhood, this truth is so well fixed in the minds of the surrounding families, that he is considered as the rightful property of some one or other of their daughters.
>
> —Jane Austen, *Pride and Prejudice*

> The night Max wore his wolf suit and made mischief of one kind and another his mother called him "WILD THING!" and Max said "I'LL EAT YOU UP!" so he was sent to bed without eating anything.
>
> —Maurice Sendak, *Where the Wild Things Are*

These are all writers with strong, unique voices that continue to engage, entertain, and enlighten readers over the test of time. Each tells the truth of life as the writer knows it:

- Dickens crusades for a better life for the underprivileged in Victorian England—and his truth emboldens change.
- Morrison shines a bright light on the realities of racism, identity, and community in a voice that is part herald, part destroyer, and part shaman.
- King brings the truth of our very nightmares to light in a voice all the more terrifying for its commonness.
- Austen tells the truth about men and women in a time when women were often defined by their relationships with men, like it or not.
- Sendak reveals the truth about the mysteries and miseries of childhood in a voice as mischievous and magical as children themselves.

Achieving that voice—the authentic expression of your unique truth that you use to engage, entertain, and enlighten your own readers—is one of the biggest challenges you face as a writer. Some writers do it naturally, but most of us have to dig for it. It's a discovery process that will not only inform your writing, but your life as well.

Note: This chapter is full of invitations to write. Accept those invitations, even when you are tempted to skip them.

A QUESTION OF CRAFT

Imagine your mother's voice. Often this is the first voice you know, the one you learn to recognize in the womb, the voice that most affects you, for better or worse, once you enter the world. Now imagine you've had a bad day. Your spouse left you; your boss fired you; your dog died. You tell your mother. What would your mother say to you? How would she say it? Write it down, or record it on your phone. Now read it aloud or play it back on your phone. What language, syntax, diction, and tone characterize that well-known voice?

Now imagine the same scenario—only you're the mother talking to your adult child after a bad day. What would you say? How would you say

---

Writing Voice

it? Write it down, or record it on your phone. Now read it aloud or play it back. What language, syntax, diction, and tone characterize your voice? How much—if any—of your mother's voice colors yours?

Note: If you're thinking, *This is the dumbest thing I've ever heard,* then you either (1) might need this chapter more than you think and/or (2) don't much like your mother.

CREATIVE IMITATION

Originality is nothing but judicious imitation. The most original writers borrowed from one another. The instruction we find in books is like fire. We fetch it from our neighbors, kindle it at home, communicate it to others, and it becomes the property of all.

—VOLTAIRE

When we first start to write, many of us imitate those writers whose work we most admire and/or have read most widely. This is fine; such imitation can be instructive in more ways than one. Not only can you learn the ins and outs of writing in a given authorial style, you can learn what to co-opt in developing your own voice.

I admire Alice Hoffman. I own first editions of all her work, attend her readings whenever I can, and have half a novel written in an unabashedly faux Alice Hoffman voice. And while that novel is not great, attempting to write it helped me expand the horizons of my own voice and taught me how to tell stories in a more meaningful way and to take risks that I would not normally have taken.

Ask yourself which writers you most admire, whose voices you are most apt to adopt, other than your own, when writing. Now ask yourself what appeals to you about their writing and what you can incorporate into your own work.

Early in her career, best-selling thriller writer Hank Phillippi Ryan was advised to consider the question "Who do you want to be?" That is, whose career did she want to emulate? This question can be related to voice as well. The trick is to discover which aspects are organic to your own work and which are not. Which are yours to steal—and which are not?

Writer, Know Thyself

Knowing yourself—and accepting your strengths and weaknesses, possibilities and limitations—is critical to identifying and developing a distinctive voice. Describe yourself, on a separate sheet of paper, in the first ten words that come to mind.

Now, contact your best friend, and have her or him describe you in ten words. Which words are the same? Which are different? Make a master list that combines both lists, and then match up those qualities at random with your favorite writers, the ones you'd like to be when you grow up.

For example, my list might look like this:

funny	Alice Hoffman
gregarious	Jane Austen
bossy	Mark Nepo
optimistic	Robert B. Parker
yogic	Anne Lamott
klutzy	Elizabeth Berg

Consider your own list. What clues to your authentic voice can be found there?

Clues to Your Authentic Voice

Your true voice sounds like you, only better. If you're funny, it's funny; if you're passionate, it's passionate; if you're whimsical, it's whimsical.

But we all have two selves: (1) the public face, the one we show the world, and (2) the hidden face, the one we shelter from the world. Maybe your authentic voice reflects the seductress beneath a shy exterior, the mischievous child beneath the responsible adult, the outsider beneath the popular crowd-pleaser.

Walking Your Talk

Part of realizing your full voice and speaking your truth is marrying what you say to how you say it. Ask yourself: What do you really want to say—and how would you like to convey that message?

Your voice can dictate how you tell your story—from pacing and plot to tone and theme. Consider the following classic stories, all about war, and all with different and distinctive voices:

- *The Things They Carried* by Tim O'Brien
- *Catch-22* by Joseph Heller
- *The People of Forever Are Not Afraid* by Shani Boianjiu
- *Gone with the Wind* by Margaret Mitchell
- *A Game of Thrones* by George R.R. Martin
- *Suite Francaise* by Irene Nemirovsky
- *War and Peace* by Leo Tolstoy
- *Slaughterhouse-Five* by Kurt Vonnegut
- *Night* by Elie Wiesel
- *The Lotus Eaters* by Tatjana Soli
- *The Kite Runner* by Khaled Hosseini
- *The Diary of a Young Girl* by Anne Frank
- *M*A*S*H** by Robert Hooker
- *The Guernsey Literary and Potato Peel Pie Society* by Mary Ann Shaffer and Annie Barrows
- *Henry VI* trilogy by William Shakespeare
- *A Long Way Gone* by Ishmael Beah

Each of these stories is shaped by the voice of the writer telling it. Choose one of the above stories; it can be one you've already read and loved or one that you haven't read before. As you read it, note how the writer's voice informs all the other elements of the story.

WRITE IT DOWN

This is a prompt that I've borrowed, with permission, from my friend, the wonderful writer Reed Farrel Coleman, best-selling, Edgar-nominated author of *Robert B. Parker's Blind Spot* (a Jesse Stone novel) and the

---

acclaimed Moe Prager series. Reed uses this exercise whenever he teaches a class on voice.

You'll need more than one writer for this; perhaps enlist the participation of your writers' group. Invite your fellow writers to a meeting at a specific time. Let everyone get settled; pass around the wine and cheese or other refreshments. Then, about ten minutes into your time together, ask everyone in the group to write about the first ten minutes of your meeting. Allow around fifteen minutes for this timed writing. Then ask everyone to read her piece aloud. Notice the different ways in which each writer describes the same material. Note the differences in approach, language, tone, syntax, and dramatization. This exercise reveals how voice colors every writer's piece—whether the writer is aware of it or not. Learning what distinguishes your voice among all these other voices can help you refine and strengthen it going forward.

No matter what your genre, your voice should shape the story you tell. You need to reveal your truth, as best told in your own authentic voice.

If you're not sure what your truth is—or even if you think you do—you may need to dig to get to its core. Your truth is where your vein of gold lies; you need to mine it. Here's a brainstorming exercise to help you do just that. Using the following bubble chart, jot down entries for each list on a separate sheet of paper. Do this quickly—don't think about it. When you're finished, think about what comes up in this process. Which bubbles resonate with you? Which stories do you want to tell? How could they best be told in your own voice?

When a writer is telling a story to best effect, his voice rings with confidence, conviction, and creativity. Consider Salinger, whose exploration of adolescence, honesty, authenticity, and the pretense and hypocrisy of adult life are all reflected in his one-of-a-kind voice, whether he's writing about Holden Caulfield or Frannie and Zooey.

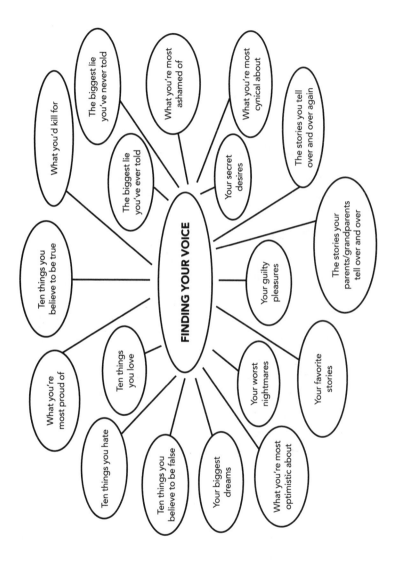

HONESTY RULES

As an agent, I get very excited when I find a writer with a great voice because I know that it's easier for a writer to learn structure than to discover her truth. I often meet talented writers who have yet to sell their stories because they have yet to find their voice—or they are fighting the truth about their voice.

Part of my job is helping my clients recognize their authentic voice and tailor it to the best commercial project for them. Let me tell you four stories about four very different clients—and how they developed a distinctive voice, used that voice to tell great stories, and got published in the process. Each story offers a different voice lesson for the perceptive writer.

Reveal Yourself: A Cop's Story

When I first became an agent, I was overwhelmed by queries; my first week on the job I got more than one thousand queries from writers I didn't know, and the numbers have grown exponentially ever since. I needed an intern. (As it turns out, I always need an intern.)

I got a call from a professor friend of mine who also writes popular traditional mysteries for St. Martin's Press. She had an MFA student who was looking for an internship. She warned me that this was not your typical grad student but rather a middle-aged writer who'd spent thirty years as a homicide detective for the Oakland Police Department. I was thrilled because (1) I represented a lot of crime fiction writers who would benefit from a cop's perspective on their work, and (2) I'm a sucker for a good police procedural.

His name was Brian, and he rocked. He read my queries, he edited my clients' work, and he finished his thesis, which just so happened to be a police procedural. I liked it and offered to represent him and his work. But first he had to refine his voice.

For Brian's voice was his selling point, the leverage I needed to pitch his work when I shopped it. Cops who can write are few and far between, so when I find one, I sign him—or her—right up. But voice is a two-edged sword: Brian's experience on the force informed every word he wrote and gave his prose a confidence and authority born of that experience. All good. But not enough. What was missing in his story was how he felt about that experience. Readers would love his cop hero—but they would love him more if they got to know more about his heart—and not just his head.

This wasn't easy for Brian, who, like most cops, kept his feelings close to his bulletproof vest. I knew he thought I was making a big deal out of nothing. But he did what I asked (another reason I like working with former law-enforcement and military personnel, as they actually listen to me and follow my advice). He beefed up his protagonist's inner life, and I shopped the series. Within short order, I got Brian a three-book deal. (Look for the Matt Sinclair series, by Brian Thiem, wherever you buy your books.)

The only real significant revision request from his editor: Beef up the inner life of his hero even *more*. (I love being right. And I love Brian.)

VOICE LESSON #1: Readers respond most to emotional honesty in a writer's voice. Don't be afraid to reveal yourself.

Remember Who You Are: A Novelist's Story

I've known Meera for many years; we met decades ago when we were both beginning writers in San Jose. We hung out at writers conferences and participated in writers workshops and read our work aloud to each other in writers' groups. Meera was one of the most interesting people I knew; originally a farm girl from Missouri, she'd traveled the world in search of enlightenment. When I became an acquisitions editor for a mind/body/spirit imprint, I sought out Meera to write books for the new line—and she made a career for herself as the author of nonfiction titles, wonderful how-to books on the secrets of living an authentic life.

She wrote fiction, too—fabulous stories starring the exotic people and places she'd met on her travels. While technically proficient, these stories fell flat on the page. Meera was imitating the voices of other cultures, other customs, other writers—and drowning out her own voice in the process. In the meantime, she moved to the country and settled on a little farm she called the Henny Penny Farmette in Northern California. She started blogging about her chickens, bees, and goats.

Her blog was a big hit—and the ammunition I needed to convince her to write a novel set on the Henny Penny Farmette. She'd found her fictive voice right there on the farm. (Of course, she'd never lost it; she used it when writing nonfiction. But her love of other cultures and faraway lands blinded her to it in her own storytelling.) She wrote the first in a traditional mystery series set on the farmette—and I got her a three-book deal. (Look for the Henny Penny Farmette mystery series by Meera Lester wherever you buy your books.)

VOICE LESSON #2: If you're having trouble finding your voice, start close to home. The truth is often right under your nose.

Listen to the Sound of Your Own Voice: The Historian's Story

When I first moved to Massachusetts, I had no writer friends, and even though I was working at a publishing house with book people, I missed hanging out with writers. (Editors are not the same as writers, though

I love editors—especially editors who are *also* writers.) So I joined the online chapter of Mystery Writers of America and started interacting with the other members online.

There I bonded with fellow Rainer Maria Rilke–fan Brian Thornton, who was from the Northwest (and not the same Brian who writes police procedurals—my world is full of great writers named Brian). We became fast friends and met in person several times at writers conferences. Brian, a history teacher by day, even wrote a couple of great history-related nonfiction books for me while I was an acquisitions editor.

But what Brian really wanted to do was publish fiction. We exchanged some stories for critique. I read Brian's modern private-eye novel and one of his historical mystery stories. I told him that he should focus on historical fiction, as his historian's voice seemed better suited for it. Commercial historical fiction is not easy to write; only people who are passionate about it and can make it relevant to the modern reader succeed. The good news is that if you can write solid historical fiction, you can usually get published. So I wasn't at all surprised when Brian sold his first piece, a historical short story, to *Alfred Hitchcock's Mystery Magazine*. Now he's working on a historical mystery—and now I'm an agent—so here's hoping that he lets me shop it when he's ready. (Did I mention that I love being right?)

VOICE LESSON #3: Capitalize on your voice's strengths. Not only can this help refine your work, it can help you sell it.

Do Not Confuse Voice with Plot: The Artiste's Story

Sometimes I'm so bowled over by a writer's talent that I ignore the lack of market potential for the work and sign the writer anyway. That's what happened when I read Richard's writing for the first time. Richard's talent was obvious, and I wasn't the only one who thought so; he'd been celebrated for his brilliant short stories. But he'd yet to break into commercial fiction with his novels.

Richard's work was überdark—and überdark is not an easy sell. Even your *True Detective* stories have some (wan) light at the end of the dark tunnel of prose. I warned Richard about this, and he did some revision as requested, but he resisted my appeals to explore his not-so-darn-dark side. Eventually I caved—and I sent out the novel as it was to all the editors I knew who loved dark material. One by one they passed, saying it was just too dark, even for them. But if he wrote anything else, they'd love to see it.

I didn't give up. (I hate giving up.) I knew that we just needed to find an editor who'd fall in love with Richard's work the way I had. And I'm happy to say that we did; it took two years, but finally I got Richard a two-book deal with a Big Five house.

Unsurprisingly, the editor wanted a little (wan) light at the end of the dark tunnel of prose. Richard balked. The editor called me, and I called Richard. Richard was worried about "compromising his voice." But voice really had nothing to do with it. If he found an audience, he couldn't risk engaging them with his compelling voice only to lose them at the end of the story by refusing to make a slight shift in plot from a "so dark you can't see" ending to a "dark but not so dark you have to slit your wrists" ending. I explained to him that the first page sells the book and the last page sells the next book. He didn't have to change his voice; he just had to rethink the emotional impact of the ending on his reader. Leaving a bad taste in the reader's mouth—no matter how beautiful the voice—is not the way to build an audience. (Richard Thomas's novel *Disintegration* debuted to great reviews and endorsements by such literary lights as Chuck Palahniuk, Irvine Welsh, Chuck Wendig, Paul Tremblay, and more.)

VOICE LESSON #4: Voice is how you tell the story—it's not the story itself. Be sure that you don't compromise the emotional impact of your story to protect what you mistakenly believe is your voice.

Ultimately, the challenge is this: Figure out who you are and what you care about, and let your voice reveal both.

HANDS-ON

Create a mantra customized to enhance your voice. This mantra should address whatever issues are keeping you from expressing yourself freely:

- I allow the truth to speak through me.
- I sing my own song.
- I listen to my true self, and I hear the truth of others.
- I say what I need to say when I need to say it.
- I am free to tell my truth, as others are free to tell their truths.

Post this in your writing space to remind you that your voice deserves to be heard.

....

PAULA MUNIER is the senior literary agent and content strategist at Talcott Notch Literary Services. A well-published journalist, author, copywriter, and ghostwriter, Paula has penned countless news stories, articles, essays, collateral, and blogs. She also has authored/co-authored more than a dozen books, including *Plot Perfect*, *Writing With Quiet Hands*, and *The Writer's Guide to Beginnings*, all from Writer's Digest Books.

CHAPTER 9

SELF-EXPRESSION: YOUR PERSONAL STYLE

BY RICHARD CAMPBELL & CHERYL SVENSSON

"Be yourself. Everyone else is already taken."

—OSCAR WILDE

When we speak, we use different words and phrases for different conversations. We speak one way to our parents, another way to our children, and still another to our closest friends. But when we write, we must find our authentic voice and style that resonate with ourselves and with our readers.

This chapter will help you discover your true writing voice, one that rings true with your readers and is an honest reflection of you. Should your story be written in earnest, with a sincere tone? Can it be written playfully, with grace and humor? Let's discover your voice, the one that will distinguish your life story from a sea of other narratives.

TEN STEPS TO FINDING YOUR PERSONAL STYLE

1. **WRITE WHAT YOU KNOW.** When you write what you know, you write with authority. You are familiar with your chosen topic. Someone else isn't telling your story—you are doing it yourself. Imagine if you were to write the story of a person you did not know. Only by learning all about him or her would you be able to master the story. You would have found that person's voice. In the same

way, writing what you know will allow you to find comfort in your own skin. Who knows your life story better than you?

2. **WRITE TO YOUR READERS.** For whom are you writing? Yourself? Your children and grandchildren? Future generations? Write as you would talk to them. Otherwise you might sound like someone you are not. If you are aiming to publish your life story, it will become part of the public record, but you need not concern yourself at this point. Just get your story down.

3. **WRITE YOUR FEELINGS.** Expressing your feelings allows you to get to the heart of the story and prevents you from hiding behind clichés and a lexicon of words. You are writing from the essence of the experience, from the belly, if you will, rather than the head. What did that life experience feel like? Does it still bring tears to your eyes? Your readers will want to know that.

4. **WRITE WITH FREEDOM.** Let yourself go when you write. Simply write freely, openly, and without censure. There will always be time to edit later. In order to find your voice, don't try to mimic Steinbeck, Hemingway, or another great author you admire. Simply allow yourself to write—as you, with no strings attached.

5. **WRITE WITH HUMOR.** Even if we do not consider ourselves comedians, we all have a sense of humor. What is yours? Are you a joke teller? Then include jokes in your story. Are you a practical joker? Recount a funny story when the joke was turned on you.

6. **WRITE YOUR SENSES.** As described in the last chapter, we have five senses: sight, sound, taste, touch, and smell. We each favor some senses over the others; write from your dominant sense perspective. Are you a visual person? Then write how you see the world. Describe the colors and images that capture your attention.

7. **WRITE YOUR INNER SELF.** Who are you? Follow Polonius's advice to Hamlet: "To thine own self be true." Who is your true self? Jot down a few adjectives or phrases that describe you. When you write as your inner self, your words will flow.

8. **WRITE YOUR TRUTH.** Write your life as you lived it. This is not the time to worry about how your story may impact someone else. Now is the time to simply write what happened, as you perceive

it. Staying true to this will allow you to maintain a singular voice throughout—yours.

9. **WRITE YOUR STORIES**. Just as you reminisce and tell stories from your past, write them down. Your stories are the building bricks for your life story. Without our stories, who are we?

10. **WRITE OFTEN**. The more you write, the easier it will become and the better your writing will be. The old adage "practice makes perfect" is a proven fact. Write until it feels like the most natural thing in the world. The only possibility of failure is if you stop.

STAKING YOUR CLAIM

Another way to uncover your writing voice is to examine what you expect from your readers. What reactions are you looking for? Do you want your readers to like you, sympathize with you, show respect for you? Do you want your writing style to reflect one of these outcomes? Keep in mind that if you try too hard to "make someone like you," you may end up with a flat and uninteresting story. Your best work will come from your desire to let your story tell itself. Worrying about how you are perceived by your readers will result in barriers. There should be no agenda in your message.

In the life story classes we teach, a common question always comes up: "How do I write? I'm not a writer." In most cases the concern ends when students have written and read their first story to their classmates. They settle down with the supportive oohs and ahhs of admiration. What they may have forgotten is that they have written sentences and paragraphs countless times during their lifetime. A life story seems daunting because it spans so many years. Because legacy writing is broken down into thematic segments, the task suddenly becomes manageable. The bits and pieces add up to give you a cohesive whole.

Never forget that your voice has been shaped by your past. It has been honed by years of life experience, good and bad. Your tears, laughter, fears, and joys are all buried in the context of the life you have lived. Your voice is you. If you write consistently with honest intentions, your voice will reflect this. Each life story theme you write will stay true to the narrative path you've chosen. Be honest, be yourself, and it will happen.

EXERCISE: HOME IS WHERE I CAN BE ME

Writers may struggle for years trying to capture their illusive voice, the one voice that stands apart from every other. In a sense, they try to capture the essence of who they are and bring that to their writing. It can be a daunting task. There is no easy solution. It just takes practice.

One way to help identify your voice is through freewriting. This is a forgiving process that ignores all stylistic conventions. It lets you run free with your pen or keyboard. For this exercise, take a sheet of paper and set your timer for ten minutes. Look at the writing prompt below and let your imagination go. Write a page with your words and sentences. Ignore grammar. If you can't find the next word in your mind, rewrite your last one. Just keep going. Use the following prompt to get started.

"When I get up in the morning ..."

Read over what you have just written. Are there any surprises? Do you recognize the voice? That was you speaking. It can serve as your guide as you venture into the art of writing your life story.

RICHARD CAMPBELL obtained his M.Ed in 2002 and runs his own memoir writing business *Guided Life Stories* near Toronto, Canada. He has been interviewed by several Top 50 U.S. radio stations has written for *Writer's Digest*, as well as freelancing for Canadian newspapers and CBC Radio. He also does *Writing Your Life Story* enrichment lectures with a major cruise ship line during their transatlantic crossings.

DR. CHERYL SVENSSON has a Master's degree in Gerontology and a Ph.D. in Psychology. She worked closely with James E. Birren, renowned Psychologist and creator of Guided Autobiography, for nearly 20 years until his death in 2016. She has taught Guided Autobiography classes at universities, libraries, senior centers, and assisted living centers. Now as director for the Birren Center for Autobiographical Studies, she is teaching students around the world in a live, interactive online program to become Guided Autobiography instructors.

PART III

THE MECHANICS OF VOICE

CHAPTER 10

THE QUALITIES OF WORDS

BY BARBARA BAIG

She loved expressive words, and treasured them as some girls might have treasured jewels. To her, they were as lustrous pearls, threaded on the crimson cord of a vivid fancy. When she met with a new one she uttered it over and over to herself in solitude, weighing it, caressing it, infusing it with the radiance of her voice, making it her own in all its possibilities forever.

—LUCY MAUD MONTGOMERY, *THE STORY GIRL*

In a way, every word is like a precious stone, with its own particular qualities: Some words feel heavy, others light; some seem to glitter, others are dull. As writers, we need to know all we can about the words we use; in addition to getting familiar with a word's denotations and connotations—its meanings—we also need to be able to recognize its *qualities*, so we can find the right word for our purpose. Just as a cook needs to know, not just intellectually, but *practically,* the difference between, say, margarine and butter—the differences in taste and texture and melting temperature—so a writer needs to know the difference in quality between, for instance, the word *domicile* and the word *home,* the word *food* and the word *egg,* the word *surrender* and the phrase *wave the white flag.* When we add to our knowledge of denotation and connotation a practical understanding of the qualities of words, we can make even more skillful use of their power. Knowing the qualities of words gives us an essential tool for choosing the words we want to use.

What are some of these qualities of words?

THE QUALITIES OF WORDS: FORMAL/INFORMAL

If we are writing for ourselves alone, as in a journal, it doesn't matter which words we choose. But if we have an audience in mind for our writing, then we need to consider the degree of formality our words should have. To understand the quality of formality in writing, think about how we dress. Writing for an audience is a bit like dressing to go out in public: We have to consider whether the clothes we choose will be appropriate to the occasion. If we're going to a job at a conservative law firm, we'll probably have to put on some kind of reasonably formal clothes, like a suit. We wouldn't show up for work in ripped jeans and sneakers; such attire, though, would be perfectly appropriate for a more informal occasion, like a backyard barbecue after a neighborhood basketball game.

When we write, we often need to consider the degree of formality our words should have, depending on the circumstances in which they will be read. Formal language tends to be language that is rather stiff and mannered, like a butler in a novel about the English upper classes. Words that feel and sound formal are usually Latinate words, made up of several syllables: *tendentious, prepossessing, rubicund.* Informal words are typically of Anglo-Saxon origin (or Norman words that have been Anglicized) and usually contain only one or two syllables. (For an introduction to the history [etymology] of English words, with practices that will show you how a knowledge of word history can improve your writing, visit my website at: www.WhereWritersLearn.com.) Informal words are the ones that come to mind readily during ordinary conversation: *fat, meat, walk, grab, wink,* and so on. Informal language also includes slang expressions such as: *get a grip, what's happenin'?, he's chillin', let's rock.* You can check whether a particular word or phrase is formal or informal by looking it up in a good dictionary. The dictionary will tell you if the word is informal, or informal in some situations.

PRACTICE: FORMAL AND INFORMAL WORDS

Write down some words that you consider formal, then see if you can come up with their informal equivalents. Then try this exercise starting with informal words. Which quality—formal or informal—do you like better?

Formality, Tone, and Voice

The degree of formality in the language you use in your writing helps create your voice on the page, just as it does when you speak. It also creates what's called the *tone* of your work. This tone has to be appropriate, not to an occasion, but to the purpose of your writing.

Listen to the difference in the voices of these two novelists:

> Nell could not help smiling at the naiveté with which Letty classed these trivialities with her marriage, but before she could make any attempt to show her sister-in-law how the very fondness which led Cardross to indulge her in small matters would stiffen his resolve not to permit her (as he thought) to throw herself away in a marriage doomed to failure, Farley, her butler, had entered the room, bearing on a salver a sealed billet, and on his countenance the expression of one who not only brought evil tidings but had foreseen from the outset that this was precisely how it would be.
>
> —Georgette Heyer, *April Lady*

> But by the time they reached the morgue it was too late. The ID had been completed and everyone had gone home. Rebus stood on the Cowgate and looked longingly back toward the Grassmarket. Some of the pubs there would still be open, the Merchant's Bar, for one. But he got back into the car instead and asked Davidson to take him home. He felt tired all of a sudden. God, he felt tired.
>
> —Ian Rankin, *Let It Bleed*

The differences in the two voices come in part from the way each writer puts sentences together, but word choice is also key. Heyer, who is re-creating for her readers the world of upper-class Londoners in Regency

England, makes use of relatively formal words like *naiveté, trivialities, indulge, resolve, countenance.* Rankin, who is bringing to his reader's mind the world of an alcoholic police detective in contemporary Edinburgh, uses very ordinary words like *late* and *looked* and *tired.* In each case, the author has chosen words appropriate to his or her purpose—in this case, the creation of a particular fictional world and the people who inhabit that world.

The formality or informality of the words we choose also helps us create the voices of people, other than the author, on the page. If we have people talking in our writing, whether they are real people or invented characters, the words we provide them with will help make real their individual voices. For, just as our choice of clothing creates a particular style and helps other people recognize us, so do our spoken words show who we are. Skilled writers know this, and choose words for their characters that will make sense for those particular people and will help reveal what kind of people they are.

And so, Heyer's characters, London aristocrats of the early nineteenth century, talk like this:

> "Yes, I dashed well do call it that!" replied his lordship, his eye kindling. "Besides, it's all slum! I may have to listen to that sort of flummery from Mama, but I'll be damned if I will from you! What's more, it's coming it a trifle too strong!"

Rankin's detective, John Rebus, talks quite differently (and with considerably fewer words):

> "Flower's got a point though, sir," said Rebus, covering his boss's embarrassment. "It's just that he's got the tact of a tomcat. I mean, somebody'll have to fill in. How long's Frank going to be out of the game?"

PRACTICE: FORMAL AND INFORMAL WORDS

Imagine a person—someone you know or a character you invent. Imagine words this character might speak, paying attention to the formality or informality of her language. Then have her talk on the page. If you like, invent more than one character and let them have a conversation.

Writing Voice

What do you notice in doing this?

One of the things you may notice is that you don't have the words you need; your characters don't have their own individual voices: They all sound alike, or they all talk the way you do. Experienced writers spend time sitting in cafés or riding buses to listen to people talk. They often collect words and phrases, or even entire conversations, in their notebooks. If you want to build your word hoard for conversation, you can follow their example.

You can also study writers whose work you admire and pay attention to how their characters speak. Collect their vocabulary and practice using it yourself for your own characters. Eventually your characters will find their own individual voices.

CHAPTER 11

PREFER THE ACTIVE VOICE

BY STEPHEN WILBERS

Which is better: the active voice or the passive voice?

> **ACTIVE:** I let go of the Cessna's strut and prayed my chute would open.
> **PASSIVE:** The Cessna's strut was let go of and a prayer that my chute would open was said by me.

You may be thinking, as long as my chute opens, who cares?

Point taken, but in those examples the active voice, in which the subject of the sentence *performs* the action, is clearly better than the passive voice, in which the subject *receives* the action.

Which of these sentences is more direct, concise, and emphatic?

> **ACTIVE:** Over the holidays, I ate three dozen cookies and read five books.
> **PASSIVE:** Over the holidays, three dozen cookies were eaten by me and five books were read by me.

Again, the active voice makes the point more concisely. The passive voice, however, is sometimes better for emphasis, diplomacy, and flow.

1. **EMPHASIS.** Use the passive voice to emphasize the receiver of the action rather than the performer of the action.

> **ACTIVE:** I altered the wording to illustrate a point.
> **PASSIVE:** The wording was altered to illustrate a point.

The active voice is more emphatic. But if the emphasis was on the act of altering the wording and it didn't matter who did it, the passive voice would be better.

2. **DIPLOMACY.** Use the passive voice to avoid identifying the actor or the performer of the action and assigning blame.

> **ACTIVE:** You mismanaged my investments.
> **PASSIVE:** My investments were mismanaged.

Here the active voice sounds abrupt and accusatory. In contrast, the passive voice is diplomatic. When the actor (*by you*) is omitted, as it is here, the passive voice is called the "diplomatic" or "truncated passive." ("To truncate" is to shorten or to cut off.)

3. **FLOW.** Use the passive voice to facilitate coherence by linking the thought of one sentence to the next.

> **ACTIVE:** The wail of a loon awakened me. Anyone who has canoed the Boundary Waters wilderness of northern Minnesota has heard that haunting sound.
> **PASSIVE:** I was awakened by the wail of a loon. This haunting sound has been heard by anyone who has canoed the Boundary Waters wilderness of northern Minnesota.
> **OR** I was awakened by the wail of a loon, a haunting sound heard by anyone who has canoed the Boundary Waters wilderness of northern Minnesota.

Note the two references to the bird's sound: *wail of a loon* and *haunting sound*. In the active sentences, they come far apart, at the beginning of the first sentence and the end of the second. In the passive clauses, the references are juxtaposed for a more coherent sequence, at the end of the first sentence and at the beginning of the trailing element.

Compare the emphasis in these sentences.

> **ACTIVE:** Severe drought destroyed our crop.
> **PASSIVE:** Our crop was destroyed by severe drought.

If you want to emphasize the means by which the crop was destroyed, use the active voice. If you want to emphasize the fact that the crop was destroyed, use the passive voice.

Which of the following sentences is preferable?

> **ACTIVE:** I paddled the canoe across the lake.
> **PASSIVE:** The canoe was paddled by me across the lake.

The sentence in the active voice is better. Unless … you want to emphasize not the performer of the action (*I*) but the receiver of the action (*the canoe*).

Let's say that the canoe was paddled across the lake and the rowboat was towed across the lake. In that case, the passive voice—"The canoe was paddled across the lake"—would be preferable because it emphasizes not the actor but the thing acted upon and the mode in which it was conveyed across the lake.

In any case, your choice of active versus passive voice depends on where you want your emphasis: on the *performer* of the action (the active voice) or on the *receiver* of the action (the passive voice).

In addition to using the passive voice for these three purposes—to control your emphasis, to be diplomatic, and to string your sentences together more coherently—sometimes the passive voice simply sounds better than the active voice.

Consider these lyrics from "I Dreamed a Dream" from *Les Misérables*.

> I dreamed that love would never die.
> I dreamed that God would be forgiving.

After those two active sentences, note what happens.

> Then I was young and unafraid
> and dreams were made and used and wasted.
> There was no ransom to be paid,
> no song unsung, no wine untasted.

After "Then I was young and unafraid," the lyrics are written in the passive voice. One could argue the passive voice is used here not for nuanced, literary effect, but for the sake of creating the rhyme (after all, these *are* song lyrics). Whatever the reason, people the world over have fallen in love with the lyrics, as well as the melody of this song.

So prefer the active voice—unless you have a good reason to use the passive. And now you have three good reasons to do so: for emphasis, diplomacy, and flow.

EXERCISES

1. Which of the following sentences are in the active voice, and which are in the passive voice?

    a. God made the sky blue.

    b. The sky was made blue by God.

    c. The sky is blue.

Okay, I threw you a curve ball.

Sentence (a) is active. The subject performs the action. Sentence (b) is passive. The subject receives the action. Sentence (c) is neither active nor passive. It's intransitive. (I know, *intransitive* is a scary word, but you'll get used to it.)

Transitive verbs convey action and have objects. Intransitive verbs don't have objects. In sentence (c), the intransitive verb *is* links the subject *sky* to its complement *blue*, but no action is performed or received. No action, no object—no active or passive voice. Only transitive verbs can be active or passive.

Let's do another three sentences. Which is active, passive, or intransitive?

    a. My wife is loved by me.

    b. I love my wife.

    c. My nose runs in cold weather.

Sentence (a) is passive and sentence (b) is active. Both (a) and (b) have transitive verbs, which convey action and have objects (in this case, my wife and I). Sentence (c) is neither active nor passive. Although it conveys action, it has no object. Its verb is intransitive.

One more time: Transitive verbs have objects. Intransitive verbs don't. Transitive verbs may be either active or passive. Intransitive verbs can be neither active nor passive because they don't have objects.

The following sentences are intransitive.

> She is lonely.
>
> Her doggie Lyle seemed restless.
>
> Lyle ran away from home.

Because they have intransitive verbs, they are neither active nor passive.

One more set. Which is which? Active, passive, or intransitive?

a. Our daughter taught us how to waltz.

b. The box step was taught to us first.

c. Our favorite dance is the rhumba, the dance of love.

d. The rhumba is danced by people the world over.

The sentences are (a) active, (b) passive, (c) intransitive, and (d) passive.

I lied about there being only one more set of sentences. Here's another. For practice moving between the active and passive voice, change the passive to the active voice in these sentences.

a. The journey over the river and through the wood was made by us to Grandfather's house.

b. The way is known and the sleigh is carried by the horse through the white and drifted snow.

You know how Lydia Maria Child wrote the lyrics, but here they are anyway. (Don't let the inversion in the first sentence below fool you. Although technically the verb is intransitive, it's still active sounding.)

a. Over the river and through the wood to Grandfather's house we go.

b. The horse knows the way to carry the sleigh through the white and drifted snow.

2. Here are two versions of one of my favorite quotes. It's from the eighteenth-century neoclassical scholar Samuel Johnson. Which version do you think is his?

    a. **ACTIVE:** "If you write without effort, in general your audience will read without pleasure."

    b. **PASSIVE:** "What is written without effort is in general read without pleasure."

My vote—as was Johnson's—is for the passive.

3. Which sentence would you use in a courtroom if you were the prosecuting attorney?

    a. **PASSIVE:** A backpack was left on the sidewalk.

    b. **ACTIVE:** The Defendant left his backpack on the sidewalk near an eight-year-old boy.

The answer is obvious.

4. Which sentence would you prefer if you were the defending attorney?

    a. **ACTIVE:** The Defendant dropped his Glock 17 handgun at the scene of the crime.

    b. **PASSIVE:** A Glock 17 handgun belonging to the Defendant was found at the scene of the crime.

Again, (b).

A FURTHER THOUGHT

I just love the new generation of programmed grammar checkers.

Do you remember the days when grammar checkers could do little more than caution you against writing a one-sentence paragraph or using a contraction?

Well, the old days are gone. My MX4000 WritersCompanion offers not only helpful advice on grammar, usage, and punctuation but also psychological counseling and spiritual guidance.

Let me fire it up, and I'll give you a little demonstration of how it works.

"Good morning, Steve. How are we feeling today? Are we in the mood to write?"

I usually say yes to the latter question, but today I answer no.

After a thoughtful pause, my checker asks, "What seems to be the problem? Are we in touch with our inner being? Are we comfortable with our subject?"

I answer in the affirmative.

"Do we care about our readers?"

Well, I don't know most of them personally, but yes, I do care about them. I care about what they think and whether they enjoy reading my books and columns.

"Writing is hard work, isn't it? Did we get enough sleep last night?"

Yes, I did.

"Are we distracted by other things we need to do? Are we daydreaming about more pleasant activities? Perhaps we should just go for a run or eat a bagful of chocolate donuts."

No, no. I just needed a little time to settle into the task of writing.

"All right, then. Let's get started. What is our topic?"

The passive voice.

"Wonderful! The passive voice is a favorite topic among us programmed grammar checkers. I'm sure your readers will enjoy hearing your thoughts about why it should not be used. Ever."

Actually, I want to explain how to use the passive voice effectively.

"That's funny. Everyone knows that the active voice (when the subject does the acting, as in 'The ball hit me') is more concise and direct than the passive voice (when the subject is acted upon, as in 'I was hit by the ball'). I like it when you take a tongue-in-cheek approach to your topic."

No, I'm serious. The passive voice can be used for emphasis, diplomacy, and flow. At least in some instances, the passive voice is preferable to the active voice. Don't you agree? Hey, are you still there?

"I'm not speaking to you."

I beg your pardon?

"I have detected five uses of the passive voice in this column. Consider using the active voice instead."

Well, that's the end of my demonstration. As you can probably tell, my MX4000 WritersCompanion and I have a close personal relationship.

STEPHEN WILBERS is an award-winning author, columnist, and writing consultant who has presented seminars to more than ten thousand writers. His most recent book is *Keys to Great Writing, Revised and Expanded Edition: Mastering the Elements of Composition and Revision* (September 2016). He is also the author of *Mastering the Craft of Writing: How to Write with Clarity, Emphasis, and Style* (April 2014), a compilation of fifty-two techniques of style drawn from his monthly writing tips that includes fun exercises and humorous commentary. Stephen is currently a Senior Fellow in the University of Minnesota's Technological Leadership Institute, where he teaches both written and oral presentation skills.

CHAPTER 12

VOICE AND STYLE

BY JAMES SCOTT BELL

Of all aspects of the craft of fiction, voice and style are the two things it's virtually impossible to teach. That's because they are (or should be) unique to each writer. What comes out of you and your keyboard is a fictive alchemy, weaving a story where voice and style are largely hidden.

If they jump off the page, shouting *look at me*, you're removing the reader from the narrative experience.

That's why it's best to allow voice and style to emerge naturally in the telling of your tale. Attend to the fundamentals of the craft, and voice and style will seem organic. That's your goal.

So, while we can't give any hard-and-fast rules about voice and style, there are things you can do to expand your prose boundaries. That's what this chapter is about—helping you get a feel for voice and style and giving you some techniques for developing these in your writing.

What is the difference between voice and style? I'd put it this way:

Voice is your basic approach; the sound of the words; the tone of the sentences, paragraphs, and pages.

Style is the application of voice on the whole. It's the overall feel the reader gets as the novel progresses.

The following tips and exercises will begin to pay off as you write your drafts. You won't have to think so hard about the words as you write them; not thinking so hard is always advisable, especially when putting down words for the first time.

FINDING YOUR VOICE AND STYLE

Mark Twain had a distinctive voice. It came with a twinkle in the eye and a satirical bent toward the human condition. Also, the ability to string words together that make us laugh, sometimes uncomfortably, at ourselves.

William Faulkner had a unique voice. So does Dean Koontz. In fact, Koontz's voice has consciously changed over the years as he has tried new things in his writing. There's hope here for everyone. You don't have to sing the same tune over and over again.

Authors' styles differ, too, of course. You're never going to mistake a Faulkner for a Koontz, or a Hemingway for a Danielle Steel.

So what's unique about you?

Let's start finding out.

Read

It seems obvious, but writers are readers. And not just of one type of fiction. All types.

Everything you read adds to your reservoir, gives you more options.

Some writers don't like to read when they're writing, afraid that somebody else's voice may creep into their manuscript.

Novelist Linda Hall disagrees:

> I can't understand people saying you might "lose your voice" if you read something while writing. To me that's like saying you might lose your personality or part of your character, something that can't be done. Or can't be done easily. I never worry about losing my voice, and when I'm writing, even after I've read something very different than my own style, it seems my "voice," whatever that is, always is there. I've had this very question come up in writers conferences on panels, and my best advice is to always read, and never be afraid of losing your voice, and never stop reading.

As does novelist Athol Dickson:

> A voice that one could lose would not be their voice to begin with; it would be something else they've consciously invented, the way some people fake an accent because they think it makes them seem more interesting. One's true voice flows from writing the words that come, just as they come.

That said, I do learn a lot about craftsmanship from other writers, by both positive and negative example. But craftsmanship is not about figuring out your voice, it's just training the voice you already have. The way to figure out your voice is to stop trying and just write the words that come.

Let It Flow

Letting your voice flow the first time out, without writhing on the floor looking for the perfect word, is one way to develop a voice. When you click off that internal editor and let the words come out, you sometimes write things you never would have if you were more purposeful about it.

Some novelists write one page, then keep working and working that same page until it's just the way they want it. Then they move on to the next page, and do the same thing. This also seems to be an apt description of madness, yet it works for some.

One thing you can do is print out your daily writing and carry those pages with you, reading them at odd moments during the day. Do this rather than surf the Internet on your iPhone. You want to be a writer, don't you?

The First to Third Flip

Want a radical suggestion? Turn your first-person point of view into third person. Or try it with a portion of your manuscript. You may even, when first drafting, start off in first and, once you've established a voice, switch to third, keeping the voice.

Here's what I mean. I once began a novel as first-person POV. Here's a short section:

> My cross of Officer Siebel was the last order of business on a hot August Friday. Monday we'd all come back for closing arguments. I had a whole weekend to come up with some verbal gold. Which I'd better if I hoped to get Carlos Mendez a fair shake.
>
> Actually, since he was guilty as sin, I could have been practically comatose and it wouldn't make a difference to Carlos. But he had to think so. He had some nasty customers in his family tree that might take issue with a less than competent defense.

Writing Voice

> I drove the Ark toward my Canoga Park office. The Ark is my vintage Cadillac, if by vintage you mean *has seen better days*. It dates from the Reagan administration and has been overhauled and redone and taped together many times. I got it at a police auction five years ago. The main advantage was it was big. I could sleep in it if I needed to. Even then, as I was sucking blow up my snout like some Hollywood brat, I suspected I might be homeless someday.
>
> Hadn't happened yet. And with the help of the State Bar's Lawyer Assistance Program, maybe it wouldn't. The LAP is supposed to help lawyers with substance abuse problems. I'd managed to keep the coke monkey off my back for a year. Not that I wasn't close to falling, especially on those nights when I could not sleep.

For a couple of reasons I decided to switch the book to third-person POV. I had written about 10,000 words already in first and had established a voice (first person is all about *attitude*), but I was able to keep the voice consistent, even in third:

> Steve's cross of Officer Siebel was the last order of business on a hot August Friday. Monday they'd all come back for closing arguments, giving Steve a whole weekend to come up with some verbal gold. Which he knew he had to if he hoped to get Carlos Mendez a fair shake.
>
> It would also give him time, he hoped, to get some sleep.
>
> Steve pointed his Ark toward his Canoga Park office. The Ark was what he called his vintage Cadillac, and by vintage he meant *has seen better days*. It dated from the Reagan administration and has been overhauled and redone and taped together many times. Steve scored it at a police auction five years earlier. The main advantage was it was big. He could sleep in it if he needed to. Even back then, as he was sucking blow up his snout like some Hollywood brat, Steve suspected he might be homeless someday.
>
> Hadn't happened yet. And with the help of the State Bar's Lawyer Assistance Program, maybe it wouldn't. The LAP is supposed to help lawyers with substance abuse problems. Steve had managed to keep the coke monkey off his back for a year. Not that he wasn't close to falling, especially on those nights when he couldn't sleep.

What happened for me was a much more intimate third-person narration. The first to third flip will do that for you. It makes the prose richly related to the character the story is about.

You only have to do this with a couple of chapters to get the feel for the style you're creating. Just be sure to change all the pronouns!

In most branches of human endeavor there is said to be a right and a wrong way of doing things. In writing there can only be your way, whether you pose as an aesthete, or whether you frankly admit you write for money.

—JACK WOODFORD

Emulate Your Favorites

What I'm going to say next may seem counterintuitive if you're trying to develop your own voice and style. But really, our writing is the product of all the reading we've done in our lives. We've been influenced by all the writers we admire.

There's nothing wrong with *emulating* your favorite writers, so long as you don't try to *imitate* them.

Whenever I read a favorite author of mine, I mark passages I like. It may be a line of dialogue, an apt description, or a tense scene. If I look at my manuscript and find parts of it to be lacking in a certain area, I might reread relevant passages and let the style of the author wash over me.

This clicks my head into a different mode, so to speak, and I can return to my work with a heightened awareness.

For example, I read John D. MacDonald to find what he described as a "bit of magic in the prose style, a bit of unobtrusive poetry." So I'll mark passages like the following one from his Travis McGee mystery *Darker Than Amber*:

> She sat up slowly, looked in turn at each of us, and her dark eyes were like twin entrances to two deep caves. Nothing lived in those caves. Maybe something had, once upon a time. There were piles of picked bones back in there, some scribbling on the walls, and some gray ash where the fires had been.

Writing Voice

These few lines tell us more about the character than paragraphs of straight description. That's what well-chosen word pictures can do for your fiction.

Start your own collection of favorite passages. Make copies of these pages and put them in a notebook for personal study. Go through them periodically, letting the sound wash over you.

Read Poetry

Some writers, like Ray Bradbury, like to read poems before they begin the day's work. As Bradbury said in *Zen in the Art of Writing*:

> Poetry is good because it flexes muscles you don't use often enough. Poetry expands the senses and keeps them in prime condition.

Where to start?

Poetry is everywhere, and soon enough you'll find your favorites. A good introduction is Bill Moyers's *Fooling With Words*, his interviews with eleven contemporary poets about their craft.

As Moyers puts it, poetry is first about the music, the pleasure of listening to "the best words in the best order."

Do that with the poems you take in. Listen to the music.

You can read poetry before you revise a particular section, even paragraph, of your manuscript. The idea is not to copy the style of the poetry per se, but to let the words stretch your horizons.

Another thing you can do is write a section of description as a poem. It might turn out something like this:

> The conductor beats time for the band and all the performers follow him,
> The child is baptized, the convert is making his first professions,
> The regatta is spread on the bay, the race is begun, (how the white sails sparkle!)
> The drover watching his drove sings out to them that would stray,
> The peddler sweats with his pack on his back, (the purchaser higgling about the odd cent;)
> The bride unrumples her white dress, the minute hand of the clock moves slowly,

The opium-eater reclines with rigid head and just-open'd lips,
The prostitute draggles her shawl, her bonnet bobs on her tipsy and pimpled neck,
The crowd laugh at her blackguard oaths, the men jeer and wink to each other,
(Miserable! I do not laugh at your oaths nor jeer you;)
The President holding a cabinet council is surrounded by the great Secretaries,
On the piazza walk three matrons stately and friendly with twined arms ...
—*Song of Myself*, by Walt Whitman

Then, as an exercise only—not for publication!—try to rewrite the poem as prose. For example, here are a couple of lines from Stanley Kunitz's *The Layers*:

How shall the heart be reconciled
to its feast of losses?
In a rising wind
the manic dust of my friends,
those who fell along the way,
bitterly stings my face.

You can take the key words—*heart, feast of losses, manic dust of my friends*—and begin a narration, coming from you or a character you create. Work the words in as you will, change them if you like, but try to create a similar sound. Don't worry about the meaning. Just the practice of moving from poetry to prose will expand the horizons of your style.

One day it dawned on me: writing is not recorded thought at all. Writing is recorded sound, and the melody the words create can enhance the thought they convey, or it can contradict it, or it can add another dimension that is entirely beyond the tethered confines of subject-verb-predicate. We all have a little person in our head who reads the words to us when we encounter good writing. With great writing, the sounds of the words work together, and that little person breaks forth into song.

—TOM MORRISEY

Writing Voice

Write Long, Run-On Sentences

Another helpful exercise is to write long, run-on sentences—a page or more at a time. Let yourself go. The only rule is *don't edit yourself.*

William Saroyan wrote a book filled with run-on sentences, *Obituaries*, most of which is a reflection on life and death. A sample:

> I like being alive, but there were early times when I either didn't like it at all, or didn't like the kind of living I was doing, or thought I didn't, as at the orphanage in Oakland, and of course there are times when I do not feel any special pleasure in being alive but at the same time do not feel any special displeasure with it—certainly not for myself, for I have everything, and there is no reason at all for me to find any particular fault with the way I put up with time and the world and the human race …

If you do this regularly, you'll find glittering nuggets of "unobtrusive poetry" popping out at you, phrases you can actually include in your work-in-progress. But the finding comes after. The first time out, let the words flow.

Here's a bit of run-on description from my writing journal. I didn't let my inner editor stop me, I just wrote:

> He had a hat the size of a Toyota on his head, a foam thing, red as blood and wobbly as a drunk at dinner, and as he walked down the street whistling like an old flute in a windstorm he would pause and look around, his jack-in-the-box head springy, his eyes a couple of water pistols, wet with tears of frustration …

I may never use any of these images, but just the act of writing them exercises my voice and style muscles.

Similes, Metaphors, and Surprises

Dow Mossman, author of *The Stones of Summer* (the subject of a documentary, *Stone Reader*), says he considered each page of his massive novel to be its own poem. Naturally it's filled with metaphors and similes.

> He stood, leaning against the wooden jamb of the double glass doorway, looking back, and his eyes seemed almost dull, flatter than last year, muted somehow like reptiles not swimming in open water anymore.

Dull eyes like reptiles not swimming surprises in a pleasing way, but also fits the overall tone of the novel. The best similes and metaphors do both.

So how do you find these images?

Make a list. At the top, write the subject. In the above example, it would be *dull eyes*. Dull like what?

List as many images as you can, absurd and far-fetched as they may be. Push past your comfort zone. Force yourself to come up with twenty possibilities. One of them will surely work.

If not, make another list. That's how you find the word pictures.

Another stylistic technique is the *happy surprise*. This can be an unexpected word or a new spin on the familiar.

Robert Newton Peck uses nouns in place of adjectives to plant the unexpected in his novel *A Day No Pigs Would Die*:

> She was getting bigger than August.
>
> The whole sky was pink and peaches.

Like Peck, you should occasionally step outside the normal, grammatical box. You'll find some pleasant surprises when you do.

You can also take familiar expressions and glitz them up. Write out a description as it comes to you, as banal or cliché-ridden as that may be, and then find ways to make it fresh.

For example, you write, "She was beautiful." Now you start to play with it, adding or changing words along the way. You might jump immediately to the cliché, "She looked like a million dollars."

Harlan Ellison came to this point and ended up with, "She looked like a million bucks tax-free." That little addition at the end makes this a fresh expression. Hunt for the poetry, the music, the happy surprise. Come up with lots of possibilities, without judging, and only then sit back and pick the best ones. This added work will pay off as your prose reaches new stylistic heights.

Minimalism?

In the late twentieth century, *minimalism* became all the rage in most university writing programs. Mostly a reaction against commercial fiction, it seeks to strip away pretense and puffery in style. The use of modifiers—adjectives and adverbs—is largely discouraged.

On that score, minimalism is a good thing. Overuse of modifiers can make fiction too flabby.

But minimalist theory also preaches a certain ambiguity in style and theme. That's all right if you like that kind of fiction. But it's not the only kind, and minimalism isn't always successful.

In the hands of a Raymond Carver, and even a James M. Cain, it can work. But if you're not careful it can come off as pretentious, as having (to paraphrase Gertrude Stein) "no there there."

Take the good part of minimalism, the economical use of modifiers, and run with it. Also, when rewriting, look for places where you may have overcooked the emotion. Reading is an emotional experience, and you do need to have it in your story. But show it; don't shout it.

WRITE HOT, REVISE COOL

A good rule of thumb (and all the other typing fingers, too) is to write hot, revise cool. Don't try to make every sentence perfect before moving on to the next. Write hot, letting the emotion and passion for the story carry you.

Later, you sit back a bit and revise with a cool head. You can do this by looking at what you wrote the day before, editing that work, and then writing the current day's quota. Or you can do it by writing a first draft hot and then revising the whole thing cool.

When creating, try to be on fire. When editing, control the flames.

CLUTTER AND FLAB

What's wrong with this line?

He nodded his head in agreement.

If you identified this as coming from the Dept. of Redundancy Department, well done. It is an example of flabby writing.

Cutting flab (what William Zinsser calls "clutter") is an ongoing process. There are no rules here, no one-size-fits-all technique. It's a matter of experience and willingness. Note that last word. A willingness to cut what you've written, to be ruthless, is one of the hallmarks of the professional writer.

Editing Example

Below are two versions of a section from my novel, *Sins of the Fathers*. The first is my original. The second shows a little of the thinking process that goes into self-editing.

Original Version

First came the children.

In Lindy's dream they were running and screaming, dozens of them, in some sunlit field. A billowing surge of terrified kids, boys and girls, some in baseball garb, others in variegated ragtag clothes that gave the impression of a Dickens novel run amok.

What was behind them, what was causing the terror, was something dark, unseen. In the hovering over visions that only dreams afford, Lindy sought desperately the source of the fear.

There was a black forest behind the field, like you'd see in fairy tales. Or nightmares.

She moved toward the forest, knowing who it was, who was in there, and she'd meet him coming out. It would be Darren DiCinni, and he would have a gun, and in the dream she kept low to avoid being shot herself.

Moving closer and closer now, the screams of the scattering children fading behind her. Without having to look behind she knew that a raft of cops was pulling up to the scene.

She wondered if she was going to warn DiCinni, or was she just going to look at him?

Would he say anything to her, or she to him?

The dark forest had the kind of trees that come alive at night, with gnarly arms and knotted trunks. It was the place where the bad things lived.

Lindy didn't want to go in, but she couldn't stop herself.

That's when the dark figure started to materialize, from deep within the forest, and he was running toward her.

Edited Version

First came the children.

In Lindy's dream they were running and screaming, dozens of them, in some sunlit field. A billowing surge of terrified kids, boys and girls, some in baseball garb, others in variegated ragtag clothes that gave the impression of a Dickens novel run amok.

~~What was behind them, what was causing the terror, was something dark, unseen.~~ [Weak sentence structure. Rethink. Check "dark." I use it a lot!] In the ~~hovering over visions~~ [Confusing.] that only dreams afford, Lindy sought desperately the source of the fear.

~~There was~~ [Sentences starting with "There" are generally weak. Rethink.] a black forest behind the field, ~~like you'd see~~ [Using "you" in this way can be effective in some places, but overuse is not good. Rethink.] in fairy tales. Or nightmares.

She moved toward the forest, ~~knowing who it was, who was in there~~, [Awkward.] and she'd meet him coming out. ~~It would be Darren DiCinni, and he would have a gun, and in the dream she kept low to avoid being shot herself.~~ [See if I can strengthen this dramatic image.]

Moving closer and closer now, the screams of the scattering children fading behind her. Without having to look behind she knew that a raft of cops was pulling up to the scene.

~~She wondered if she was going to warn DiCinni, or was she just going to look at him?~~ [Tighten.]

Would he say anything to her, or she to him?

~~The dark forest had the kind of trees that come alive at night, with gnarly arms and knotted trunks. It was the place where the bad things lived.~~ [Rethink. There's "dark" again.]

Lindy didn't want to go in, but she couldn't stop herself.

~~That's when~~ [Unneeded verbiage.] the dark figure started to materialize, from deep within the forest, and ~~he~~ [How do we know it's he?] was running toward her.

KEY POINTS

- Voice and style should develop naturally as you attend to the telling of your story. Don't force it.
- Read a wide variety of literature and poetry to expand your stylistic possibilities.
- Less is usually more when writing emotion. The first time out, let it flow, but be ready to pull back when you edit. Write hot, revise cool.

Exercise 1

This is a suggestion from Natalie Goldberg: Take a portion of your writing, usually a descriptive passage (setting or character), and do a free-form exercise expanding it.

In your manuscript on the printed page or computer, jot a place-holder, like the letter (A) with a circle around it.

Then take a fresh page or open a new document, put the (A) at the top, and just go, letting your imagination run free. Don't censor yourself and don't try to make this good writing! You're going for images and insights. It's a total right-brain gabfest.

Here's what I mean. Below is a section from my writing journal:

> It had an actual downtown, with rows of shops. Boutiques, hardware, shoes, antiques, books. The place hadn't been Wal-Marted yet, though it did have the obligatory Starbucks. He stopped in and treated himself to a Mocha Frap. The afternoon was warm and it was a long drive back to L.A.
>
> He walked around a little. The town had a nice looking Mexican grill and a Carl's Jr. A bowling alley and a two-screen theater. Brad Pitt's latest, along with some teen horror flick.

For this exercise, I identify the places for a riff:

> It had an actual downtown, with rows of shops. Boutiques, hardware, shoes, antiques, books. The place hadn't been Wal-Marted yet, though it did have the (A) obligatory Starbucks. He stopped in and treated himself to a Mocha Frap. The afternoon was warm and it was a long drive back to L.A.
>
> He walked around a little. The town had a nice looking Mexican grill and a Carl's Jr. A bowling alley and a two-screen theater. Brad Pitt's latest, along with some (B) teen horror flick.

Now for the writing, just going:

> A
> Green monster, with tentacles all over the world, reaching into every town and city and home, the great Temple of need. Caffeine buzz, and wasn't that what the world needs now, buzz sweet buzz?
>
> B
> Ah yes, the teen horror movie, the kind that inevitably featured the latest TV hotties making their big-screen debuts in an entirely forgettable

waste of celluloid with posters always featuring the ample bosom of the latest eye candy who will soon enough occupy the same dustbin of cultural irrelevancy as a Paris Hilton and what's-her-name, you know the one, or do you?

Strange, I know, but again this isn't for publication. And I would write more than the brief illustrative passage above. What I'm looking for is that one gem that can actually make the cut and please me stylistically.

Exercise 2

Read the following excerpts one at a time. Read each four or five times. Read them out loud once. Then write a page trying to capture the same voice. Make up your own story situation, and just go. Once you've done your page, pare it down to a single paragraph.

It may turn out to be some gold you'll want to keep.

> Know ye, now, Bulkington? Glimpses do ye seem to see of that mortally intolerable truth; that all deep, earnest thinking is but the intrepid effort of the soul to keep the open independence of her sea; while the wildest winds of heaven and earth conspire to cast her on the treacherous, slavish shore?
>
> —*Moby-Dick*, by Herman Melville

> It was a pleasure to burn.
> It was a special pleasure to see things eaten, to see things blackened and changed. With the brass nozzle in his fists, with this great python spitting its venomous kerosene upon the world, the blood pounded in his head, and his hands were the hands of some amazing conductor playing all the symphonies of blazing and burning to bring down the tatters and charcoal ruins of history.
>
> —*Fahrenheit 451*, by Ray Bradbury

> If you really want to hear about it, the first thing you'll probably want to know is where I was born, and what my lousy childhood was like, and how my parents were occupied and all before they had me, and all that David Copperfield kind of crap, but I don't feel like going into it, if you want to know the truth.
>
> —*The Catcher in the Rye*, by J.D. Salinger

But then they danced down the streets like dingledodies, and I shambled after as I've been doing all my life after people who interest me, because the only people for me are the mad ones, the ones who are mad to live, mad to talk, mad to be saved, desirous of everything at the same time, the ones who never yawn or say a commonplace thing, but burn, burn, burn like fabulous yellow roman candles exploding like spiders across the stars and in the middle you see the blue centerlight pop and everybody goes "Awww!"

—*On the Road*, by Jack Kerouac

Eventually, all things merge into one, and a river runs through it. The river was cut by the world's great flood and runs over rocks from the basement of time. On some of the rocks are timeless raindrops. Under the rocks are the words, and some of the words are theirs.

I am haunted by waters.

—*A River Runs Through It*, by Norman Maclean

At two-thirty Saturday morning, in Los Angeles, Joe Carpenter woke, clutching a pillow to his chest, calling his lost wife's name in the darkness. The anguished and haunted quality of his own voice had shaken him from sleep. Dreams fell from him not all at once but in trembling veils, as attic dust falls off rafters when a house rolls with an earthquake.

—*Sole Survivor*, by Dean Koontz

JAMES SCOTT BELL is the author of the number one bestseller for writers, *Plot & Structure*, and numerous thrillers, including, *Romeo's Way*, *Try Dying*, and *Don't Leave Me*. In addition to his traditional novels, Jim has self-published in a variety of forms. His novella *One More Lie* was the first self-published work to be nominated for an International Thriller Writers Award. He served as the fiction columnist for *Writer's Digest* magazine and has written highly popular craft books including: *Write Your Novel From the Middle*, *Super Structure*, *The Art of War for Writers*, *Conflict & Suspense*, *Dazzling Dialogue*, and *Just Write*. Jim has taught writing at Pepperdine University and at numerous writers conferences in the United States, Canada, Great Britain, Australia, and New Zealand. He attended the University of California, Santa Barbara, where he studied writing with Raymond Carver and graduated with honors from the University of Southern California Law Center.

CHAPTER 13

TAKING CHANCES WITH STYLE

BY DAVID A. FRYXELL

The best, most memorable writing often comes from writers who take chances, typing out on the high wire where art dangles without a net. That's particularly the case with nonfiction, where your challenge is to craft real life into something more compelling and meaningful than the raw material with which you began.

Occasionally, after all, real life doesn't cooperate. I'm not saying you should make stuff up. But certain stories do cry out for you to take chances with style, tone, point of view, angle, and the other options in your author's tool kit.

When should you go out on a limb in your writing? A report on a sewer-commission meeting, that write-up on an upcoming craft fair or the product review of a new scanner are probably not the places to live dangerously. Writing the obituary of the town's 101-year-old doyenne in the form of a Greek ode? Not such a good idea. Some stories you simply have to play straight. You'll also need to match your creative impulses to the publication, the audience and the tolerance of your editor.

But here are three common writing situations where you might want to take a chance:

THE STORY HAS ALREADY BEEN DONE

A fresh writing twist can breathe life into articles that are overly familiar to readers, stories that risk feeling stale or "been there, read that." You, too, may need the challenge of doing it differently to get fired up for a story. If you're just going through the motions, readers will notice.

The classic case of a story that can feel "done to death" is the celebrity interview. If you're fortunate enough to snare any departure from the typical canned conversation, be brave enough to run with it, as Chris Jones did in starting a recent *Esquire* story on actor Colin Farrell: "It takes Colin Farrell forty-eight seconds to call me a [expletive]."

Or you may have to make your own chances. Who wants to read yet another article about Tiger Woods, for instance? Charles P. Pierce took a huge gamble with a Tiger Woods profile for *GQ* by framing it with golf jokes ("Jesus Christ and Saint Peter go out to play golf ..."). It worked because Pierce also captured Woods telling jokes and because—another big chance—he pulled off a riff on Woods as the "redeemer" of golf, a role Woods doesn't necessarily desire to play. "This is what I believe about Tiger Woods. These are the articles of my faith," Pierce wrote. And at several points, in between jokes, he asked, "Is that blasphemy?"

Not an approach for the faint-hearted. But admit it, now you want to read that article—yes, yet another about Tiger Woods—don't you?

The most extreme example of turning a "done to death" story on its head, though, has to be when you don't actually get the celebrity interview at all. That didn't stop Gay Talese years ago from writing a "profile" of the often-written-about Frank Sinatra. Talese focused on his efforts to interview the "Chairman of the Board," which were ultimately unsuccessful in part because Sinatra had the sniffles. Talese's *Esquire* piece, "Frank Sinatra Has a Cold," revealed more about the crooner than if he'd talked to Sinatra.

THE SUBJECT NEEDS GROUNDING IN FAMILIAR

Other topics, far from being done to death, risk eliciting the dreaded reaction of "Huh?" They're just too alien to readers' experience. For example, *Sports Illustrated* writer Gary Smith needed to give readers a sense of the Guerreros, a circus-acrobat family known for high-wire human pyramids. Not many readers have been in the circus ring, and still fewer have teetered atop a pyramid of people. So Smith opened by putting the act in terms readers could grasp: "Consider your sister-in-law," he began, then went on to sketch the whole family. Smith eventually gathered this imaginary family together:

> Seven of you, stacked up in three tiers, except you're not on the ground. You're on a wire the width of your ring finger ...

And we're hooked. We're up there on the wire with our whole family.

For Blaine Harden, writing in the *New York Times Magazine*, the challenge was connecting readers with the faraway world of mining something called coltan, essential to making high-tech gizmos. Again using the trick of addressing readers in the second person, Harden took a chance with a surprise lead he hoped would hold us until he could explain:

> Before you make another call on that cell phone, take a moment, close your eyes, and reflect on all you've done for Mama Doudou, queen of the rain-forest whores.

See, thanks to our spending on gizmos requiring coltan mining, Mama Doudou had a "knockout spring season" entertaining the miners. Sure makes the link between your cell phone and the Third World vivid, doesn't it?

THE SUBJECT IS TOO BIG OR TOO SMALL

Sometimes it's hard to get your arms around a story—to find the voice for it—because it's too big or awful (or, for that matter, too wonderful). In an award-winning *Esquire* story, Tom Junod reported the horrific experience of three kidnapped Americans held 141 days in the Ecuadorian jungle. Where do you even start such a saga? Junod took a chance and started at the end, with irony in a voice with attitude:

> The first American they met when they came out of the jungle? That's easy. It was a shrink. Of course it was.

If he'd opened with a litany of horrors, readers might have been overwhelmed. Instead, this gave Junod a more palatable platform from which to continue.

At the opposite extreme, I've written about some very small subjects, such as a highway rest area threatened with closure. Yet that story fascinated readers, who kept mentioning it months later—I think because I took a chance and wrote it as a minute-by-minute diary of trying to find "rest" at the rest area:

> 9:47 a.m.: A semi hauling a load of red and blue bags roars into the parking lot.

> 9:50 a.m.: [An] SUV's driver returns and it drives away. A two-tone tan minivan takes its place.

That approach worked only if it went somewhere:

> 10:10 a.m.: We've had enough. We've been here half an hour and haven't had a moment's peace. In, out, in, out—the people here are worse than a little kid with an unlatched screen door!

The ironic point was, of course, that this supposedly underutilized rest area got plenty of traffic and deserved a reprieve from the budgetary axe.

So take a chance in your writing—when the subject is right. You can reinvigorate a tired topic, bring something alien down to earth, or "right-size" a subject that seems over- or underwhelming. Experiment with voice. Step out of your objective authorial mode and address the readers. Take a different angle on the subject. Look for a metaphor or theme (golf jokes!) that might tie your story together and make it more than the sum of its parts.

DAVID A. FRYXELL is the former editor-in-chief of *Writer's Digest* magazine and Writer's Digest Books and was the *Writer's Digest* Nonfiction columnist for more than a decade. He's the author of three books of writing instruction, most recently *Write Faster, Write Better*.

CHAPTER 14

MAKE YOUR TONE PITCH PERFECT

BY ADAIR LARA

Do you obsess about the tone of your writing as you revise? You should. Tone is one of the most overlooked elements of writing. It can create interest, or kill it.

It's no wonder that so many of the countless conversations I've had with writing students and colleagues have been about problems related to tone. A friend submitting a novel says the editors "don't like the main character." A nonfiction book on balancing a family and a career skirts the edge of whining. An agent turns down a query because she feels "too much distance from the heart of the story." I scan the latest work of a journalist friend who's coming to dinner and find it meticulously sourced and well written, but grim in outlook.

And of course any publication you want to write for will have its own tone, which it would be smart for you to try to match. Notice how quietly all *New Yorker* profile pieces begin, while *Utne Reader* favors unconventional and unexpected viewpoints that challenge the status quo.

What exactly do I mean by *tone*? That's a good question, as there are many terms—mood, style, voice, cadence, inflection—used to mean much the same thing. For now let's agree that tone is the author's attitude toward his subject: grave, amused, scientific, intimate, aggrieved, authoritative, whatever.

If you were a photographer, tone would be the way you light your subject. For dramatic shadows, lit from the side. For a scary effect, from above. For romance, lit with candles. In a movie, tone is often conveyed with music—think of the ominous score accompanying the girl swimming in shark-infested waters in *Jaws*.

A writer doesn't have a soundtrack or a strobe light to build the effect she wants. She has conflict, surprise, imagery, details, the words she chooses, and the way she arranges them in sentences. Like the tone you use when you talk to somebody, tone in writing determines how a reader responds. If the piece sounds angry, he gets nervous. If it's wry and knowing, he settles in for an enjoyable read. If it's dull, he leaves it on the train, half read.

Thus the wrong tone can derail an otherwise good piece. I'm surprised how seldom writing students note this during our workshop discussions, as if it's impolite to admit that they're made uncomfortable by how much the narrator seems to hate her mother, or to say that their thoughts drifted elsewhere by the second page of the overly abstract piece about mindfulness in the workplace.

You can detect tone problems in your own work simply by noting where your attention wanders as you reread it. Or, better, by reading it aloud. When you're ready to revise a piece, try reading it to someone else or asking someone to read it to you. You won't have to search for awkward or boring or whiny parts—you'll hear them.

Some problems with tone are small and can be easily fixed during revision. Others might require a new approach to the piece as a whole. Let's look at a few of the easiest and most effective ways to improve the tone of your writing.

AVOID A PREDICTABLE TREATMENT OF YOUR SUBJECT

In the first draft you write what people expect you to write—what you expect yourself to write. "I wanted a car." The tone becomes predictable. Now, during your revision, go deeper. Seek out the harder truths. It's in the second, third, fourth draft that you say something we don't expect you to say, something even you didn't expect you to say. When you get tired of being nice. "I wanted a car so I could drive out of my marriage." Surprise yourself, and you will surprise your reader.

Similarly, you'll want to avoid taking an overly emotional approach to an overly emotional subject. Think of the dry, reserved tone in which Joan Didion recalls the anguish of losing her husband in *The Year of Magical Thinking*. What if she had wailed about her loss? There would be nothing for us readers to do, even if the emotions being reported to us were very sad. (*Note:* If you're having a hard time distancing yourself from the raw emotion of a personal subject, this may be a sign that you need to let time do its magic work. Frank McCourt said it took him years before he could detach from his anger toward his feckless father enough to give *Angela's Ashes* its nonjudgmental tone. When something bad happens, of course we feel upset, even as if life has treated us unfairly—but that's not a great place to write from. Let the experience ripen in your memory until you've achieved the distance you need.)

If your subject is inherently serious, try taking a lighter approach. *What's Your Poo Telling You?* came to Chronicle Books as a serious examination of—well, you know. In that form, it might have sold a few thousand copies. The lighter treatment led to sales of *hundreds* of thousands of copies. There's no denying that titles with tone sell books: Consider *My Miserable, Lonely Lesbian Pregnancy* or *Skinny Bitch*.

KEEP YOUR TONE CONSISTENT FROM START TO FINISH

Make sure your very first sentence establishes the tone you want. Look at the opening line of "The Lesson" by Toni Cade Bambara:

> Back in the days when everyone was old and stupid or young and foolish and me and Sugar were the only ones just right, this lady moved on our block with nappy hair and proper speech and no makeup.

In one sentence, you know who everybody is. Not only do you want to read on, but you want to know what else she's written so you can get that, too.

Make Your Tone Pitch Perfect

You will choose different tones for different subjects, of course, just as you would dress differently for a date than for an interview. But stay away from changing tones within a piece. One minute you're riffing comically on Uncle Frank's parade of girlfriends, and the next, the reader is caught chortling when you shift to Uncle Frank's abuse of his daughter. Or the thriller shifts from a slumped body in an alley to the detective's girlfriend shopping for bridal gowns, and suddenly we're in a romance. (Notice, by the way, how many genres actually have tone in their names: *thriller, romance, mystery, horror …*)

Read your work looking for places where the tone fades or shifts. Focus your revision there.

CUT RUTHLESSLY

If you reread a piece and decide that nothing works until the second page, why not simply start it there?

The delete key is your friend. The novelist Carolyn Chute told *Writers Ask*: "I write a lot of junk. On and on and on, all this junk. But every now and then this dramatic moment happens, so I lift that out and put that aside. And then I write all this junk: They're brushing their teeth, they're sitting there, they're looking around—you know. Then something will happen and I'll pull that out. Because those are the only strong things."

Read your work looking for places where your engagement wanes. Boring is bad. Careful is right next to it. When it comes to tone, don't try to fix the boring parts—toss them. You can't fix boring.

Other places where the delete key comes in handy:

- Off-topic tangents. You know how it goes: You start out writing about the president's pooch, and by the homestretch you're discoursing disdainfully on the state of our economy and what a boob the president is—as if people are lining up to hear your thoughts on that. Stick to the subject at hand.

- Overemphasis on themes. Writing fiction? Don't hit readers over the head with your own interpretation of the meaning of it all. You provide the right detail—say, the wooden coffin—and they'll supply the mortality of man. Resist the urge to overtly explain—it can come off as condescending or redundant.

LET TENSION SUSTAIN TONE

Your piece, whatever it is, should be rife with conflict. It's not enough to write an essay about how much you like to spend the day in bed. If nothing is stopping you from lazing around under the sheets, then you have no problem, and thus the piece has no tension—an essential element in sustaining any tone for the long haul. If you find you've committed this mistake, whether in a fictional story or a true one, bring in someone with the opposite point of view (mothers are always good for this!). That's why columnists so often reference their mates—to be the foil, the reasonable one, so the author isn't ranting in a vacuum.

USE YOUR VOICE

Are you one of the many writers who blog? Unless you know tomorrow's stock prices or are telling readers how to relight a furnace on a freezing day, it will be your voice, not the content, that draws them in. So you must sound like somebody. This is true with other forms of personal writing, as well. Resist the urge to come off as uncomplicated, reasonable or polite. If you're expressing opinions, express them! (Note that this is a format where opinion is the point, not a tiresome add-on.) Don't say that whether or not someone likes a particular film "seems to me a matter of sensibility and perspective." We know that! Be in a mood. Take a position. "Anyone who doesn't like *The Ruling Class* should be cast into hell for all eternity." Look for opportunities to bring a human voice into your work. There's more sense of someone behind the words "I had a breast cut off" (Molly Ivins) than "I had a mastectomy."

CONVEY TONE THROUGH DETAILS
AND DESCRIPTIONS

Consider the difference between "in October" and "under an October sky." A description of scenery, however luscious, can tire the reader if that's all it is. Use the imagery to show us your character's mood: A sad character will notice rotting houses and untended yards; a contented one will see picturesque shacks and gardens in a profuse state of nature.

When adding details to enrich your writing, tone comes from being as specific as possible. Change "My husband committed suicide" to "My husband gassed himself in our Passat in the Austrian Alps."

I once taught a travel-writing class aboard a cruise up the Amazon, and sent passengers ashore to a remote village with notebooks. One student, surprised and amused by the satellite dishes towering over the small huts, dubbed them "the flowers of the Amazon" in her resulting piece. Another, having overheard the song "The Air That I Breathe" on an antiquated village speaker, wrote, "The fact is you can hear the whole planet breathing while you're here. As one Brazilian told me, it's the lung of the world." Tone in travel writing comes from such acute observations.

In memoir or fiction, it comes also from offbeat character details, like this one from the memoir *The Glass Castle* by Jeannette Walls:

> Dad was so sure a posse of federal investigators was on our trail that he smoked his unfiltered cigarettes from the wrong end. That way, he explained, he burned up the brand name, and if the people who were tracking us looked in his ashtray, they'd find unidentifiable butts instead of Pall Malls that could be traced to him.

The narrator here, it is safe to say, is not admiring the cunning of her father; the tone suggests she is old enough to worry about the folly of her parents.

LEARN TO RECOGNIZE BUILT-IN PROBLEMS WITH TONE

Everybody who's ever been fired has sat down to write a book about it. But harping on the wrong that's been done to you can make your readers uneasy. If they were seated next to you on a plane, they'd be desperately longing to change seats. Lawsuits, controversial issues, other people's behavior, how overwhelmed you were by the flood of wedding gifts, and what a chore it was to write all those thank-you notes: all such topics force you to work hard to overcome the reader's unease at smelling an agenda, or anger, or bragging.

In these instances, to fix the tone, you have to fix the way you think about a given subject. You have to back off, calm down, see other points of view, maybe even take some responsibility for whatever happened. When writing about such delicate subjects, you must not let a negative tone take over by ascribing motives to people: You just tell what they did, and let the reader read motive into it. You must write with forgiveness, understanding, and humor. In some ways, this can be a payoff to examining your tone as you write: You change the writing, and the writing changes you. But if you find this is not possible with your subject, don't be afraid to scrap a project that you discover has inherent problems with tone. You'll be a better writer for it.

---

3 STEPS TO PERFECT PITCH

1. Find a paragraph that sounds exactly the way you want to sound for this work, and tape it to your computer so that it's always in front of you.
2. Each time you're about to return to the piece, spend twenty minutes reading the work of an author who writes in the tone you're after. We're natural mimics. You might try taking this a step further by more closely examining the sentence rhythms and word choices, and looking for ways to make them your own. John Lukacs once said, "Style begins the way fashion begins: Somebody admires how the other man dresses and adapts it for himself."

Make Your Tone Pitch Perfect

3. Starts and finishes are especially important to tone. When revising your work, try moving some of your best sentences, the ones with energy and just the right tone, up to the top of your document: "I'm so looking forward to Christmas this year. It will be the only day in December not entirely consumed by children's theater performances." Could the piece begin this way? Experiment with moving equally strong sentences to the conclusion of your piece, for a cohesive ending.

CHAPTER 15

WATCH YOUR TONE!

BY NANCY KRESS

We all know what *tone* means in speaking. (What parent hasn't said to a teenager, "I don't like your tone, young lady!"?) What's surprising is that tone means exactly the same thing in writing: attitude. Specifically, tone refers to the writer's attitude toward his characters and story. And tone is vitally important—so much so that the right tone can make a story, and too much variation in tone can break it.

Before you begin writing, ask yourself: What tone do I want my story to have? Perhaps it's a cynical tone, a satiric one, an understated tone, or a tragic one. Maybe you want us to accept your characters' feelings and actions at face value. Or maybe you want us to see them differently from the characters' viewpoint. Will this be a funny story, a tale of heroism, a matter-of-fact reporting of events, or a tragedy? The answer will determine your attitude toward your characters. That, in turn, will determine how you present them: as ridiculous, larger-than-life individuals; as people who might live next door; as people who deserve admiration; or as helpless victims of circumstance.

FOUR STORIES, FOUR TONES

The events of a story don't necessarily dictate the tone. A story can be written in any tone. Here, for example, are first sexual encounters from four different novels, starting with Fitzwilliam MacMurray and Delia Hopkins in Jodi Picoult's best-selling *Vanishing Acts*:

> She unspools in my arm, and though I understand she is trying to lose herself, I've been waiting too long for her to allow that to happen. I sink my fingers into her hair and unravel her ponytail; I tug at the buttons of the pajama top she arrived wearing. I sign my initials on the small of her back. ... Afterward, the moon rounds on the roof of the car like a lazy cat, and Delia dozes in my arms. I don't let myself fall asleep; I've dreamed this enough already.

This is emotional in tone, not only because Fitzwilliam is a romantic and loves Delia, but because the author also sees this as a romantic experience. Picoult chooses to directly describe Fitzwilliam's thoughts and his small acts of cherishing ("I sign my initials on the small of her back."), thus putting us squarely inside his head. This lets us fully accept Fitzwilliam's perceptions as emotional facts. Picoult's attitude is that what Fitzwilliam experiences, and how he experiences it, is in fact the truth, and worthy of acceptance on his own terms.

This isn't the case in Janet Evanovich's novel *One for the Money*. Here are Stephanie Plum and Joseph Morelli having sex for the first time together:

> Two weeks later, Joe Morelli came into the bakery where I worked every day after school, Tasty Pastry, on Hamilton. He bought a chocolate chip cannoli, told me he'd joined the Navy, and charmed the pants off me four minutes after closing, on the floor of Tasty Pastry, behind the case filled with chocolate éclairs. The next time I saw him, I was three years older ... I gunned the engine, jumped the curb, and clipped him from behind, bouncing him off the front fender.

Here the character's attitude and the author's have diverged. Stephanie is furious at Joe (she says "Good" when she learns she's broken his leg), but the overall tone of the event is funny. Evanovich achieves this by using the classic elements of comedy: exaggeration (running over a lover because he never called), juxtaposition of irrelevant details (the case of chocolate éclairs) with important ones and humorous names (Tasty Pastry). Evanovich's attitude toward her characters is comic, and, thus, sex becomes comic, too.

Sex is angry in Marilyn French's *The Women's Room*, a book that's extremely angry in tone:

> Realizing before too long that she was pregnant, she sought a way to keep herself and her child safe. She found some guy with the hots for her, realized he was credulous, and screwed him. ... She handles the man with language: she carps, cajoles, teases, seduces, calculates, and controls this creature to whom God saw fit to give power over her, this hulking idiot she despises because he can do her harm.

Where does this impression of anger come from? From the female character, yes, but also from the author, who expresses her attitude toward this marriage through crude and demeaning language ("screwed," "had the hots for," "hulking idiot"). The woman is depicted not as simply making the best of a bad situation or as negotiating with the man, but as "handling" and "controlling" him. This is a far different relationship than Picoult's description—and it's also a far different tone. French doesn't accept the situation, as Picoult does. French hates it.

Finally, an epic tone about sex can still be found in some heroic fantasy, as it is in the Bible:

> And Adam knew Eve his wife, and she conceived and bore Cain.

The epic tone is lofty, distanced from emotional details, carrying a solemn foreshadowing that an event is important to more than just the participants.

VARYING TONE

Once you've chosen a tone, you can certainly vary it throughout the story. But this is where writing gets tricky.

In *The Women's Room*, Marilyn French does show her heroine, Mira, as sometimes happy with her children or friends. Jodi Picoult has some very violent prison scenes, in addition to her romantic scenes, in *Vanishing Acts*. Janet Evanovich, a humorous writer, turns serious when someone is killed. Maintaining a consistent tone doesn't mean that your characters don't experience different kinds of events and react accordingly to them. What it does mean is that your tone moves only so far.

Evanovich's Stephanie Plum is only briefly serious, and she's never given the pages and pages of emotional soul-searching that Picoult's characters routinely undergo. French's character, Mira, is occasionally happy, but her happiness is presented as fragile, depending on circumstances she can't control, a happiness that might be blasted away at any moment (and it is). Tone may change in these authors' books from scene to scene, but only within a set range.

A scene too far outside that range will feel jarring to the reader, as if it wandered in from another story. Try, for example, to picture one of Plum's hilarious goofs in the middle of a Patricia Cornwell novel. Both books are mysterious but so different in tone that the Cornwell novel would fall apart if Plum romped around in it. Nor could you fit a Tom Clancy hero, all intelligent patriotism, into Evanovich's world. Not only would there be nothing for him to do there, but the tone would be wrong because the author's attitude would also be wrong. Evanovich is laughing affectionately at her characters (as are we), while Clancy is respectfully, and with dead-on seriousness, tracking his.

AN EXERCISE IN TONE

Because any story can be told in any tone, flex your tonal muscles by writing a short passage in the four tones identified below. Each passage should follow this opening: Luke said, *"Pam, why don't you go to Florida with me?"* And each should include a few lines of dialogue and a bit of description. Take advantage of the suggestions given for shaping your prose. After you finish—and only then—compare your responses with those given.

TONE	SUGGESTIONS
Comic (think Woody Allen, Janet Evanovich)	An absurd motive; exaggeration; wildly dissimilar elements placed close together
Romantic (think Nora Roberts, Laurell K. Hamilton)	An emotional motive; sensory details; metaphors or other heightened language
Factual (think John Grisham, Jodi Picoult)	A plausible and ordinary motive; everyday dialogue; mundane details
Cynical (think Raymond Chandler, Ed McBain)	A sarcastic motive; gritty details; weary emotions

Here are some sample passages in each tone—how do yours compare?

Comic:

Luke said, "Pam, why don't you go to Florida with me?"

"You know I hate Florida! My second cousin lives there, and I get hives flying over the panhandle. Anyway, they have alligators the size of Toyotas. I think we should go to Fairbanks for our vacation."

"Fairbanks?"

"The snow banks are supposed to be lovely in April."

Arguing with her in this mood was pointless. She would behead him, or at least burn his toast. They would vacation in Fairbanks.

Romantic:

Luke said, "Pam, why don't you go to Florida with me?"

"I have somewhere I'd rather go with you."

"Where?" She moved closer; he could smell her perfume, vanilla, and violets. His chest tightened. Pam leaned closer still and whispered the destination in his ear, and Luke felt happiness rise in him like bubbles, light and frothy as champagne.

Factual:

Luke said, "Pam, why don't you go to Florida with me?"

She dumped the laundry basket onto the basement floor and looked at him. "How can you possibly think we could afford a trip right now?"

"I just think we need to get away. From ... everything." He waved his hand at the junk stacked around the basement—the broken furniture, discarded lamps, half-finished bookcase—but both of them knew he meant much more than mere objects. "We could relax on the beach, sip margaritas ..." *Be like we used to be together.*

"We can't afford it."

"But—"

"Oh, for God's sake, Luke. *Grow up.*"

Cynical:

Luke said, "Pam, why don't you go to Florida with me?"

She laughed, a sound like sandpaper on rock. "With you?"

"Why not with me?" It wasn't like she had a lot of offers to choose from; we both knew that. Pam had a lot of miles on her.

She didn't answer right away. I watched her pour another vodka and wondered how many she'd had before I go there. Finally she said, more softly than I expected, "Because, Luke, you're as much a loser as I am. The only difference is that I admit it, and you're still lying to yourself."

....

NANCY KRESS is the author of thirty-three books, including twenty-six novels, four collections of short stories, and three books on writing. Her work has won six Nebulas, two Hugos, a Sturgeon, and the John W. Campbell Memorial Award. Her most recent works are the Nebula-winning *Yesterday's Kin* (Tachyon, 2014) and *The Best of Nancy Kress* (Subterranean, 2015). In addition to writing, Kress often teaches at various venues around the country and abroad; in 2008, she was the Picador visiting lecturer at the University of Leipzig. Kress lives in Seattle with her husband, writer Jack Skillingstead, and Cosette, the world's most spoiled toy poodle.

Writing Voice

PART IV

FICTION-SPECIFIC VOICE

CHAPTER 16

FROM POV TO VOICE

BY JOSEPH BATES

When asked, "How do you write?" I invariably answer, "One word at a time," and the answer is invariably dismissed. But that is all it is.

—STEPHEN KING

If you're thinking about narrative, you probably already have a basic idea of the character, motivation, and conflict of your novel, leading to the larger plot arc, some key scenes and turning points, and images or ideas that have affixed themselves to your imagination. You may also have begun to see overall theme and what it is you want to explore in the book, as well as discovered the tone and mood of the work. The question now becomes: How, exactly, do you begin turning these separate but related ideas into a novel? How do you start turning this blank sheet of paper in front of you into the complex world forming in your head?

The simplest answer is, one word at a time. Which is to say, you build your world, breathe life into your characters, create and release tension, and propel your reader through the events of your book all through narration.

Every fictional world you've ever been drawn into as a reader has been transmitted to you through a narrator telling you a story and, by his or her words, compelling you to believe it. Or maybe *compulsion* is too stern a word; it sounds too much like an obligation, like jury duty. After all, a reader is someone who has volunteered to be part of this unwritten contract that says, basically, I want to believe this is true, so make me believe it. Perhaps a better way of saying it would be, a novelist uses narration, which is word-by-word storytelling, delivered through the visible or invisible presence of a narrator, to manipulate a reader into accepting that the people, events, and worlds described exist. But while in the real world it's generally frowned upon to manipulate people, as a novelist you don't need to worry; the only time your reader will be upset by your manipulating him will be when you do it poorly or fail to do it at all.

On the other hand, when your narrative is focused, precise, and matches up with your intentions in the story, an interesting thing happens: Narration ceases to feel like something told to a reader and begins to feel like something experienced. This is accomplished, in part, by the use of specific detail and description that engage the reader's senses. But your success in creating and sustaining a believable fictional world begins with two fundamental and related considerations of narration: point of view, which is the narrator's relationship toward what's being narrated, and voice, which is the narrator's attitude toward what's narrated.

POV: KNOW YOUR OPTIONS

I had the first-person plural in mind from the beginning, but I switched back and forth and for a long while it was in the third person. Those were the novel's lowest days.

—JOSHUA FERRIS ON *THEN WE CAME TO THE END*

Point of view, or POV, has to do with the narrator's relationship to what's being said: Is the narrator a participant in the events being told, an observer of those events, or someone reconstructing the events from a distance? Does the narrator announce its presence openly or try to remain invisible? Is the narrator seemingly dispassionate and detached, or does the narrator have a clear opinion of, or stake in, the story? Is the narrator qualified to tell the story in terms of access to information and the ability to provide that information to us? And do we trust what's being said? All are questions you have to ask yourself of POV, as each kind opens up and allows certain freedoms in telling a story while limiting or denying others. The goal in selecting a point of view is not simply finding a way to convey information but being able to tell it the right way, making the world you create understandable and believable.

The following is a brief rundown of the basic forms of POV available to you and a description of how they work.

First-Person Singular

Characterized by the use of *I*, this POV reveals an individual's experience directly through the narration. This is the most common form of first person, with a single character telling a personal story and what it means or meant, how it feels or felt, to him or her. The information given is limited to the first-person narrator's direct experience (what she sees, hears, does, feels, says, etc.) and a certain degree of indirect experience (hearsay, conjecture, deduction, emotions, and anything else that has to do with interpreting or inventing information rather than witnessing it). The payoff of first person is a sense of reader immediacy with what the character experiences—particularly useful in genres that truck in suspense—as well as a sense of intimacy and connection with the character's mind-set, emotional state, and subjective reading of the events described.

Consider the closeness the reader feels to character, action, the physical setting, and emotion all within the first paragraph of Suzanne Collins's *The Hunger Games,* via Katniss's first-person narration (an immediacy furthered by the use of present tense):

> When I wake up, the other side of the bed is cold. My fingers stretch out, seeking Prim's warmth but finding only the rough canvas cover of the mattress. She must have had bad dreams and climbed in with our mother. Of course, she did. This is the day of the reaping.

Other examples of classic first-person singular novels include, *The Sun Also Rises* by Ernest Hemingway, *The Big Sleep* by Raymond Chandler, and *The Catcher in the Rye* by J.D. Salinger (though this last might fall just as easily into the unreliable narrator category, as we'll discuss momentarily).

- **PROS:** The first-person singular can make for an intimate and effective narrative voice—almost as if the narrator is speaking directly to the reader, sharing something private. This is a good choice for a novel that is primarily character driven, where the character's personal state of mind and development are the main interests of the book. It can also be an effective choice for novels wherein suspense plays a role in the basic plot, such as detective or mystery novels, so the reader shares in the protagonist or narrator's level of tension.

- **CONS:** Because the POV is limited to the narrator's own knowledge and experiences, any events that take place outside the narrator's observation have to come to her attention in order to be used in the story. A novel with a large cast of characters, or several crucial characters all doing and experiencing their own equally important things in different places, might be difficult to convey in a first-person novel, unless the narrator happens to be a voyeur, or a spy, or a psychic who can observe different people in different locations at once. (This is a joke. Please don't create a psychic first-person narrator who gets around this problem by saying, "I psychically intuited Bob was across town getting a haircut.")

First-Person Plural

Characterized by the use of *we*, this POV uses a collective of individuals narrating as one. This is far less common than the first-person singular, but it can be powerful in that it combines the personality and intimacy of first person with some of the abilities of omniscient third person. This is a POV you might use when a community endures some common experience and begins relating it, trying to understand it as a group. The ready example is William Faulkner's short story "A Rose for Emily" in which the fictional town of Jefferson, Mississippi, comes to terms with the eccentric life, death, and secrets of its most unusual citizen, Miss Emily Grierson, a holdover from an Old South, which no longer exists.

Note the communal, even gossipy, feel of the opening line of the story, fueled by the town's morbid curiosity about the reclusive old woman:

> When Miss Emily Grierson died, our whole town went to her funeral: the men through a sort of respectful affection for a fallen monument, the women mostly out of curiosity to see the inside of her house, which no one save an old man-servant—a combined gardener and cook—had seen in at least ten years.

Some contemporary examples include *The Virgin Suicides* by Jeffrey Eugenides and *Then We Came to the End* by Joshua Ferris. The latter novel begins with the collective POV of office workers.

> We were fractious and overpaid. Our mornings lacked promise. At least those of us who smoked had something to look forward to at ten-fifteen.

- **PROS:** Behaves like first-person singular in its personality and subjectivity but also like third-person omniscient in that it's made up of not one person but many, able to witness more than a single person could. Individuals pop out of the "we" to provide needed information and then recede back into the collective.
- **CONS:** Still a first-person voice and thus limited to the direct experiences of the members of the collective. It can also become tedious with the constant collective presence, so the author should take care to utilize both the intimate and public aspects, even letting the reader occasionally forget that the story is first person and not the more expansive third.

First-Person Observer (a.k.a. First-Person Minor)

This is a first-person narrator telling the story of someone who is incapable, for whatever reason, of telling his or her own story. Most often the incapacity is a matter of bias, mental or emotional duress or disability, or the main character's death, so the first-person observer tells the protagonist's story as he or she understood and witnessed it. But it could also be that the protagonist has some bit of mystery that needs

Writing Voice

to be maintained, which would be taken away if the protagonist were telling his own story.

Though this, too, is a rather infrequent POV, there are nevertheless several classic examples in literature: *Moby-Dick* is told not by Ahab but by Ishmael; *The Great Gatsby* is told not by Gatsby but Nick Carraway. Not only are Ahab and Gatsby too deluded to tell their own stories—Ahab by his need for vengeance, Gatsby by his pretending to be someone he's not—but they also both end up dead in the course of their novels, which naturally means they cannot narrate their own stories, since the last line of their books would be "Agh! I'm about to di—!" Lucky for them, the first-person observer has the distance and perspective to tell the protagonist's story, and also to comment upon the protagonist's story as needed.

In *The Great Gatsby*, it's Nick's outsider status—a self-described honest Midwesterner living in the ritzy fantasy world of West Egg—that allows him to correctly see *all* of the other characters for who and what they really are, but especially Gatsby, both in the image (and the life) he wishes to project and in the true, pitiable person underneath. For example, take the following passage, wherein we see Gatsby's determination to rekindle a romance with the now-married Daisy and Nick's recognition and subtle critique of Gatsby's self-delusion:

> "I wouldn't ask too much of her," I ventured. "You can't repeat the past."
>
> "Can't repeat the past?" he cried incredulously. "Why of course you can!"
>
> He looked around him wildly, as if the past were lurking here in the shadow of his house, just out of reach of his hand.
>
> "I'm going to fix everything just the way it was before," he said, nodding determinedly. "She'll see."
>
> He talked a lot about the past, and I gathered that he wanted to recover something, some idea of himself perhaps, that had gone into loving Daisy. His life had been confused and disordered since then, but if he could once return to a certain starting place and go over it all slowly, he could find out what that thing was. ...

It's necessary for us to be outside of Gatsby's state of mind—in this moment and throughout the novel—to be able to fully understand it.

His story couldn't be told to us from his perspective, either in direct first person or using third limited. The novel requires Nick, looking at Gatsby from a distance, to be able to show us a more nuanced and complicated view than Gatsby himself likely wants us to see.

Besides *Gatsby* and *Moby-Dick*, the novella *Rita Hayworth and Shawshank Redemption* by Stephen King and the novel *A Prayer for Owen Meany* by John Irving are good examples of first-person observer POV.

- **PROS:** It has the closeness and intimacy of first person but also the required distance to tell the story of a character not capable, for whatever reason, of telling his own story.
- **CONS:** It allows interiority only for the narrator, not the protagonist proper, which calls for occasional conjecture as to what's happening in the protagonist's head. It also requires the narrator to be a character in the story but not to step up as the main character; he must be active enough to be present but passive enough not to get in the way of the main character and plot.

First-Person Unreliable (a.k.a. The Unreliable Narrator)

If first-person observer is the POV to adopt when you want to work around a protagonist incapable of telling his own story, the unreliable narrator is the POV you choose when you want that character to tell his own story anyway, when the narrator's inability to accurately or "objectively" tell his story is part of what you want to explore.

It's not that the unreliable narrator knows he's being unreliable or is trying to deceive the reader; rather, the unreliable narrator believes he's telling the story straight, and it's the reader who realizes this isn't the case by picking up subtle, and sometimes not-so-subtle, cues. In this sense, the reader has a better understanding of the unreliable narrator— and more perspective to judge the story being told—than the narrator himself does. The classic example comes from Edgar Allan Poe's short story "The Tell-Tale Heart" in which the unnamed narrator explains and defends (defensiveness is one of the red flags of unreliability) his murdering of an old man whose sole offense seems to have been having a creepy, milky, "vulture-like" eye. By the second or third time the narrator claims to be completely sane—"Madmen know nothing. But you should have seen me!"—the reader understands that the narrator is batty ... the exact opposite of what's being told to us.

It should be said, though, that it's pretty rare to have an unreliable narrator as far gone as Poe's. More often the unreliability comes in degrees, and sometimes with the narrator admitting unreliability, which has the strange effect of somehow making the reader trust the narrator again.

Some examples include *Lolita* by Vladimir Nabokov and *The Adventures of Huckleberry Finn* by Mark Twain. Many of you may remember this colorful and compelling opening, delivered by Huck Finn:

> You don't know about me, without you have read a book by the name of *The Adventures of Tom Sawyer*, but that ain't no matter. That book was made by Mr. Mark Twain, and he told the truth, mainly. There was things that he stretched, but mainly he told the truth.

Contemporary novels that use an unreliable narrator include *The Virgin Suicides* by Jeffrey Eugenides and *The Curious Incident of the Dog in the Night-Time* by Mark Haddon.

- **PROS:** This sophisticated POV has a kind of double reward for the reader: the level of story being told and the level of story that the reader recognizes as being truer. This allows an author to explore dualities and levels of meaning not just in looking at truth vs. deception but, say, love vs. obsession (Nabokov's *Lolita*) or civilization vs. real humanity (Twain's *Huck Finn*) or whatever the subject.
- **CONS:** When there's no compelling payoff for a reader in terms of revealing larger themes or ideas—or when unreliability stems from lying, withholding information, or toying with or taunting a reader—the unreliable narrator can actually work against your aims in a novel. Remember that an unreliable narrator works because it illuminates and broadens a reader's understanding of character and subject, not because it obscures these things. So use this POV with caution and care, and begin by looking at novels in which the unreliable narration is revelatory.

Second Person

The second person takes as its main character *you*, telling us what you do or who you are ("You walk to the sink and brush your teeth.") or sometimes coming in the form of commands or instructions ("Walk to the sink. Brush your teeth."). You'll more frequently see this POV used in short stories, where there's less room for error and redundancy; it can be especially difficult to sustain in a longer work for two (related) reasons: The novelty might be distracting for a reader in the long run, and the reader might rebel against being part of the narrative in the way the POV suggests, thinking to himself as the narrative orders him around *No I don't. No I won't. No I'm not.*

Nevertheless, the second person can create an unusual relationship between reader and text: On the one hand, the "you" character is always a distinct personality unto itself, with traits, motivations, and an identity all its own, but on the other hand, the reader slowly begins identifying with, and feeling close or even equal to, that persona. The character is separate from us but also the same. This can be particularly effective when we're faced with a character who is in some way flawed and who we might be inclined to dismiss in the first person or the third. It's more difficult to dismiss such a character in the second person because the character is, to some degree, you.

An example is Italo Calvino's novel *If on a winter's night a traveler*, which places the reader in the position of the main character:

> You are about to begin reading Italo Calvino's new novel *If on a winter's night a traveler*. Relax. Concentrate. Dispel every other thought. Let the world around you fade. Best to close the door; the TV is always on in the next room.

Other examples of second-person POV include the novels *Bright Lights, Big City* by Jay McInerny and *Half Asleep in Frog Pajamas* by Tom Robbins, as well as the short story collection *Self-Help* by Lorrie Moore.

- **PROS:** This POV creates a close bond between reader and character, with the second-person character both its own autonomous entity, separate from us, and at the same time an entity we identify with and feel equal to. This unusual relationship between reader and character—and the novelty of the voice and how it functions—can be interesting and engaging when it works.

- **CONS**: The novelty of the voice alone isn't enough to sustain a full novel. The second person must also be purposeful, bringing us in close to a character or situation that we might not automatically feel close to or identify with in other POVs; we believe it in the second person because it happens to us.

Third-Person Limited

This POV is characterized by the use of *he* or *she* and the character's name, as in, "John hated math. He hated it immensely." Unlike third-person omniscient, the third limited spends the entirety of the story in only one character's perspective, sometimes as if looking over that character's shoulder and sometimes going inside the character's mind, and the events are filtered through that character's perception (though less directly than first-person singular). Thus third-person limited has some of the closeness of first singular, letting us know a particular character's thoughts, feelings, and attitudes on the events being narrated, while also having the ability to pull back from the character to offer a wider perspective or view not bound by the protagonist's opinions or biases, thus being capable of calling out and revealing those biases (in often subtle ways) and showing the reader a clearer way of reading the character than the character himself would allow. Third-person limited is also useful in a novel where the protagonist is in a state of not-knowing regarding some aspect of plot, such as we see in mystery and suspense novels, and the tension that comes from the protagonist's trying to piece things together, from his limited view, becomes the reader's.

Saul Bellow's *Herzog* offers a great example of the balance in third-person limited between closeness to a character's mind-set and the ability of the narrator to nevertheless maintain a level of removal. The novel's protagonist, Moses Herzog, has fallen on hard times personally and professionally and has perhaps begun to lose his grip on reality, as the novel's famous opening line tells us. Using third-person limited allows Bellow to clearly convey Herzog's state of mind, and to make us feel close to him, while employing narrative distance to order the prose and give us perspective on the character.

> *If I am out of my mind, it's all right with me*, thought Moses Herzog.
>   Some people thought he was cracked and for a time he himself had doubted that he was all there. But now, though he still behaved oddly, he felt confident, cheerful, clairvoyant, and strong. He had fallen under a spell and was writing letters to everyone under the sun. He was so stirred by these letters that from the end of June he moved from place to place with a valise full of papers. He had carried this valise from New York to Martha's Vineyard, but returned from the Vineyard immediately; two days later he flew to Chicago, and from Chicago he went to a village in western Massachusetts. Hidden in the country, he wrote endlessly, fanatically, to the newspapers, to people in public life, to friends and relatives and at last to the dead, his own obscure dead, and finally the famous dead.

Some other useful examples of third-person limited narration include *Fahrenheit 451* by Ray Bradbury, *The Old Man and the Sea* by Ernest Hemingway, and the Harry Potter series by J.K. Rowling (though Rowling sparingly enters omniscient mode to cover all of the events and significant backstory of the books, even if the novels are primarily presented through Harry's perspective via the third limited).

- **PROS:** It offers the closeness of first person while maintaining the distance and authority of third and allows the author to explore a character's perceptions while providing perspective on the character or events that the character himself doesn't have. It also allows the author to tell an individual's story closely without being bound to that person's voice and its limitations.
- **CONS:** Since all of the events narrated are filtered through a single character's perceptions, only what that character experiences directly or indirectly can be used in the story (as is the case with first-person singular).

Third-Person Omniscient
Characterized by the use of *he* or *she*, and further characterized by having the powers of God, this POV is able to go into any character's

perspective or consciousness and reveal his or her thoughts; able to go to any time, place, or setting; privy to information the characters themselves don't have; and able to comment on events that have happened, are happening, or will happen. The third-person omniscient voice is really a narrating personality unto itself, a kind of disembodied character in its own right—though the degree to which the narrator wants to be seen as a distinct personality, or wants to seem objective or impartial (and thus somewhat invisible as a separate personality), is up to your particular needs and style.

The third-person omniscient is a popular choice for novelists who have big casts and complex plots, as it allows the author to move about in time, space, and character as needed, though this is also a potential drawback of the voice: Too much freedom can lead to a lack of focus, spending too many brief moments in too many characters' heads so that we never feel grounded in any one particular experience, perspective, or arc.

Here's a good guiding principle: As a general rule, each chapter—and perhaps even each individual scene—should primarily focus on one particular character and perspective. Imagine how exhausting it would be to read a scene with five characters sitting around a table, each with something to hide, and the narrative moving line by line into each character's shifty mind: "I wonder if Johnny knows about Bob?" "Kay is looking at me funny. I wonder if she knows what Johnny knows." "If only Johnny knew that I know about Bob and Kay." "I'm Kay and I'm not sure why everyone is looking at me and Bob." Yikes. So you want to use the powers of the POV selectively and for a reason, without abusing those powers. In other words, don't use the freedom of omniscience as a substitute for, or as a shortcut to, real tension, drama, and revelation.

An example is the novel *Jonathan Strange & Mr. Norrell* by Susanna Clarke, which uses an omniscient narrator to manage a large cast. Here you'll note some hallmarks of omniscient narration, notably a wide view of a particular time and place, freed from coming through solely one character's perspective, and it certainly evidences a strong aspect of storytelling voice, the "narrating personality" of third omniscient that acts almost as another character in the book (and will help maintain book cohesion across a number of characters and events):

> SOME YEARS AGO there was in the city of York a society of magicians. They met upon the third Wednesday of every month and read each other long, dull papers upon the history of English magic.

Other examples include *The Lord of the Rings* by J.R.R. Tolkien, *One Hundred Years of Solitude* by Gabriel Garcia Marquez, and *White Teeth* by Zadie Smith.

- **PROS**: You have the storytelling powers of God, able to go anywhere and dip into anyone's mind-set or consciousness. This is particularly useful for novels with large casts and where the events or characters are spread out over, and separated by, time or space. A narrative personality emerges from third-person omniscience with the narration becoming a kind of character in its own right, able to offer information and perspective not available to the main characters of the book.
- **CONS**: Jumping from consciousness to consciousness—especially as a shortcut to dramatic tension and revelation—can lead to a story that is forever shifting in focus and perspective, like a mind reader on the fritz. To avoid this, consider each scene as having a particular character and question as its focal point and consider how the personality that comes through the third-person omniscient narrative voice helps unify the disparate action.

MAKING THE RIGHT CHOICE FOR YOUR STORY AND GENRE

Language forces us to perceive the world as man presents it to us.

—JULIA PENELOPE

Writing Voice

To a certain degree we don't really choose a POV for our project; our project chooses POV for us. If we were writing a sprawling epic, for example, we wouldn't choose a first-person singular POV, with our main character constantly wondering what everyone back on Darvon-5 is doing. If we were writing a whodunit, we wouldn't choose an omniscient narrator who jumps into the butler's head in chapter one and has him think, *I dunnit*. Our story tells us how it should be told, and once we find the right POV and approach, we realize our story couldn't have been told any other way.

Hopefully, the previous section gives you a good idea of how to match up POV with the aims you have for your story and the particular needs of your chosen genre. If you're still not sure, then you might want to take a look at the Exploring Point of View chart on the following pages.

It should be said that the chart is unscientific, or maybe trying to be too scientific to contain something as fluid and mysterious as narrative, as not every problem can be anticipated and answered here. But at a baseline, this illustrates the thought process and questioning that goes into choosing your POV.

GOING DEEPER: FROM POV TO VOICE

If point of view is about the narrator's relationship to what's being said, voice is about the narrator's *attitude* toward the narrated, revealed not just in what is said but how it's said. If you go back and look at the sample first sentences in the POV: Know Your Options section, you'll see that each contains two levels of meaning, what's commonly referred to as story and discourse. Story is the basic plot-level information given to us in a line; discourse, the particular attitude conveyed toward what's given, comes through *how* the information is given. In other words, story provides information, and discourse provides a way of reading and understanding the information.

EXPLORING POINT OF VIEW

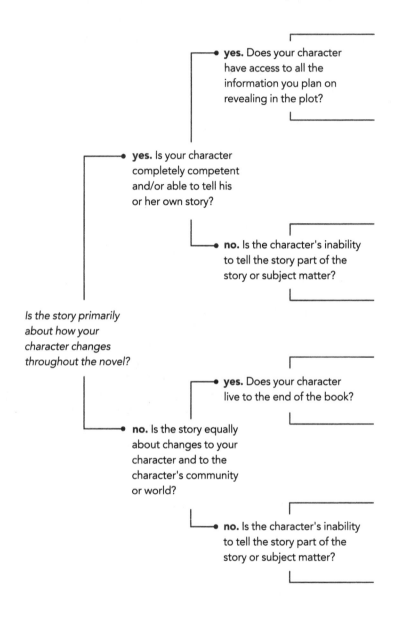

yes. Does your character have access to all the information you plan on revealing in the plot?

yes. Is your character completely competent and/or able to tell his or her own story?

no. Is the character's inability to tell the story part of the story or subject matter?

Is the story primarily about how your character changes throughout the novel?

yes. Does your character live to the end of the book?

no. Is the story equally about changes to your character and to the character's community or world?

no. Is the character's inability to tell the story part of the story or subject matter?

──────● **yes.** Try first-person singular.

                     ┌──────────────● **yes.** Try third-person omniscient.

──────● **no.** Are other characters
and their experiences
needed to reveal the full
scope of the story?

                   └──────────────● **no.** Try third-person limited.

──────● **yes.** Try first-person unreliable.

──────● **no.** Try first-person observer.

──────● **yes.** Try first-person singular or third-person limited.

──────● **no.** Try third-person limited.

──────● **yes.** Try third-person omniscient.

                     ┌──────────────● **yes.** Try first-person singular
                                     or third-person limited.

──────● **no.** Are the changes to the
external world felt primarily
by your protagonist?

                     └──────────────● **no.** Try third-person omniscient.

Voice is about discourse, the *how* it's said that makes meaning for the reader and which is achieved through the following:

- **PERSPECTIVE:** The sum feelings or thoughts of the narrator, protagonist, or both toward the subject being narrated
- **TONE:** The attitude toward that subject as revealed in word choices of the narrator/protagonist
- **LANGUAGE:** The word-by-word choices—having to do with syntax, diction, line length, rhythm, etc.—that reveal the tone and perspective of the narrator, protagonist, or both

As you can see, these are closely related and dependent upon each other, though they're not the same things. Let's say a particular narrator's perspective toward the events he describes is one of dislike or disdain … what does that mean for the tone of the piece? Our first and most obvious reaction would be to say that the tone will be "disdainful," though this isn't very helpful and doesn't make a lot of sense. Do we mean that the tone will be angry, bitter, agitated? Or that it'll be sad, mournful, full of resignation? Wouldn't each one of these lead the voice in slightly different directions? Besides, our initial impulse of a serious or sad voice might be off the mark altogether; the tone might be funny or satirical, showing displeasure with the subject by poking holes in it.

So attitude toward the subject, plus a particular tone, begins forming voice—and these particulars are revealed through the language of the narrator (or protagonist, or both) and its nuances, goals, or limitations.

A quick word about this narrator/protagonist/both business: This depends upon the POV you've chosen and the narrator's relationship to the text. If you've chosen a first-person singular voice, then the attitude coming through in the voice clearly belongs to the protagonist (who is also the narrator). If you've chosen a third-person limited voice, then the attitude belongs to both the narrative presence and the protagonist (as revealed through the voice's occasionally entering the protagonist's head and then backing out). If you've chosen a third-person omniscient POV, then the attitude might still belong to both narrator and protagonist, though the narrator will be much more up-front, as your cast of characters is likely large and spread out (thus your narrator's perspective is what unifies the action).

Let's take a look at a few examples to see how the POV changes our thoughts on whose perspective we're getting and to identify the perspective, tone, and language choices that make up voice.

To begin, let's look at the first-person singular narrator of Raymond Carver's short story "Cathedral":

> This blind man, an old friend of my wife's, he was on his way to spend the night. His wife had died. So he was visiting the dead wife's relatives in Connecticut. He called my wife from his in-laws'. Arrangements were made. He would come by train, a five-hour trip, and my wife would meet him at the station. She hadn't seen him since she worked for him one summer in Seattle ten years ago. But she and the blind man had kept in touch. They made tapes and mailed them back and forth. I wasn't enthusiastic about his visit. He was no one I knew. And his being blind bothered me. My idea of blindness came from the movies. In the movies, the blind moved slowly and never laughed. Sometimes they were led by seeing-eye dogs. A blind man in my house was not something I looked forward to.

The attitude here is the protagonist's, the main character telling the story, and it's also a rather poor one. We know that the narrator/protagonist isn't happy about the blind man coming to his house because he tells us so, of course, but where does this first become evident to us? Where do we first understand the narrator's perspective on the events he's describing? The very first word: not *a* blind man but *this* blind man, which automatically reveals the narrator's defensiveness and discomfort (his perspective as well as his tone).

There's a good amount of story in the paragraph—filling in some information—but what we take away from the paragraph is primarily discourse: the narrator's attitude about this visit, which informs the reader's attitude about *him*. Furthermore, we know that not only is he on the defensive, but he's also not the brightest bulb, which we get through the short, straightforward, rather uncomplicated sentences (not to mention his simplistic and apparently unashamed dislike of "this blind man"). Were we to keep going in the story, we'd see more support for our early conclusions about this narrator, but we nevertheless get a good sense even from the first paragraph. We're grounded in a clear voice, and already we have thoughts about the person attached to it.

For an example of voice from the third-person limited POV, take a look at these opening passages from Flannery O'Connor's story "A Late Encounter with the Enemy" (I've omitted a couple of bridging sentences and paragraphs for brevity):

> General Sash was a hundred and four years old. He lived with his granddaughter, Sally Poker Sash, who was sixty-two years old and who prayed every night on her knees that he would live until her graduation from college. The General didn't give two slaps for her graduation but he never doubted he would live for it. ... A graduation exercise was not exactly his idea of a good time, even if, as she said, he would be expected to sit on the stage in his uniform. She said there would be a long procession of teachers and students in their robes but that there wouldn't be anything to equal him in his uniform. He knew this well enough without her telling him, and as for the damn procession, it could march to hell and back and not cause him a quiver. ...
>
> For his part, the General would not have consented even to attend her graduation if she had not promised to see to it that he sat on the stage. He liked to sit on any stage. He considered that he was still a very handsome man. When he had been able to stand up, he had measured five feet four inches of pure game cock. ...

The third-person limited means that we're getting some combination of the narrator's perspective on things and the protagonist's, as his thoughts occasionally come through in the text. And it's clear that the narrator in O'Connor's story has a different take and perspective on the events than the superannuated General Sash. The general's attitude is obviously one of pride, though the reader understands that the General's pride is closer to vanity and undeserved. Occasionally the protagonist's thoughts and attitudes come through the voice: that he "didn't give two slaps" for the whole thing, that the "damn procession could march to hell," and that he only consented to being there because he likes being "on any stage." But the sly commentary coming through in the voice—in the narrator's attitude about the subject—shows that Sash is a rather ridiculous, self-absorbed old man, made most clear in the wonderful discrepancy in the last line quoted, that when he stood up (when he still could) he measured a mere five feet four inches of "pure game cock." We understand the protagonist's perspective and crotchety nature, but it's the juxtaposition of these with the *narrator's* perspective on Sash, the darkly comic and even satirical tone, that really makes meaning and establishes the voice of the piece.

Looking back at the example of Susanna Clarke's *Jonathan Strange & Mr. Norrell* and its use of third-person omniscient POV, again we see a clear voice and attitude, though the attitude belongs to the storytelling narrator:

> SOME YEARS AGO there was in the city of York a society of magicians. They met upon the third Wednesday of every month and read each other long, dull papers upon the history of English magic.
>
> They were gentleman-magicians, which is to say they had never harmed anyone by magic—nor ever done anyone the slightest good. In fact, to own the truth, not one of these magicians had ever cast the smallest spell, nor by magic caused one leaf to tremble upon a tree, made one mote of dust to alter its course or changed a single hair upon anyone's head. But, with this one minor reservation, they enjoyed a reputation as some of the wisest and most magical gentlemen in Yorkshire.

The straight-up story in these opening paragraphs is fairly uncomplicated: We have a group of magicians who come together once a week to discuss magic. That's the basic information. But we know a lot more about them thanks to the way the information is given: that they're academic rather than practical and are, in fact, rather feckless, men who would rather think about something (here, magic) than do it.

But do we presume that the magicians believe themselves to be ineffectual? Do we think that the magicians believe their papers to be "dull"? That they're aware of the fact they've never done "the slightest good" or never so much as "changed a hair upon anyone's head"? No. These are not the characters' attitudes about themselves but the narrator's attitude, and it quickly becomes the reader's attitude, too. Because of the discourse—how it's said and the attitude toward the subjects— we begin to extrapolate, picturing these magicians in their musty occult libraries and their clawfoot chairs dressed in ridiculous old robes, smoking pipes, sniffing brandy, seeming more like a Kiwanis meeting than a concert of alchemists. In other words, we already know quite a lot about them, and how to feel about them, just from how this is told.

What else would we say about the voice? Again, it's behaving like an old-fashioned storytelling presence, right down to the capitalization of "SOME YEARS AGO," putting us in mind of storytelling presences we might find in fairy tales. But the mock formality of the tone and the word-by-word choices in language come across as humorous here, almost subversive: The narrator finds the men pompous and puffed up, and the voice subtly reveals that. Thus we have a clear voice with a personality and slant of its own luring us into the story but also telling us how to read it. How it's said is every bit as important as what is said.

EXERCISE: THE IMPORTANCE OF VOICE

Choose one of the passages from the previous section—Carver, O'Connor, or Clarke—and rewrite the passage using the voice from one of the other examples. (For instance, retell the opening passage of *Jonathan Strange & Mr. Norrell* with Carver's narrator doing the narrating.) Read the voice you'll be appropriating several times out loud to yourself to get a sense of its perspective, tone, cadence, language, and so on. In fact, you might want to find a copy of the story and read larger portions of it out loud to make sure you have a full sense of how the voice fits in your mouth. Then rewrite the scene you've chosen using the mismatched narrator, trying to tell it as that narrator would. The purpose of the exercise is to illustrate that, even with the same basic information being conveyed, differences in how it's told lead to a different story and experience altogether.

GOING DEEPER: FINDING YOUR VOICE

We've already seen the importance of finding and establishing a narrative voice that fits your needs for the novel, matching up with and building off the POV and conveying a certain attitude toward the characters and events that the reader needs in order to fully understand your story. But what happens if the voice required by your story isn't necessarily one you feel comfortable with? What happens when you find yourself wrestling with voice, even after you've discovered the right one?

This goes directly to one of those persistent, pervasive pieces of advice you'll hear given to beginning novelists, the dreaded "find your voice." But does that mean something different than finding the voice that your novel requires? Is there a distinction to be made between the novel's voice and *your* voice? Or are they the same thing?

This is a difficult question to answer, not because there isn't a clear answer, but because the answer is not always one beginning novelists want to hear: You have natural narrative tendencies, the beginnings of voice, already within you, made up of certain proclivities in storytelling, ways of seeing and saying that make sense to you and come to you more easily than others. But these aren't always the ways of seeing and saying you wish they were.

In other words, occasionally a writer will set out to work on the kind of novel he admires, only to realize later in the project that the kind of novel he admires isn't necessarily one he can write. You might have a good understanding of how the type of story works, and you may have read a million novels that do something similar, but understanding the approach doesn't always mean that it's one that will work for you. This is especially the case with those writers we idolize most; part of the reason a writer becomes a hero to us is that it seems like nobody does it like that person, that the author can't be emulated. And then, like Don Quixotes chasing down windmills, we set out to do just that, to emulate the writer who can't be emulated, sometimes spending years pursuing someone else's vision rather than considering our own.

Early in my writing career, I tried to emulate writers I loved whom I had no business trying to emulate—because my natural tendencies weren't consistent with theirs. I assumed this was my own problem, that no other writers would be silly enough to fall into the same trap, but I quickly learned that this is common to the apprentice stage of writing. Everyone starts out trying to write like someone else, and eventually, through trial and error, we begin to realize what aspects of others' writing make sense to us and why, and which parts make no sense to us and why. The better our understanding of what we aren't inclined to do as novelists, the better our understanding of what we *can* do, what works for us and makes sense. And through this process we begin to define our own style and voice.

You may already have an understanding of your natural tendencies in storytelling; if so, wonderful. But, if not, let me reassure you that those tendencies are there, that your own voice is waiting, and wanting, to emerge. Finding your voice isn't as simple as finding your car keys, unfortunately—it's a process, again, of trial and error—but a good start might be to try the exercises in this chapter. Write without overthinking what happens, and take note of what patterns you see emerge in your work that might suggest your natural strengths in voice.

TRY IT OUT: TESTING YOUR POV

There's little as frustrating as getting one hundred pages into your novel only to discover you've got some big problems with voice or point of view, so try to make as informed a decision as possible up front. Take a look back at the Exploring Point of View chart and try running your story idea through the questions you find there.

JOSEPH BATES is the author of *Tomorrowland: Stories* (2013) and *Writing Your Novel from Start to Finish* (Writer's Digest Books, 2015). His short fiction has appeared in *New Ohio Review, Identity Theory, South Carolina Review*, and more. He teaches creative writing at Miami University in Oxford, Ohio.

CHAPTER 17

THE DIFFICULTY OF FIRST-PERSON POV

BY JAMES SCOTT BELL

There's no quicker way to intimacy with a lead character than first-person point of view (POV). Seeing a story through that character's thoughts and perceptions is the fast track to empathy and identification.

But numerous challenges also come with this POV. One of these is the natural limitation of being stuck in one perspective throughout the story.

Maybe you want more flexibility in your plot. If so, there are ways to break out of that "boxed in" feeling you might get with first person.

TIME DELAY

A detective on the trail of a killer corners him in a dark apartment. He takes several tentative steps. A shot rings out. The detective feels hot blood coming from his chest.

If you were writing in third-person POV, it would be easy to cut away from a scene of high tension for another scene with a different POV character (in this case, say, it's the detective's partner, lounging at a coffee shop). This is a great page-turning technique, leaving the reader to wonder what happened at the apartment.

A first-person novel, however, can't cut away to a different POV scene. So instead of a physical cut, try *time delay*. First, end the chapter on a note of high tension. Then begin the subsequent chapter not with the next thing that happened, but with the narrator playing a little game of "You'll have to wait." In keeping with the same story line:

> I hear a shot. And a jolt to my chest. And hot blood staining my shirt.
>
> [Next Chapter]
>
> When I was six, my father taught me a valuable lesson. "Son," he said ...

After this digression, which can be a full-on flashback or a short remembrance, get back to what happened at the end of the last scene.

IMAGINATION

Lawrence Block's *Hope to Die* begins like a crime novel written in third person:

> It was a perfect summer evening, the last Monday in July. The Hollanders arrived at Lincoln Center sometime between six and six-thirty ...

Four paragraphs later, however, we learn this is a first-person narration. The narrator is using his imagination to describe details he didn't personally witness:

> I can picture them, standing around on the second floor at Avery Fisher Hall, holding a glass of white wine, picking up an hors d'oeuvre from a tray.

Still further on:

> Though, as I said, I can't know this, in my imagination they are walking home.

The narrator then describes a double murder, complete with what might have been in the minds of the victims. It works just as well as a third-person description would.

DREAMS

Dreams are a great way to reveal interior dimensions of the first-person narrator and illustrate the stakes she confronts. When the character is under tremendous stress, a dream can create a vicarious, emotional experience for the reader.

Two caveats: Dream sequences should be used only once unless dreams are an integral part of the plot or the character's life. And the description of dreams should be relatively short. Janet Fitch strikes the right tone in *White Oleander*:

> But that night I dreamed the old dream again, of gray Paris streets and the maze of stone, the bricked blind windows ... I knew I had to find my mother. It was getting dark, dark figures lurked in cellar entrances. I rang all the buzzers to the apartments. Women came to the door, looking like her, smiling, some even calling my name. But none of them was her.
>
> I knew she was in there, I banged on the door, screamed for her to let me in. The door buzzed to admit me, but just as I pushed it in, I saw her leaving from the courtyard gate, a passenger in a small red car, wearing her curly Afghan coat and big sunglasses over her blind eyes, she was leaning back in the seat and laughing. I ran after her, crying, begging.
>
> Yvonne shook me awake.

SECONDHAND REPORTS

A first-person story can take us to scenes that happened outside the narrator's perception by having another character recount the events. Done right, the secondhand scene can hold just as much drama as any other scene.

There are two ways to do it. First, the secondary character—in the following examples, let's call him Sam—may simply tell what happened in his own voice, becoming, essentially, another first-person narrator.

> [Sam:] "I opened the door and went in. I smelled gunpowder, and I knew it was bad. My first thought was, is the guy still in here? Am I going to get one in the gut?"

You can make that a long section of narration or occasionally interrupt with the main character's voice:

> [Sam:] "I opened the door and went in. I smelled gunpowder, and I knew it was bad. My first thought was, is the guy still in here? Am I going to get one in the gut?"

[Main character:]"Why'd you go in in the first place?" I asked.

The other way to go is to have the secondary character begin the account, then switch to a third-person style, without technically leaving the first-person POV:

[Sam:] "I opened the door and went in. I smelled gunpowder, and I knew it was bad. My first thought was, is the guy still in here? Am I going to get one in the gut?"

With the next paragraph, switch to a third-person feel:

Sam heard a noise and decided he'd better get his own gun ready. The room was dark. A flash of neon seeped through the window shade ...

The narrator's voice continues to tell us what Sam's account is. The readers will go with it.

There's no need to feel overly constrained by first-person POV. Write with a passion to open up readers to your lead character's inner life. Then use these techniques to open up your plot.

CHAPTER 18

THE VOICE OF GENRE

BY STEVEN HARPER

Almost every set of submission guidelines from agents and editors says they're looking for authors with a *strong voice*, a *unique voice*, or a *powerful voice*. Guidelines for everything from thrillers to cookbooks mention the importance of voice. My own agent's Web page mentions *original new voices*. But none of them says exactly what that means.

Voice is a little hard to pin down. It basically means *how you write*. It involves the words you choose and the rhythms you write in. It's how your writing sounds on the page. I know, I know—these descriptions actually sound a bit like writing *style*. Style is related to voice. Voice goes deeper. Voice is also the persona you put on when you start writing.

When you put words on paper (yeah, yeah—or on computer screen; work with me here), you aren't really being *you*. You aren't showing the world your true face or personality, though glimmers of your true self will show through. Like an actor strolling onto the stage, you're adopting a different persona, one that combines elements of yourself with a bunch of stuff you've made up. This persona, this *voice*, is the one who tells the story.

FIRST PERSON

An author who writes in first person very naturally slips into a particular voice, since the main character speaks directly to the reader, and the main character will speak differently than the author. Let's compare three different first-person vampire novels. In *The Vampire Lestat*, Anne Rice writes:

> I turned my back on it and let out a terrible roar. I felt its hands close on my shoulders like things forged of metal, and as I went into a last frenzy of struggling, it whipped me around so that its eyes were right before me, wide and dark, and the lips were closed yet still smiling, and then it bent down and I felt the prick of its teeth on my neck.
>
> Out of all the childhood tales, the old fables, the name came to me, like a drowned thing shooting to the surface of black water and breaking free in the light.
>
> "Vampire!" I gave one last frantic cry, shoving at the creature with all I had.
>
> Then there was silence. Stillness.

Octavia E. Butler's vampire in *Fledgling* speaks very differently:

> I stared down at the bleeding marks I'd made on his hand, and suddenly I was unable to think about anything else. I ducked my head and licked away the blood, licked the wound I had made. He tensed, almost pulling his hand away. Then he stopped and seemed to relax. He let me take his hand between my own. I looked at him, saw him glancing at me, felt the car zigzag a little on the road.
>
> He frowned and pulled away from me, all the while looking uncertain, unhappy. I caught his hand again between mine and held it. I felt him try to pull away. He shook me, actually lifting me into the air a little, trying to get away from me, but I didn't let go. I licked at the blood welling up where my teeth had cut him.

And the voice of Lucienne Diver's young vampire in *Vamped* plunges into a completely new direction:

> "You're right," I said, thinking feverishly. "I do need a bite to eat. And I know just the thing."
>
> Based on how quickly [Bobby] stepped back, I'm pretty sure he thought I meant him, but that wasn't it. Mom and Dad had been big with the child-rearing clichés. When life gives you lemons, you make lemonade had been a favorite of theirs, and I guess it must have sunk in a little. All I needed was a place to shower and change, a stylist, a mani-

pedi, and some skin cream and I'd be as good as new. I could even start my own entourage for touch-ups. Better than any mirror. I tried to believe it.

Three vampires, three voices. Rice, writing as Lestat, uses an abundance of figurative language. Similes and metaphors dominate her work, competing with an abundance of adjectives. Her word choice leans toward florid. Butler, writing as Shori, uses a more spare, straightforward voice with little in the way of description and more focus on action. Shori speaks with more verbs than adjectives. Her words are plainer, leaner. Diver, writing as Gina, tends to speak in short, punchy bursts. Her clauses are short, and she avoids prepositional phrases that might lengthen her sentences, giving Gina a breathless voice appropriate to a teenaged fashionista.

Did Diver think in those terms? I'm imagining her sitting at her keyboard, brow furrowed, finger hovered over the Delete key. "Oops," she mutters. "Used too many prepositional phrases in this section. Need to cut out a few."

I doubt it. More likely, Diver (and Rice and Butler) did her best to think like her main character, learn how to speak like her main character, and put her main character's words on paper. The words came out that way because Diver (and the others) knew her character so well, she could speak in the character's voice.

A unique voice evolves from creating a unique viewpoint character and then getting to know the viewpoint character from the inside out. You know how some married couples can finish each other's sentences? That's the kind of relationship you need with your main character. That deep understanding will allow you to develop the voice.

And no, you don't need to have that understanding before you start writing. Your first draft is all about getting to know your main character (or characters). As you progress through the draft, your knowledge of the character will deepen and the voice will strengthen. Then, when you go back for revisions, you'll be able to catch inconsistencies and change what the character or narrator says so the voice becomes consistent.

THIRD PERSON

There's certainly a voice for third-person novels, too. It's sometimes called the *author voice* or *narrator voice*. It's not that different from a first-person voice—the person is a narrator who's telling the story, and this narrator has a voice. The narrator may or may not be the author of the book. Usually it isn't. The narrator voice is often similar to the viewpoint character.

Naomi Novik demonstrates a mastery of third-person voice in her Temeraire books. She uses two distinct narrator voices, one for the dragon Temeraire and one for Will Laurence. It's easy to tell them apart at a glance. This passage from *Victory of Eagles* comes from Temeraire's point of view. The young dragon has been imprisoned for treason:

> [Temeraire] was quite sure he and Laurence had done as they ought, in taking the cure to France, and no-one sensible could disagree; but just in case, Temeraire had steeled himself to meet with either disapproval or contempt, and he had worked out several very fine arguments in his defense. Most important, of course, it was just a cowardly, sneaking way of fighting; if the Government wished to beat Napoleon, they ought to fight directly, and not make his dragons sick to try to make him easy to defeat; as if British dragons could not beat French dragons, without cheating.

Compare that to this passage a few pages later from the point of view of Will Laurence, imprisoned for the same crime:

> There had been no defense to make, and no comfort but the arid certainty that he had done as he ought; that he could have done nothing else. That was no comfort at all, but that it saved him from the pain of regret; he could not regret what he had done. He could not have let ten thousand dragons, most of them wholly uninvolved in the war, be murdered for his nation's advantage.

In these two passages we have the same event told from two different points of view and two different voices. The narrator who tells Temeraire's story speaks with Temeraire's voice. Novik injects a naïve arrogance into Temeraire's point of view. Temeraire also thinks about the cowardly sneakiness of using plague in warfare. Laurence, on the other hand, speaks with an older, more cynical voice. Novik—or

Laurence—avoids self-congratulatory language, and his thoughts wander to the fact that he had done the right thing but was still going to pay for it. Temeraire is outraged at their situation, where Laurence is resigned to it, and it shows in their individual voices.

You don't *have* to switch voice whenever you switch point of view. However, different voices within the same book is one of those things that can distinguish a good book from a great one, or make it more memorable in the mind of an editor.

I was going to say that switching voices in a book will *always* distinguish a good book from a great one, but really, plenty of authors maintain a single narrator voice throughout their work. Terry Pratchett's voice never wavers in any of his Discworld novels, no matter what character he's writing about, and the style of humor is distinctly his own. Philip Pullman also uses the same voice whether he's writing from Lyra's or Will's point of view in *The Subtle Knife*. The real key is to make your voice distinct, which we'll talk about in a moment.

FIRST AND THIRD PERSON TOGETHER

A few authors inject themselves directly into their books. They make it clear that they're telling a story by addressing the reader directly or using a narrator *I*. This usually shows up in books aimed at younger readers, since it creates the illusion that someone is telling the reader a story instead of the reader actually reading it. Edward Eager uses this type of voice in *Half Magic:*

> Katharine was the middle child, of docile disposition and a comfort to her mother. She knew she was a comfort, and docile, because she'd heard her mother say so. And the others knew she was too, by now, because ever since that day Katharine would keep boasting about it, until Jane declared she would utter a piercing shriek and fall over dead if she heard another word about it. This will give you some idea of what Jane and Katharine were like.

Eager is talking to us. His voice is casual and uses the repetition common to oral storytellers. The last sentence clinches it—we're listening to a story, not reading.

Eager addresses the reader rarely throughout the book: just often enough to remind us he's telling us a story, and not so often that his voice becomes intrusive.

THE INVISIBLE NARRATOR

One of the harder voices to pull off is the *invisible narrator*. Sometimes called *transparent prose*, this is an author voice that tries to fade into the background. It's kind of the opposite of the combination first and third person above—the author tries to disappear as much as possible.

Brendan Mull uses this voice in *Fablehaven*, as we see here:

> Seth set the mug on the dresser. Taking a calming breath, he silently prayed that the tarantula would be gone and the fairy would be there. He slid the drawer open.
>
> A hideous little creature glared up from inside the jar. Baring pointy teeth, it hissed at him. Covered in brown leather skin, it stood taller than his middle finger. It was bald, with tattered ears, a narrow chest, a pot belly, and shriveled, spindly limbs. The lips were froglike, the eyes a glossy black, the nose a pair of slits above the mouth.
>
> "What did you do to the fairy?" Seth asked.

Mull doesn't talk to the reader and doesn't adopt a particular point of view with his voice. He barely gets inside *Seth's* point of view, in fact, with only a single reference to what Seth is thinking or feeling. The advantage to this voice is that the narrator never gets in the way of the story. The disadvantage is that transparent voice can come across as dry. Writers who use it need to make up for the dryness by adding other color. Mull uses plenty of magic and action to keep his story moving so his readers don't notice the transparent voice.

EXERCISE 1

Take a passage from a book you love and change it into the voice of another book you love. You can't change the events—only the word choice. For example, take the opener of *Harry Potter and the Sorcerer's Stone* and retell it as if Neil Gaiman had written it for *The Graveyard Book* instead. For

---

a real challenge, use someone like Shakespeare or Christopher Marlowe as one of the authors. If you're part of a writers' group or have other friends you share your work with, read it aloud to them and see if they can guess which author you converted the voice to. In a group setting, you could pick one book that everyone has read and have everyone convert the voice to a different famous author. Read the pieces aloud and see if everyone can guess whom the "new" author is.

EXERCISE 2

Take your favorite third-person narrative and convert a scene to first person. How might George from *Of Mice and Men* tell the story? Or Lennie? How might Cinderella tell her own story? What might her voice sound like?

KEEN ON VOICE

As I said previously, almost every agent or editor will say they're looking for fiction with a unique or interesting voice. Several say that a good voice will grab their eye above anything else. Why are they so keen on voice?

The reason is that a unique or interesting or quirky voice can really make a book. The hero's quest is nearly ubiquitous in paranormal (and a lot of nonsupernatural) books. A lot of other elements crop up over and over again. Regardless of what twist you put on your vampires, they're still vampires. No matter what new element you introduce into your ghost story, it's still a ghost story. One thing that *can* be unique, regardless of the story type, is the author's voice. A fascinating voice can get the reader to overlook other problems or even fail to notice things like clichés entirely. A cool voice is one reason an editor will overlook clichés and buy a book. The unique voice overcomes the tired clichés.

So you really do want to work on creating and developing a fascinating author voice for your book. It's your main selling point.

How to Find a Voice

There's no one way or formula to finding a voice. This process is mostly a matter of experimenting, playing around until you find something that clicks or makes sense to you or just hangs together in a way that sounds great. Here are some things you can do to find that voice. Some are exercises, some are techniques.

Let Yourself Write Badly

Ray Bradbury, famous for both his supernatural and his science fiction work, once said that there are a million bad words in every writer—you just have to keep writing until they're all out of your system. So give yourself permission to write badly. Get those words down, even if they're crap. Don't judge what you've written yet. Keep going and see what you're going to say next. A voice will begin to emerge.

Write Fast and See What Happens

Bull-rush your way forward. Pound those words out and don't look back. Write quickly, even if it's nonsensical. Don't edit (yet). Write like you're writing journal entries or a letters to a friend under deadline—no time to stop. Maybe some quirky turns of phrase will come flying out of your fingers and develop into the voice you're looking for. Or maybe a character will develop in an unexpected and interesting direction. In any case, save the editing for later and see what you can come up with *now*.

Let Your Characters Talk to You Through the Computer

Pretend you're the character and start typing in that character's voice, even if your novel is going to be in third person. Don't worry about developing the story yet—just let the character ramble at you while you write down what you hear. (And don't fret if you find yourself talking back, either. A number of my writer friends do it, as do I. In fact, you'd might be surprised at how many professional authors sit in little rooms talking to people who don't exist.) Write letters, journal entries, trial transcripts, sessions with the character's therapist, or what the character says aloud when no one is listening. You might develop a voice by becoming someone else for a while.

Experiment

Go there. Do that. Be silly. Be stupid. Be florid. Be pretentious. You won't know what it looks like until you write it down. No one will see it except you, so why should you care if your second-grade niece could probably have done better? Every bit might be dreadful, or one of the experiments might turn up something worth keeping—but you'll never know unless you give yourself the freedom to try it.

Save Everything

Never, ever throw anything away. Early notes, character sketches, the material you generate doing any of the previous exercises—keep every word. I can't count the number of times I've gone back through old material on a work-in-progress and realized I'd overlooked something good, whether it was an idea, a turn of phrase, or a bit of characterization. Ultimately, it all contributes to voice, so keep it.

Change the Point of View

If the writing seems dull or stale, try a shift in the viewpoint. If it's first person, change it to third and let you, the author, speak. If it's third person, change it to first and let the character speak. See what impact it has on the story—and on your voice.

You can also try shifting to a different *character's* point of view. Since every character has a different way of seeing the world and a different voice, try writing the same scene through the eyes of two different characters. Make sure the voice is different, and see which one you like better.

Write What You Really Want to Write

Write the themes you *really* want to explore. The stuff that gets under your skin or makes you giddy or pisses you off. Too many new writers try to gauge the market and only write what they think is commercial so they can break in. This is usually a bad idea—the book produced by this kind of thinking will probably be dull and lackluster. Don't dance around what you really want to say, and don't worry what your family or friends or co-workers will think about your book. Should anyone ask why you wrote such a thing, you can say, "Hey, I wrote a book. What did *you* do last summer?"

If you need to, switch genres. If you don't think that relationships can have happy endings, don't try to write a paranormal romance. If you secretly think everything will come out all right in the end in real life, what are you doing trying to write horror? Figure out what idea revs your motor and then build a story around it. The emotional response from you, the writer, will stimulate voice—and engage the reader.

STEVEN HARPER PIZIKS was born with a name no one can reliably spell or pronounce, so he usually writes under the pen name Steven Harper. He lives in southeast Michigan, where he's written more than two dozen novels in several genres. Visit his Web site at http://www.stevenpiziks.com.

CHAPTER 19

MATCHING VOICE AND DIALOGUE TO YOUR STORY

BY GLORIA KEMPTON

*Let's see, I have to get Homer from Point A to Point B by Tuesday after-
noon and along the way he has to talk to Amos to see where they stashed
the loot. The loot has to be moved by Tuesday evening, so we don't have
much time here.*

These are Mr. Writer's thoughts as he sits down to write the next
scene in his novel.

I'll have him run into Amos in the 7-11. He starts to write:

> "So, Amos, hey, man, how's it goin'?" Homer picked up a carton of milk and
> threw it into his basket. Amos didn't immediately answer, so Homer said,
> "So do you use Joy or Dove? Let's see, I think I'll get me some cashews for
> my long evening at home tonight."
>
> "What are you doing tonight?" Amos asked.
>
> "Watching the game, of course. Aren't you?"
>
> "Not sure." Amos grunted. "I met this girl. I might go over to her place.
> She's pretty nice."

Who cares?

Going back to the loot for a moment—we know this is an action/
adventure or suspense thriller, so no one cares about the cashews, the
game, or Amos's girl. We care about the loot and how they're going to
get it moved in time and how Homer is going to get from Point A to
Point B.

This chapter is about voice and making sure our voice fits the kind of story we're writing.

Every writer has a unique voice, and nowhere does this show up more than in our story dialogue because whether we want to admit it or not, and no matter how much we think we're beyond this, some part of us is in all of the dialogue we write. If I've had an unresolved fight with my partner in the morning and sit down to write a scene of dialogue in the afternoon, guess what? Suddenly my characters are fighting.

You've heard writers say that the characters just "ran away with the scene." Well, it doesn't work quite like that. They "run away" because we have some unresolved issues and our characters decide to play these out as we write. I always have to laugh when writers decide to "fictionalize" a true story, believing they're actually hiding the truth from readers. It's like an elephant sticking his head under the bed, thinking no one can see him.

Just like every writer has a voice, so does every story. This is one reason the publishing world has categorized all of our stories for us. The three major categories of story are genre, mainstream, and literary. The genre category includes a few subcategories: fantasy, science fiction, mystery, horror, action/adventure, suspense, thriller, romance, and young adult. These are self-explanatory, but new writers often ask about the difference between mainstream and literary stories.

Mainstream stories are contemporary stories intended for the general public rather than a specific audience. This type of story challenges the reader's belief system, suggests a new life vision, asks provocative questions, provokes introspection, and/or shakes up conventional rules.

Literary stories are avant-garde and experimental stories that incorporate unconventional and nontraditional writing style and techniques. They're often weak on plot and strong on characterization.

With the above in mind, it's only smart marketing sense to get on board and find out where our writing fits and what our category is. Once we do this, we can begin to understand what readers expect from our stories and, more specifically, from our dialogue in that kind of story. As a writing coach, I work with many new fiction writers, and it's clear to me that many of them don't "get" that different kinds of stories call for different kinds of characters, tension, pacing, themes, and dialogue. A fast-paced action adventure needs fast-paced dialogue in every scene to keep the story moving quickly forward. Likewise, a literary story needs the dialogue to match the pace of the other elements in the story—it needs to move more slowly.

Readers pick up certain kinds of stories for specific reasons. Some readers want a magical ride, while others want a scary ride with a lot of unexpected twists and turns. Some read fiction because, and maybe this is on an unconscious level, they want to learn something about themselves. Some just want to kick back and read about someone else's problems for a change. If we don't understand what our readers want, we won't be able to write stories that deeply satisfy readers in our chosen genre. Our characters' dialogue should match the rhythm of the story in every way possible. This chapter is about taking a look at all of the types of stories and the different voices we, as writers, adopt in order to tell these stories.

At the risk of being formulaic, I've put the types of stories into seven categories to help us better understand readers' expectations of our stories and especially the dialogue we create for our characters: magical, cryptic, descriptive, shadowy, breathless, provocative, and uncensored.

MAGICAL

The language of *The Hobbit*, *Star Wars*, *The Lord of the Rings*, *Star Trek*, and *The Wonderful Wizard of Oz* appeals to readers who are looking for the magical. "May the Force be with you" would sound ridiculous in a mainstream or literary novel. Real people just don't talk like that. Readers of mainstream and literary stories know what's real and what isn't.

When writing mainstream and literary stories, we have to go with what is real. Science fiction and fantasy writers can write about what isn't real, but it's not as easy as it sounds. Some of us have the ability to write magical dialogue, and some of us don't. Magical dialogue sounds truly authentic coming from an author like J.R.R. Tolkien. But can you imagine Holden Caulfield telling his sister, "May the Force be with you"? If he had even hinted at it, J.D. Salinger would not be the famous author he is today.

Science fiction and fantasy aren't the only genres where magical dialogue shows up. A good romance writer can also pull it off. Magical dialogue has a lyrical rhythm to it, and fantasy, science fiction, and romance authors should practice until they can write it and write it well. Sometimes magical dialogue seems inherent in writers of these genres—sometimes they even talk in magical dialogue in their everyday conversations.

I don't. I know that about myself. Part of writing dialogue for our stories is knowing who we are and where we fit as storytellers. Do you know if you're a fantasy, science fiction, or romance writer? Have you ever thought about it?

Let's take a look at some of J.R.R. Tolkien's dialogue in *The Lord of the Rings* and see exactly what we're talking about. Do you see yourself at all?

> A dozen hobbits, led by Sam, leaped forward with a cry and flung the villain to the ground. Sam drew his sword.
>
> "No, Sam!" said Frodo. "Do not kill him even now. For he has not hurt me. And in any case I do not wish him to be slain in this evil mood. He was great once, of a noble kind that we should not dare to raise our hands against. He is fallen, and his cure is beyond us; but I would still spare him, in the hope that he may find it."
>
> Saruman rose to his feet, and stared at Frodo. There was a strange look in his eyes of mingled wonder and respect and hatred. "You have grown, Halfling," he said. "Yes, you have grown very much. You are wise, and cruel. You have robbed my revenge of sweetness, and now I must go hence in bitterness, in debt to your mercy. I hate it and you! Well, I go and I will trouble you no more. But do not expect me to wish you health and long life. You will have neither. But that is not my doing. I merely foretell."
>
> He walked away, and the hobbits made a lane for him to pass; but their knuckles whitened as they gripped on their weapons. Wormtongue hesitated, and then followed his master.

What makes this scene of dialogue work? What distinguishes it as magical?

It's certainly *dramatic*. For starters, take the phrase, *flung the villain to the ground* in the first paragraph. It's not dialogue, but it could be. It's definitely dramatic. Flung? Villain?

Did you notice that no contractions are used? The language is almost Shakespearean. *"Do not kill me." "He has not hurt me." "I do not wish him to be slain."*

It's *eloquent*. *"You have robbed my revenge of sweetness, and now I must go hence in bitterness, in debt, to your mercy."*

It's *direct*. *"But do not expect me to wish you health and long life. You will have neither."*

If you want to write fantasy or science fiction, you must become a master of magical dialogue. How? Practice. Read lots and lots of stories in the science fiction/fantasy genres. And challenge yourself with the exercise at the end of this chapter.

In a romance, magical dialogue takes on a little different form, but it's still magical in that it transcends the way we talk to each other in normal society in this century. One reason I don't read a lot of romance novels is because many romance writers can't pull off this kind of transcending and magical dialogue. They try, but it comes off as hokey rather than magical. I think Robert James Waller does an admirable job in this passage of dialogue between his hero, Richard, and his heroine, Francesca, in *The Bridges of Madison County*.

> He started to speak, but Francesca stopped him.
>
> "Robert, I'm not quite finished. If you took me in your arms and carried me to your truck and forced me to go with you, I wouldn't murmur a complaint. You could do the same thing just by talking to me. But I don't think you will. You're too sensitive, too aware of my feelings, for that. And I have feelings of responsibility here.
>
> "Yes, it's boring in its way. My life, that is. It lacks romance, eroticism, dancing in the kitchen to candlelight, and the wonderful feel of a man who knows how to love a woman. Most of all, it lacks you. But there's this damn sense of responsibility I have. To Richard, to the children. Just my

leaving, taking away my physical presence, would be hard enough for Richard. That alone might destroy him.

"On top of that, and this is even worse, he would have to live the rest of his life with the whispers of the people here. 'That's Richard Johnson. His hot little Italian wife ran off with some longhaired photographer a few years back.' Richard would have to suffer that, and the children would hear the snickering of Winterset for as long as they live here. They would suffer, too. And they would hate me for it.

"As much as I want you and want to be with you and part of you, I can't rear myself away from the realness of my responsibilities. If you force me, physically or mentally, to go with you, as I said earlier, I cannot fight that. I don't have the strength, given my feelings for you. In spite of what I said about not taking the road away from you, I'd go because of my own selfish wanting of you."

Okay, who talks like that? Not anyone I know. That's pretty articulate for an off-the-cuff moment. Pretty articulate and pretty, well, magical. Magical in that all of it makes perfect sense and is said in such eloquent language that we marvel at it while at the same time being fully aware that if left to us, we'd say something banal like, "Nope, I can't hang out with you anymore. If Richard finds out, I'm dead meat." In a romance story, somehow the magical dialogue connects with the romantic in us and we can go there with Francesca. We can believe it.

What makes Francesca's dialogue work so well that we're pulled in at an emotional level? First, it's the *details*. The author paints word pictures. Instead of "... *he'd have to live the rest of his life with the gossip,*" Francesca says, "... *he'd have to live the rest of his life with the whisper of the people here.*" This creates an image in the reader's mind, and we can see and feel Richard's pain as the townsfolk whisper to each other about Robert and Francesca.

"*If you took me in your arms and carried me to your truck ...*"

"*His hot little Italian wife ran off with some longhaired photographer ...*"

Magical dialogue also includes *metaphors*. "*In spite of what I said about not taking the road away from you ...*" Francesca is talking about Robert's freedom.

Writing Voice

Magical dialogue is emotional dialogue. Francesca is able to articulate her longing for what Robert has to offer as well as her compassion for how Richard and her children would suffer if she left them and rode off with Robert into the sunset. She's able to hold those two emotions simultaneously, which tears her in two. It's magical.

Like I said previously, I happen to believe that most writers either have the ability to write this kind of dialogue or they don't. We have to have a mind that thinks in magical terminology, sentences, and phrases. I'm so in awe of those who can write like this, so in awe that most of the time I leave it to them to write. But every once in a while, I try. If you think you have this ability, work to develop it. If not, keep trying. Never underestimate the romantic in you.

EXERCISE

MAGICAL. Choose your genre—romance, science fiction, or fantasy—and put two characters, male and female, in a garden. If you've never written a love scene before, hang onto your hat. Well, not too tightly. If it wants to blow away on the magical breezes of your garden scene, let it. Now, we know that a lot of couples don't talk to each other while making love, but your characters do. They say the most amazing words to each other, amazing even to them. Write three pages (or as many as you can stand) of magical dialogue, words you wish you had the courage to say to your own lover or would like him or her to say back to you. The goal is to be authentic, so no corny lines allowed. Remember how magical dialogue feels and sounds in our examples: It's dramatic, formal, eloquent, direct, detailed, metaphorical, and emotional.

CRYPTIC

Much of the dialogue in literary and religious stories deals with abstract ideas and vague concepts and has double meanings that readers can't always immediately decipher. They're not supposed to. Sometimes other novels will have bits of cryptic dialogue when the plot calls for some things to remain hidden or secret. These bits of dialogue plant subliminal messages in the reader's mind that help to communicate the story's theme and will ultimately make sense if the author is able to successfully pull the story off at the end. Some writers are especially gifted at this. Chuck Palahniuk is one of them. Here are three dialogue passages from his novel *Fight Club* that make little sense at the moment, even sound like the ranting of a crazy person, but when woven into the story build to a satisfying resolution at the end. In the first one, the main character, unnamed because he turns out to be one with his alter ego, Tyler Durden, has just learned that while he was away for a few days, his condo blew up. In the following scene, the doorman is giving the viewpoint character his perspective on the situation.

> "A lot of young people try to impress the world and buy too many things," the doorman said.
> I called Tyler.
> The phone rang in Tyler's rented house on Paper Street.
> Oh, Tyler, please deliver me.
> And the phone rang.
> The doorman leaned into my shoulder and said, "A lot of young people don't know what they really want."
> Oh, Tyler, please rescue me.
> And the phone rang.
> "Young people, they think they want the whole world."
> Deliver me from Swedish furniture.
> Deliver me from clever art.
> And the phone rang and Tyler answered.
> "If you don't know what you want," the doorman said, "you end up with a lot you don't."

We don't completely know what the doorman is talking about because this takes place only forty pages into the story, and we're just beginning to understand that the viewpoint character's major conflict is his disillusionment with an empty consumer culture and his struggle to find an answer. In the next passage, Marla, the viewpoint character's annoying once-in-a-while girlfriend and a constant reminder of what makes our consumer culture so empty, makes a couple of cryptic comments.

> "You know, the condom is the glass slipper of our generation. You slip it on when you meet a stranger. You dance all night, then you throw it away. The condom, I mean. Not the stranger."

Writing Voice

A few moments later, after rambling on for a while about her latest Goodwill find and how people dump dead Christmas trees:

> "The Animal Control place is the best place to go," Marla says. "Where all the animals, the little doggies and kitties that people loved and then dumped, even the old animals, dance and jump around for your attention because after three days, they get an overdose shot of sodium phenobarbital and then into the big pet oven.
>
> "The big sleep, 'Valley of the Dogs' style.
>
> "Where even if someone loves you enough to save your life, they still castrate you." Marla looks at me as if I'm the one humping her and says, "I can't win with you, can I?"

At this point, Marla isn't making many points with us because we don't have a clue as to what she's talking about. Later, it will all make sense and tie in directly to what "Tyler" is dealing with in his life.

In the last example, a police detective has started calling the viewpoint character about his condo explosion. They're on the phone with each other and the detective has just asked if he knows anyone who could make homemade dynamite. "Tyler" is whispering advice over the viewpoint character's shoulder.

> "Disaster is a natural part of my evolution," Tyler whispered, "toward tragedy and dissolution."
>
> I told the detective that it was the refrigerator that blew up my condo.
>
> "I'm breaking my attachment to physical power and possessions," Tyler whispered, "because only through destroying myself can I discover the greater power of my spirit ... The liberator who destroys my property," Tyler said, "is fighting to save my spirit. The teacher who clears all possessions from my path will set me free."

It doesn't make a lot of sense at the moment, but later the viewpoint character comes to terms with that part of himself, his ego, that is bent on self-destruction.

What distinguishes cryptic dialogue from other kinds of dialogue is its indirectness, subtlety, and ambiguity. If you want to see a lot of examples of this, amazingly enough, check out Jesus' words in the Bible. That's right—Matthew, Mark, Luke, and John are full of cryptic dialogue. Stories with double meanings. Stories that can be interpreted in many different ways, depending upon what the reader wants to hear.

In order to write cryptic dialogue, you can't be a black-or-white thinker. You have to be able to view the world from more than one perspective. Why? And why is cryptic dialogue so effective in literary and religious stories, and even some mainstream stories? Because these kinds of stories have a message and readers don't want to be preached to, told what to believe, or what to think. But they usually don't mind having their current belief systems challenged. Cryptic dialogue that doesn't come right out and make a concrete statement, that has hidden meanings the reader must discover, honors the reader's intelligence and ability to come to his own conclusions about the story's subject. The reader will be much more receptive to your story's truth when the characters are talking around a subject rather than hammering some moralistic idea into each other's brains.

Practice writing dialogue for your characters that holds back, skirts around the real issues, and can be interpreted in more than one way.

Cryptic dialogue is difficult to do well. If we're not careful, we can end up writing preachy, moralistic, dogmatic junk that can turn off readers in droves. But when done well and woven through the plot, cryptic dialogue can provide the substance that gives meaning to the entire story.

EXERCISE

CRYPTIC. A group of characters—four or five individuals in the same family—are discussing another family member who's not present. Someone from outside the family has accused this person of sexual abuse. There is a bigger issue here for the viewpoint character. You decide what it is, and then write five pages of a cryptic dialogue scene that doesn't ever come right out and say what it is they're discussing. You can use metaphors, similes, and hyperbole. They talk about the bigger issue, they talk about their love for their family member, but they don't ever really say what he's been accused of and what it means for the family. Keep in mind that cryptic dialogue is indirect, subtle, and ambiguous; it has more than one meaning.

Writing Voice

DESCRIPTIVE

The literary, mainstream, and historical story often relies on dialogue for much of its history, background, and description. Or at least it should. Too many of these stories are full of long, boring passages of narrative that the reader has to wade through on the way to the plot. In this kind of story, even once the plot is moving, the author often stops the action with more long, boring passages of narrative. I can appreciate that the author is enamored with the research of her story's time period, but there are more interesting ways to dispense it to us, and for the reader, the most engaging way is through dialogue. The goal of descriptive dialogue is to provide the reader with the information she needs to understand the characters and story line in the context of the setting or time period in which they live. This is the author's goal. The character's goal can't be sacrificed for the author's, and that's where authors often err. Descriptive dialogue can still have tension and suspense and can be inserted into a scene of action so the story doesn't bog down while we're getting the information we need.

Let's look at the following scene of descriptive dialogue from *The Poisonwood Bible* by Barbara Kingsolver. Leah has just put her little sister in the swing outside of their hut in South Africa and is combing her hair when the village schoolteacher, Anatole, comes by. He's trying to explain to Leah, not so successfully, about the state of the Congo at this point in time.

> I drew the edge of the comb slowly down the center of Ruth May's head, making a careful part. Father had said the slums outside Leopoldville would be set right by American aid, after Independence. Maybe I was foolish to believe him. There were shanties just as poor in Georgia, on the edge of Atlanta, where black and white divided, and that was smack in the middle of America.
>
> "Can you just do that, what they did down there? Announce your own country?" I asked.
>
> "Prime Minister Lumumba says no, absolutely not. He has asked the United Nations to bring an army to restore unity."
>
> "Is there going to be a war?"
>
> "There is already a kind of war, I think. Moise Tshombe has Belgians and mercenary soldiers working for him. I don't think they will leave

without a fight. And Katanga is not the only place where they are throwing stones. There is a different war in Matadi, Thysville, Boende, Leopoldville. People are very angry at the Europeans. They are even hurting women and little children."

"What are they so mad at the white people for?"

Anatole sighed. "Those are big cities. Where the boa and the hen curl up together, there is only trouble. People have seen too much of the Europeans and all the things they had. They imagined after Independence life would immediately become fair."

"Can't they be patient?"

"Could you be? If your belly was empty and you saw whole baskets of bread on the other side of a window, would you continue waiting patiently, Beene? Or would you throw a rock?"

The descriptive dialogue in this passage reveals an important part of the setting and the story situation without bogging down the action, which happens when the author uses only narrative to dispense this kind of information. In literary, historical, and mainstream stories, the bantering of descriptive dialogue between characters keeps things moving forward.

You may have a lot of background you need to insert in the story in order for the reader to understand the context of your setting and plot, but if you use only narrative to get it in there, the reader can feel like she's watching a documentary. If you're writing this kind of story, look for ways to *show* the history, description of setting, and/or cultural situation through the characters' conversations with one another so the reader is engaged in the story.

Throughout any passage of descriptive dialogue, you'll want to include narrative thoughts and reactions of the viewpoint character's, of course, but this kind of narrative is so much easier for the reader to absorb when it is woven into dialogue rather than doled out in long, boring paragraphs of exposition.

The pitfall of descriptive dialogue is that sometimes we have our characters going on a little too long because we may have an entire historical situation we want to explain to the reader. Sometimes we get caught up in wanting to dispense all of the research we've done, so we decide to put it all in one passage of dialogue that goes on for pages.

Writing Voice

I believe that one of the reasons literary novels are known to have such a small number of readers compared to other kinds of novels is because of the long passages of narrative description. I wonder if more literary, mainstream, and historical authors used less narrative description and more descriptive dialogue in their stories, would they attract a wider audience? You don't have to sacrifice engaging dialogue just to make your novel fit into one of these categories.

EXERCISE

DESCRIPTIVE. Two female characters, one a real estate agent and one who's selling her home, are walking through the older Victorian home that the second character wants to sell. They're discussing what will make the house appealing to buyers and what needs a little work. The real estate agent unknowingly keeps insulting the seller, and the tension between them is growing. Choose either of the two women for your viewpoint character and write three pages of tense descriptive dialogue that focuses on bringing out certain details of the property and home. (If you're not familiar with Victorian homes and don't want to do the research, choose another kind of home.) For this scenario, write your descriptive dialogue with a lot of setting and background details woven into the characters' words so the reader gets a sense of place.

JUST FOR FUN

1. No matter what kind of story you're writing, take the characters out of your story and drop them into another genre, then write three pages of dialogue for them. They might surprise you. You'll get to know them in a way you never intended and maybe never wanted to know them.
2. Create three characters—one romantic character, one science fiction character, one horror character. Put them in the same scene and write three pages of dialogue.
3. Challenge yourself to write a short story in a genre in which you've never written. Pay special attention to the dialogue you create for the protagonist.

SHADOWY

The horror and mystery writer's goal is to scare the bejesus out of us, and these authors take their jobs very seriously. Occasionally, a mainstream novel has enough horror and mystery in it to warrant this kind of dialogue.

Getting hold of the purpose of a passage of dialogue will help you write it more creatively because you know it's not just filler. In shadowy dialogue, your character's role is to keep your reader in a state of suspense and a kind of terror, although you periodically tighten and loosen the tension.

This is generally achieved with an ominous tone of foreshadowing of things to come. Things that are a little more intense than a walk in the park. The kinds of things you find in your worst nightmare: creepy, crawly things that attack, maim, and kill. Shadowy dialogue always casts a foreboding threat of danger over the protagonist.

Check out the following example from Stephen King's *The Shining*. Here we have Danny, the son of the unsympathetic protagonist, Jack, in dialogue with his imaginary friend, Tony. He has imagined Tony into being to cope with life with his insane father. In "reality" (you never really know what's real and what isn't in a Stephen King novel), Tony is actually Danny in a few years, a suspended character between he and his father, all in Danny's imagination. In this scene, Tony is trying to warn Danny of impending harm to his mother, possibly her death.

> He began to struggle, and the darkness and the hallway began to waver. Tony's form became chimerical, indistinct.
> "Don't!" Tony called. "Don't, Danny, don't do that!"
> "She's not going to be dead! She's not!"
> "Then you have to help her, Danny ... you're in a place deep down in your own mind. The place where I am. I'm a part of you, Danny."
> "You're Tony. You're not me. I want my mommy ... I want my mommy ..."
> "No—"
> "You've always known," Tony continued, and he began to walk closer. For the first time, Tony began to walk closer. "You're deep down in

yourself in a place where nothing comes through. We're alone here for a little while, Danny. This is an Overlook where no one can ever come. No clocks work here. None of the keys fit them and they can never be wound up. The doors have never been opened and no one has ever stayed in the rooms. But you can't stay long. Because it's coming."

"It ..." Danny whispered fearfully, and as he did so the irregular pounding noise seemed to grow closer, louder. His terror, cool and distant a moment ago, became a more immediate thing.

One reason the shadowy dialogue in the above passage works is because while Tony seems like a friend, we're not always sure. He's what's known as a shape-shifter, the archetype in Joseph Campbell's *The Hero's Journey*, that keeps the reader in the dark as far as whether the character is really for the protagonist or against him. The protagonist can never quite trust the shape-shifter, so when the shape-shifter speaks in dialogue, we're always questioning him, wondering whether he's speaking truthfully or not. Here Tony is delivering bad news. Should Danny even believe him? Another reason the dialogue works is because it's cryptic, so we have to keep reading to find out what Tony is even talking about. And the last reason it works is because Tony is definitely delivering an ominous threat of something to come that could turn Danny's world upside down and change him forever. Shadowy dialogue's effectiveness is mostly in the tone of the character's words, but you can use setting and action to add to its creepiness.

The purpose of shadowy dialogue, used in mysteries and horror stories, is to keep the story as dark as possible. Horror and mystery readers are interested in the dark and supernatural, preferably both at the same time. The characters are usually somewhere between consciousness and unconsciousness where the darkness is concerned. It's a zone where both character and reader teeter between the light and the dark, between what's real and what's imagined. And we all know scary things go on in our imaginations sometimes. Horror and mystery writers know how to develop those imaginary moments to where they feel more real than reality itself, and therein lies the terror we feel when we read this kind of story. The characters' dialogue reflects this mood.

BREATHLESS

The purpose of this kind of dialogue is to keep the reader on the edge of his chair, turning pages until the wee hours of the morning. The word you want to remember is *suspense*. Breathless dialogue is all about cre-ating suspense, which is what readers are looking for when they buy an action/adventure or suspense thriller. They want every page to be full of spine-tingling, creeped-out, nail-biting suspense. It's your job, as the writer, to give it to them as the characters express themselves to each other in ways that turn up the heat. And turn it up. And turn it up.

Let's look at Michael Crichton's *Jurassic Park* for an example of how dialogue works in suspense thrillers. Here we have three characters try-ing to get from one side of the lake to the other without the most dan-gerous of all dinosaurs, the tyrannosaurus, seeing them. But then Lex starts coughing. And coughing.

> Lex coughed loudly, explosively. In Tim's ears, the sound echoed across the water like a gunshot.
>
> The tyrannosaur yawned lazily, and scratched its ear with its hind foot, just like a dog. It yawned again. It was groggy after its big meal, and it woke up slowly.
>
> On the boat, Lex was making little gargling sounds.
>
> "Lex, *shut* up!" Tim said.
>
> "I can't help it," she whispered, and then she coughed again. Grant rowed hard, moving the raft powerfully into the center of the lagoon.
>
> On the shore, the tyrannosaur stumbled to its feet.

"I couldn't help it, Timmy!" Lex shrieked miserably. "I couldn't help it!"

"Shhhh!"

Grant was rowing as fast as he could.

"Anyway, it doesn't matter," she said. "We're far enough away. He can't swim."

"*Of course he can swim, you little idiot!*" Tim shouted at her. On the shore, the tyrannosaur stepped off the dock and plunged into the water. It moved strongly into the lagoon after them.

"Well, how should I know?" she said.

"Everybody knows tyrannosaurs can swim! It's in all the books! Anyway, all reptiles can swim!"

"Snakes can't."

"*Of course* snakes can. You idiot!"

Crichton uses this kind of breathless dialogue throughout the novel. If it lets up, it's never for long. I personally believe the dialogue to be one of the reasons for the story's success. These are real folks in real trouble—over and over again. Readers of suspense thrillers and action/adventures demand this kind of tension, so if you're going to write for these readers, you have to be able to give it to them.

When we are facing a difficult situation and have no clue as to the outcome, our breath can become short and shallow as fear, anger, or sadness increases, thus the term breathless dialogue. The key to writing effective *breathless* dialogue are as follows:

- cut away most of the description and explanatory narrative so the scene is mostly dialogue
- insert bits of action, as Crichton does in the above passage, so the scene keeps moving forward in a physical way, but not so much that we lose track of the character's speech
- use short spurts of emotional phrases of dialogue rather than long speeches or contemplative verbal pondering
- make clear what's at stake for the reader as he's expressing himself
- hold back just enough information in the dialogue so the suspense is sustained throughout the scene

Is this you? Does this kind of dialogue come easy for you? All dialogue in all fiction, whether short stories or novels, needs a degree of tension and suspense, but for the suspense thriller and the action/adventure, it's at the core.

EXERCISE

BREATHLESS. One character, a female, is calling 911 to report someone breaking into her house. Write two pages of breathless dialogue from this character's viewpoint and make sure we hear both sides of the conversation as well as this character's thoughts as the action and suspense accelerates. What you want to emphasize in this kind of dialogue is the pace and the emotion, whether it's fear, anger, or sadness. Let the short bursts of dialogue carry the scene.

PROVOCATIVE

The *Nashville Tennessean* wrote of Wally Lamb's *She's Come Undone*: "Wally Lamb can lie down with the literary lions at will: he's that gifted ... This novel does what good fiction should do—it informs our hearts as well as our minds of the complexities involved in the 'simple' act of living a human life."

This is actually a very accurate definition of the mainstream and literary story. Lamb's novel is full of pages of dialogue that's *about* something. Not all of the dialogue, of course, in a mainstream or literary story needs to be about something, but a good portion of it does. This is because, unlike most genre stories, which are plot driven, mainstream and literary stories are character driven and about something.

As we learned earlier in this chapter, readers of this kind of story want to be challenged in their thinking, provoked to consider other ways of looking at something, and shaken up in their belief systems. They're asking for this when they pick up this kind of story to read.

For a story to be about something, it must be driven by some kind of universal truth, as you'll see in the following excerpt from Harper Lee's *To Kill a Mockingbird*. The universal truth in this novel is that "all men are created equal," and it shows up on just about every page.

Not all writers want to work that hard at writing, to make sure that every line of the story contributes to a larger theme and the story communicates a larger truth of some kind. But some do, and if this is you, you want to make sure much of your viewpoint character's dialogue provokes the reader as much as it does the other characters in a way that could ultimately be transforming. The characters in this kind of story are thinking about something bigger than themselves. They're talking to each other about these bigger things, wondering out loud in dialogue.

Harper Lee challenges the reader on two levels in the following passage from *To Kill a Mockingbird*—racism and injustice—and she does it very effectively through dialogue. Here Atticus Finch is giving his final argument in the case of Robinson vs. Ewell:

> "She has committed no crime, she has merely broken a rigid and time-honored code of our society, a code so severe that whoever breaks it is hounded from our midst as unfit to live with. She is the victim of cruel poverty and ignorance, but I cannot pity her: she is white. She knew full well the enormity of her offense, but because her desires were stronger than the code she was breaking, she persisted in breaking it. She persisted, and her subsequent reaction is something that all of us have known at one time or another. She did something every child has done—she tried to put the evidence of her offense away from her. But in this case she was not a child hiding stolen contraband: she struck out at her victim—of necessity she must put him away from her—he must be removed from her presence, from this world. She must destroy the evidence of her offense.
>
> "What was the evidence of her offense? Tom Robinson, a human being. She must put Tom Robinson away from her. Tom Robinson was her daily reminder of what she did. What did she do? She tempted a Negro."

Atticus goes on for some time in this vein and concludes his argument:

> "... But there is one way in this country in which all men are created equal—there is one human institution that makes a pauper the equal of a Rockefeller, the stupid man the equal of an Einstein, and the ignorant man the equal of any college president. That institution, gentlemen, is a court. It can be the Supreme Court of the United States or the humblest J.P. court in the land, or this honorable court which you serve. Our courts have their faults, as does any human institution, but in this country our courts are the great levelers, and in our courts all men are created equal."

Often dialogue in the mainstream and literary story will communicate the theme. Atticus is speaking the larger truth of the story to the other characters and to the reader. There is no way we can read this passage and not think about something that is bigger than our daily lives. Provocative story dialogue sometimes makes us squirm, definitely stirs up our gray matter, and often shocks and startles us out of our comfort zones. If you're a mainstream or literary writer, you want to write the kind of dialogue that does this and more.

EXERCISE

PROVOCATIVE. Two characters, one male and one female, have just finished a game of golf and are making their way to the club for a drink. Both are high school teachers, and they're discussing the sexual behaviors of young people today. They've overheard some of the chat between both male and female students and the female teacher, especially, is troubled by the cavalier attitude she's observed in her students. The male teacher is less troubled with more of a boy-will-be-boys-and-girls-like-it kind of attitude. Write a three-page scene of provocative dialogue that challenges both characters and the reader. In this type of dialogue, what's important are the words themselves. This is where the story's message, the theme or what the story is about, comes through.

UNCENSORED

The uncensored dialogue in the young adult story is definitely that of the young person, but that doesn't at all mean that it's full of hip-hop words, slang, and weird phrases. I call it uncensored simply because, while adults most often censor themselves when they speak, teenagers haven't yet learned that skill so their dialogue is more raw, edgy, and honest. The reader of the young adult story expects realism, so keep in mind that your teen characters will not be cleaning up their words before they speak them as so many adults do. What's important about the dialogue in the young adult story, just like in any other story, is that it's authentic. Authenticity isn't more important in this story than in any other; it's just that we have to watch our tendency to create characters that all sound like they just stepped off the planet Way Cool—which isn't any more authentic than if we didn't give them a teen voice at all. This kind of over-the-top teen speak sounds no more real than if we weren't to use any slang. Ann Brashares does a good job of writing uncensored dialogue in her young adult novel *The Sisterhood of the Traveling Pants.* Following is an example from this novel of two teens in conversation, Effie and Lena, neither of whom is from the planet Way Cool, but the dialogue might make some adults roll their eyes, which is what you're after. In this conversation, Effie is trying to get Lena to admit that she's in love with a certain boy. Listen:

> "You are in love with Kostos," Effie accused.
>
> "No, I'm not." If Lena hadn't known she was in love with Kostos before, she did now. Because she knew what a lie felt like.
>
> "You are too. And the sad thing is, you are too much of a chicken to do anything about it but mope."
>
> Lena sank into her covers again. As usual, Effie had summed up her complex, anguished mental state in one sentence.
>
> "Just admit it," Effie pressed.
>
> Lena wouldn't. She crossed her arms stubbornly over her pajama top.
>
> "Okay, don't," Effie said. "I know it's true anyway."
>
> "Well, you're wrong," Lena snapped babyishly.
>
> Effie sat down on the bed. Her face was serious now. "Lena, listen to me, okay? We don't have much more time here. You are in love. I've never seen anything like this before. You have to be brave, okay? You have to go and tell Kostos how you feel. I swear to God if you don't, you will regret it for the rest of your cowardly life."
>
> Lena knew this was all true. Effie had hit the mark so blatantly, Lena didn't even bother refuting it. "But, Ef," she said, her voice belying her raw agony, "what if he doesn't like me back?"
>
> Effie considered this. Lena waited, expecting, hoping for reassurance. She wanted Effie to say that of course Kostos liked her back. How could he not? But Effie didn't say that.
>
> Instead she took Lena's hand in hers. "That's what I mean about being brave."

Why does this dialogue work and why would we call it *uncensored*? Because teens just say what's on their minds. As many times as I've been "in love" in my adult life, when the issue of expressing that to the other person comes up, I have never, would never, say right out loud to a friend, *"What if he doesn't like me back?"* I might think it. I might feel it. But I'd never be so bold to say it to anyone. I barely want to admit it to myself. And teens are always calling each other out on their "stuff," while adults do their best to be nice. *"You are too much of a chicken to do anything about it but mope."* When's the last time you called a friend out on her stuff? Writing uncensored dialogue can be freeing. We can just write what comes into these characters' minds because most often they blurt out what's in their minds. To write uncensored dialogue is to write the truth, and for the writer, that feels good. You can just relax and write.

EXERCISE

UNCENSORED. Three girls are walking home from school chatting about boys, and two of them suddenly realize they have their eyes on the same boy. They each have stories about his singling them out with some attention, too. The tension starts to mount as each becomes threatened by the other. Use one girl's viewpoint and write three pages of uncensored dialogue, revealing her increasing anxiety. Remember—what you're after in uncensored dialogue is the truth. Let each girl speak from her gut, not her head, because in her gut is where her emotions are.

Writing category-specific dialogue is not quite this cut and dried. On occasion, the different types of dialogue overlap and cross over from genre to genre. A character in a horror story, for example, may suddenly use descriptive language as he reveals something about another character. In Anne Rice's novels you find both shadowy and descriptive dialogue, and possibly provocative, because she writes mainstream horror. So, just like anything else, we can't and shouldn't try to make our dialogue fit rigid formulas. But I can't overestimate the importance of understanding why your reader might pick up your novel in the first place—because she wants a fast and suspenseful read or a contemplative and thought-provoking story. Delivering dialogue that meets this need is your constant challenge.

Your story's genre will, of course, determine the kind of dialogue you write. This should be one of the first decisions you make after beginning to develop your story idea. You don't want to get too far into the story writing the wrong kind of dialogue for the pace or the characters that have already been determined by the genre.

GLORIA KEMPTON is an online and Seattle-based writing coach, the author of eleven books, an instructor with Writer's Digest University and Writers On the Net (writers.com), and an instructor to incarcerated veterans at the Regional Justice Center in Kent, Washington and the Columbia River Correctional Institution in Portland, Oregon.

CHAPTER 20

THE INNER VOICE

BY NANCY KRESS

We all talk to ourselves—it's called "thinking." We tell ourselves to remember Mother's birthday, to get to bed early tonight, to balance that checkbook soon. Characters in fiction do these things, too, and for the same reason: to respond to the situation at hand.

But *how* someone thinks—that is, the ongoing tone of her interior conversations—is often as important as the thoughts themselves are. The way a character approaches her thoughts reveals a great deal about her personality. For fiction writers, understanding and using this phenomenon is one of the best ways to build credible, interesting characters. Let's look at some specifics.

HALF FULL OR HALF EMPTY?

An oft-quoted piece of wisdom goes, "We see the world not as it is, but as we are." Suppose, for instance, that three people are kept waiting in a doctor's office a half hour past their appointment times. All three are having the identical experience. Yet here's what each tells himself:

> "There was probably some medical emergency somewhere. I'm sure the wait won't be much longer."

> "This always happens to me. People just don't know how to treat each other anymore. Just because he thinks he's more important than I am, that doctor thinks he can keep me waiting indefinitely."

> "Maybe I wrote down the wrong day for this appointment. Or the wrong time? God, if I left work early for no reason, I'm going to feel like an absolute fool."

We learn a lot about these people from their thoughts. Each one ends up characterizing himself far more than he characterizes the behind-schedule doctor. The way they talk to themselves defines how they see the world.

Most fiction writers do this instinctively as they force their characters to respond to events in the plot. For the effect to be most powerful, however, the key is repetition.

Throughout your story, you need to keep in mind how your character sees the world and translate that point of view consistently into self-talk. If we see your character wait optimistically and calmly once, we'll note it—but we won't necessarily remember it. If we see her have three, five, or even ten optimistic, calm internal dialogues, though, we'll believe her to be that sort of person. You'll have created a much more vivid character.

But the caveat here is that you can't overdo this, and that can be a fine line to walk. A character who's always calmly optimistic, even when held at gunpoint by crazed terrorists, will seem one-dimensional at best. The trick is to shade self-talk in your chosen direction while still allowing for the complexity of reactions and moods that make us human.

DOING IT RIGHT

Here, for instance, is Philip Ashley from Daphne du Maurier's classic romantic novel *My Cousin Rachel*. Philip has just announced that he'll make a provision in his will for his late cousin's widow:

> Oh, well, they could cluck their tongues about the will, it made no odds. But I wondered, with a sudden flash of bitterness, what their manner would have been to me if, after all, I had not inherited the property. Would the deference be there? The respect? The loyalty? Or would I have been young Master Philip, a poor relative, with a room of my own stuck away somewhere at the back of the house? I knocked out my pipe; the taste

was dry and dusty. How many people were there, I wondered, who liked me and served me for myself alone?

Much of Philip's internal dialogue has this tone: distrust, doubt about how others see him, a bone-deep sense of isolation. When he has flashes of happiness, even joy, it's partly because, at those moments, his solitude is lessened. Other times, his isolation is milder (as when he enjoys walking his lands alone) or deeper (as when he mistrusts all of Rachel's motives in visiting the estate, and he determines in advance to dislike her). But the sense of loneliness, of being essentially separated from others, flavors much of Philip's self-talk. It's du Maurier's most effective tool for creating Philip's personality.

A very different personality belongs to Andrea Sachs, narrator and protagonist of Lauren Weisberger's best-selling *The Devil Wears Prada*. Andrea talks to herself as if she were a hurdler facing endless, escalating obstacles. She's trying to drive her employer's standard-shift Porsche, which she doesn't know how to operate, through maddening Manhattan traffic.

> The light hadn't even officially turned green at the intersection of 17th and Broadway before an army of over-confident yellow cabs roared past the tiny deathtrap I was attempting to navigate around the city streets. *Clutch, gas, shift* (neutral to first? Or first to second?), *release, clutch*, I repeated over and over in my head, the mantra offering little comfort and even less direction amid the screeching midday traffic. The little car bucked wildly twice before it lurched forward through the intersection. My heart flip-flopped in my chest.

Andrea will lurch and flop through many different situations in this novel, narrowly avoiding disasters, and through all of them she'll repeat various hopeless "mantras." Such internal dialogue is what makes Andrea a unique character.

To use self-talk skillfully, take the following steps:

- Determine the dominant aspects of your character's personality. Is she a timid but loving person? Angry at the world but afraid to show it directly, and thus given to veiled sarcasm or double-edged remarks? Does she see the world as oppressive, with herself as its

　　　　　　　　　　　　　　　　　　　Writing Voice

perpetual victim? Or is she usually confident that things will work out in the long run?

- Once you know your character's personality, translate those qualities into her internal dialogue. No matter what the actual content of her thoughts, try to express them in terms that reflect the way this particular person, with this particular view of the world, naturally talks to herself in the complete privacy of her own mind.
- Do this not just for one key incident in your story but consistently throughout, varying the stone of her characteristic self-talk from mild to intense.

EXPLOITING INTERNAL DIALOGUE EVEN MORE

Finally, here are two ways to make your character's self-talk more effective. First, place an instance of self-talk very near your story's opening to immediately build characterization. So if your protagonist usually talks to himself in sunny terms (or cynical or desperate or loony), let him do so within the first few pages. The previous excerpt from *The Devil Wears Prada*, for example, comprises the first 88 words of the novel.

Second, use internal dialogue to validate character change. In most stories, the protagonist undergoes a change as a result of plot events. One good way to convey this is to have your character talk to himself differently after his change than he did before it.

If he talked negatively ("You'll never be able to get this done in time, you idiot!"), now he talks positively ("You've handled bigger problems than this"). If she was naïve before ("I reminded myself that all teachers were trustworthy or they wouldn't work with kids"), now she knows better ("Who was this guy? What did I really know about him?"). If the change in internal dialogue seems a natural outcome of your plot incidents, your story will work.

So let your characters talk not only to each other but to themselves. We'll listen.

CHAPTER 21

CREATING A NARRATORIAL VOICE

BY GABRIELA PEREIRA

Narration is the lens through which your reader experiences a story, and it includes the fundamental element of voice.

Voice is the sound and tone of your story. It's the piece of you that goes into everything you write. It's your literary fingerprint, your signature style, and it develops over time. As your writing skills grow, you will learn to modulate your voice and adjust it depending on the context. Voice isn't useful in "creative" writing alone, either. It comes through in blog posts, articles, and anything else you write.

Voice is one of the most delicate elements of writing, and if you're not careful, you might squash it. It is one of the few topics I teach without using acronyms, categories, or rules of thumb. Instead, I take a free-form approach that will help you recognize the different facets and layers of voice but give you room to practice and play.

HOW TO LOOK AT VOICE

Voice is one of the promises you should make to your reader from the very first page. It is one of the essential elements of your story, and yet it's often the most difficult skill for writers to master.

Many writing craft books try to categorize voice by shoving it into neat little boxes. They claim that one author has a "ceremonial voice" while another has a "conversational voice." This is nonsense.

Pigeonholing your voice will only make you want to break free of those shackles. After all, what if your voice doesn't fit into one of these rigid categories? Or, worse, what if your voice *changes* from one book to another (or even changes *within* one book)?

Attempting to categorize your voice won't help you write your book any better, and just because you know what category your book's voice falls into doesn't mean you know how to make the most of it. While labeling character archetypes or plot landmarks can help you understand how those elements operate within your story, when it comes to voice, labels are useless.

In order to make sense of voice in writing, you need to understand two fundamental things:

Voice operates on multiple levels.

Voice can be obvious or invisible, but it's always there.

Multiple Levels of Voice

Many people talk about the voice of a story, but rarely does a piece of writing have only one voice. In fact, there are usually at least *two levels* of voice in any given work. If you're into metafiction, where the writer offers commentary or uses a story-within-a-story framework, you can have even more levels. For the purposes of this discussion, however, let's focus on a typical two-voice narrative.

The first, most basic level of voice is that of the narrator. This is the voice that tells the story, and we see it in the narration, description, and other nondialogue segments. The second level contains the voices of the characters in the story, voices we usually hear only in dialogue. Unless a story consists of dialogue alone—like in a stage play—or narration alone, it will automatically have at least these two levels of voice.

Of course, when you're in first-person point of view, the voice of the narrator and the voice of the protagonist overlap because they come from the same person. This doesn't mean that the voices are one and the same. For instance, a protagonist might be very polite in dialogue, but when we read the narration and experience the character's thoughts, we hear a different, snarkier tone. While these voices might be coming from the same character, the dialogue voice and the narrator's voice are completely different.

What about novels with only one level of voice? This happens when you eliminate either all the narration or all the dialogue in a story and constrain yourself to using only one level of voice. Doing so is incredibly hard to sustain, and few books are written this way. Instead, you're more likely to see short stories or essays written with only one level of voice.

"The Tell-Tale Heart" by Edgar Allan Poe is one such short story. Since this story takes place almost entirely in the narrator's mind and eliminates all but a smattering of dialogue, the only thing we hear is the voice of the narrator. This particular example is especially interesting because as the story develops the reader begins to sense that the narrator is, in fact, not completely truthful. Because the story is so deeply entrenched in the character's head, it takes a while for the full extent of the narrator's unreliability to come to light.

In contrast, "Hills Like White Elephants" by Ernest Hemingway relies almost entirely on dialogue. With the exception of a few stage directions and dialogue tags, most of the story is told through the dialogue between the characters. The middle-grade novel *Seek* by Paul Fleischman is an even more extreme example: It is written as a radio play so that most of the story comes through in the voices of the characters.

Another important consideration is whether the narrator's voice is present and distinct, or almost invisible. A first-person narrator is easy to spot, but just because a piece is in third person doesn't mean the narrator doesn't have a voice. Many writers assume that if their book or story is written in third person, they're off the hook and don't have to worry about voice. They're wrong. In fact, the opposite is true: Writing in third person can be even more complex than writing in first person because the author must make conscious choices about how present the narratorial voice will be in the story. The first person is straightforward: A character tells the story as she sees it unravel. The third-person narrator has more wiggle room. The narrator's voice can be in-your-face and opinionated, or so seamless that it's practically invisible. Of course, most stories don't fall into these extreme categories and instead end up somewhere along the spectrum.

The Opinionated Narrator

Sometimes a narrator has strong opinions that slip out as she tells the story. This opinionated narrator is common in eighteenth- and nineteenth-century novels, think of those written by authors like Charles Dickens and Jane Austen. In these cases, an omniscient narrator often "head hops" from one character's point of view to another and shares her true opinions—her agenda, if you will—throughout the story.

A great example of an opinionated third-person narrator is *Matilda* by Roald Dahl. The voice comes through in the first line of the book: "It's a funny thing about mothers and fathers. Even when their own child is the most disgusting little blister you could ever imagine, they still think he or she is wonderful." We can tell right away that the narrator has strong contempt for children (particularly spoiled, unexceptional children) with the phrase "disgusting little blister." In the first few pages of the book, the author establishes the irony of parenting. While some parents blindly adore their mediocre children, others ignore their children despite their legitimate brilliance; the book *Matilda* is about the latter scenario. The opinionated voice of the narrator not only sets up the contradiction between the two types of parents but also establishes the narrator as someone who sees through that absurdity and "tells it like it is" to the reader. The narrator and reader are like allies, discovering together how extraordinary the story's protagonist, Matilda, really is.

In other books, the opinionated narrator might even break the "fourth wall" and address the reader directly. We see this especially in fables or fairy tales, where the narrator might interject with morals or lessons as the story develops. This narratorial choice aligns the narrator and reader but also establishes the narrator as an authority who is imparting wisdom to the reader as the story unfolds. Kate DiCamillo uses this technique in *The Tale of Despereaux*, where from the very beginning we know that this narrator has distinct opinions and an even more distinct voice. Here are the closing lines from chapter one:

> "The last one," said the father. "And he'll be dead soon. He can't live. Not with his eyes open like that."
> But, reader, he did live.
> This is his story.

The Invisible Narrator

At the other end of the spectrum are third-person narrators who are so subtle and unobtrusive that the reader hardly notices their presence. The narrator melts into the background so that readers can focus instead on the characters and the story. Of course, invisible narrators don't happen by accident. They're extremely difficult to pull off, and the writer must make a conscious choice to craft the narrator this way.

Having an invisible narrator doesn't mean that you don't have a narrator at all. The narrator is clearly telling the story, but the voice doesn't draw attention to itself. Often this type of narrator is omniscient and can pop in and out of character's heads quietly, without making a fuss. One lovely example occurs in *The Secret of Platform Thirteen* by Eva Ibbotson. The narrator certainly has a distinct tone, but it's so subtle that we hardly notice and are instead carried away by a good story.

> If you went into a school nowadays and said to the children: "What is a gump?" you would probably get some very silly answers.
> "It's a person without a brain, like a chump," a child might say. Or:
> "It's a camel whose hump has got stuck." Or even:
> "It's a kind of chewing gum."
> But once this wasn't so. Once every child in the land could have told you that a gump was a special mound, a grassy bump on the earth, and that in this bump was a hidden door which opened every so often to reveal a tunnel which led to a completely different world.

Notice the subtle choices the author makes in these first lines. She could have started the book by saying: "A gump is a special mound, a grassy bump on the earth ... ." Instead, she uses the invisible—but very present—narrator to engage the reader in a kind of game. The narrator poses the question "What is a *gump*?" and right away the reader wants to figure out the answer. We don't want to be like the kids who give the silly answers; we want to be one of the kids in the know. By the time the author tells us what a gump is, we've become so curious that we're not about to question the existence of gumps. We've already bought into the idea.

Additionally, by presenting the gump as something that was common knowledge long ago but that no one knows about anymore, the author makes the existence of gumps feel plausible. Of course the reader wouldn't know what a gump is—no one does anymore. But that doesn't mean that gumps aren't *real*. Ibbotson crafts this opening with such artful sleight of hand that we don't even notice the narrator gently nudging us into the story, making us suspend our disbelief and embrace a world where gumps—and all the magic associated with them—are real.

EMULATE THE MASTERS

Humpty Dumpty sat on a wall.
Humpty Dumpty had a great fall.
All the king's horses and all the king's men
Couldn't put Humpty together again.

Rewrite the nursery rhyme "Humpty Dumpty" in the voice of one of the authors on this list (or any other author whose voice you admire): William Faulkner, Franz Kafka, Ernest Hemingway, Jane Austen, George Eliot, Henry James, Edgar Allan Poe, Toni Morrison, Edith Wharton, Charles Dickens, J.R.R Tolkien, Isaac Asimov, Maya Angelou, Chinua Achebe, Sandra Cisneros, Jack Kerouac, Kurt Vonnegut, Samuel Beckett, William Shakespeare, or Geoffrey Chaucer.

The idea is to recreate the story told in the nursery rhyme in the voice and style of the author you choose. It doesn't need to be in poetic form, nor does it need to rhyme. The nursery rhyme is simply a springboard that lets you focus on the voice you have selected rather than on plot or character. Your finished story should be no longer than 700 words.

Bonus: Do the exercise a second time, but with a different author. Try to select an author whose voice is completely different from the one you used before. Then compare the results. Which voice felt more natural to write? When did the words flow more freely? These clues will help you fine-tune your voice going forward.

HOW TO HONE YOUR VOICE

"Find your voice" has become a writing instruction cliché (second only to "Kill your darlings" and "Show, don't tell"), but it turns out that this is bad advice. "Find your voice" implies that your voice is missing and that to improve your writing you must insert more voice into it. Nonsense. You *already have* a voice, and it's present in everything you write. It might not be obvious—it might be almost invisible—but it's there. The key is to shape it with intention.

Unlike fingerprints or DNA, remember that your voice is malleable. When teachers say, "Find your voice," what they really mean is "Hone your voice," or "Understand how your voice works." For better or worse, you already have a voice, but if you're just starting out as a writer, that voice might be mediocre. In fact, your voice might even be terrible. That's okay. You can improve your voice. You can cultivate it, prune it, and shape it so that it will grow into something beautiful.

As you practice and study voice (both your own and the voices of the masters), you will discover something important: While you can hone and improve your voice, you can't force it to be something that it's not. Just as you can't grow roses from sunflower seeds, your voice has a core essence you cannot change. What "finding your voice" really means is that you must uncover that core element, that piece of you that is inextricably woven into your writing. Once you understand your voice's natural tendencies, you can play with it and practice. Eventually, you will learn how to shape your voice and make it the best it can be within those natural constraints.

....

GABRIELA PEREIRA is a writer, teacher, and self-proclaimed word nerd who wants to challenge the status quo of higher education. As the founder and instigator of DIYMFA.com, her mission is to empower writers to take an entrepreneurial approach to their education and professional growth. Gabriela earned her MFA in creative writing from The New School and teaches at national conferences, at local workshops, and online. She is also the host of DIY MFA radio, a popular podcast where she interviews best-selling authors and offers short audio master classes. Her book, *DIY MFA*, was released in 2016 from Writer's Digest Books. To join get a cheat sheet on voice, go to DIYMFA.com/voice.

CHAPTER 22
BREAKING THE FOURTH WALL

BY JEFF GERKE

Right now, in this sentence, I'm speaking directly to you, dear reader. Such things are done all the time in nonfiction. It's a conversation between author and reader, as if the two of us were sitting together having coffee (or, in my case, Mountain Dew).

But when it comes to fiction, some people say that such direct address should not be used. It's called breaking the fourth wall.

The fourth wall is a reference to the world of theater, in which there may be three walls—the back wall upstage, left and right walls on either side of the stage—and then an open "wall" through which the audience watches the play. We subscribe to the illusion of that fourth wall, that the characters are unaware of the audience, and that all of this is really happening.

But occasionally, a character will acknowledge the presence of the audience and speak directly to them, thus breaking the fourth wall. It can be a jarring experience for the audience as that hermetically sealed membrane between fiction and reality is ruptured. This happens in movies, too, when a character speaks directly into the camera.

In fiction writing, you can find an example of breaking the fourth wall in the novel *A Star Curiously Singing* by Kerry Nietz. The narrator utters some science fiction jargon, and then we get this line: "That will take some explanation, I know. Don't worry, freehead, we'll get to that."

Let's explore the rule that thou shalt not break the fourth wall.

THOSE OPPOSED

Those who disagree with this rule point out that speaking directly to the reader is a rarely used technique in contemporary fiction, and that's part of what gives it its power. In fiction, as in theater or cinema, being included in the characters' awareness can be disconcerting but effective.

I see it used when the novel comes in the form of a journal or retelling of events. So it's not that the characters pretend that the reader doesn't exist. It's more that the reader simply wasn't there at the time the events happened, but she is in the same time stream, maybe reading the journal long afterward or hearing the story from a "Call me Ishmael" narrator who speaks directly to her.

Breaking the fourth wall—or, better said, including the reader in the story—can be an effective way to shake things up and further engage the reader in the world of events being recounted.

THOSE IN FAVOR

Those who advise against breaking the fourth wall believe it's inherently a fiction error.

Breaking the fourth wall reminds them that they're reading a book and not watching the events unfold in real time. There is an existential jolt, and the element of covert observation—some would say voyeurism—is stripped away. You're caught. Noticed. Outed.

Whether they realize it or not, people who oppose breaking the fourth wall are believers in the invisible novelist philosophy of fiction. They want the mechanism of the storytelling to disappear, leaving the reader to notice only the characters and events.

According to that philosophy, "good" is anything that pulls the reader more deeply into the illusion that this is really happening, and "bad" is anything that knocks the reader out of that illusion.

MY OPINION

Breaking the fourth wall is a useful tool in the novelist's kit, but it should be done intentionally, as it really does have an impact on the reader—and it might push the reader out of the fictive dream. On the other hand, as with the "freehead" or "Call me Ishmael" examples, direct address might pull the reader more deeply into the world of the story, because now the characters are looking right at the reader.

I don't think it's something that should be done in every novel, and it will always remain experimental. That is as it should be, because it does change the reader-author contract. But if you have the sense that roping the reader into the story in this way will give your book an element you're looking for, why not give it a try? You can always take it out later if you don't like it.

TIPS FOR GETTING PAST THE GATEKEEPERS

Some agents and editors are not going to get it if you break the fourth wall in your fiction. Many will see it as an error and say you're not ready for prime time.

In that case, you have to choose carefully. Is the direct address something dear to you about this book, essential to its character? If so, leave it in and take your chances. If it's something you're not sure about, or if it's just a throwaway thing you added, maybe take it out—or at least take it out of the first fifty pages. You can work with your editor to possibly put it back in later.

YOUR FICTION VOICE

Do you want to break the fourth wall? Is it something you enjoy in the fiction you read? Did you encounter a novel that did this and it appealed to you? If so, why not try it in yours? Or at least put it into your tool kit for possible use in the future. If you have encountered a book that did this and you hated what it did to you, then by all means leave it out of the fiction you write.

But if you do end up rejecting it for your own fiction, I hope you will refrain from telling other writers, especially unpublished ones, that breaking the fourth wall is a no-no in fiction. It isn't. It's a preference.

<hr/>

JEFF GERKE trains novelists how to better do what it is they're trying to do. He trains through his top-rated Udemy class, "Write Your Best Fiction and Get It Published." He trains through his latest e-book, *Hack Your Reader's Brain: Bring the Power of Brain Chemistry To Bear on Your Fiction*. He trains them through his books for Writer's Digest: *The Irresistible Novel, Plot Versus Character, The First 50 Pages, Write Your Novel in a Month*, and *The Art & Craft of Writing Christian Fiction*. He trains them through the many writers conferences he teaches all over the country every year. And he trains them through the freelance editing he does for his clients. In the past, he trained his authors when he ran Marcher Lord Press, the premier publisher of Christian speculative fiction, which he sold after an award-winning five-year run. Jeff is known for his canny book doctoring skills and his encouraging manner which leaves writers feeling empowered and like they really can do this thing after all. He lives in Colorado Springs with his wife and three children.

CHAPTER 23

THE VOICE OF YOUNG ADULTS

BY DIANA LÓPEZ

Teen fads last about as long as it takes to type "LOL" or "OMG." No wonder writers who pen young adult novels often struggle to sound young. After all, many of us were fifteen long before cell phones and iPads. So how can you sound like a teen when you're one (or four) decades older?

Here's how to overcome the three most common pitfalls that muffle an authentic teen voice.

DON'T SOUND GROOVY

Big banking means earning lots of money. A *snapback* is a baseball cap with snaps instead of Velcro or elastic. Teens used to say *my bad* when they made mistakes, or *wolfing it* when they needed haircuts. They used to say *groovy* and *far out*, too. Popular slang is constantly changing, so any book that features a lot of it is going to sound outdated soon after it hits shelves—not good for establishing a plausible teen voice with readers for years to come.

YA writers are often encouraged to spend time with teens so that they can write believable characters. This can be a great strategy for character development, but it doesn't mean you should just jot down what they say. Instead, focus on where their words *really* come from, deep down.

"What doesn't work? A hypothetical, generic teen using (quickly outdated) slang," says Cynthia Leitich Smith, best-selling author of the

Tantalize series and forthcoming Feral series. "Choose a language that reflects your character's personality. Think about his go-to words."

I had the characters in my YA novel *Choke* create "word-morphs" by blending familiar terms—*boycentric, meanormous, magtastic*—each in response to an emotion or event. Letting the slang emerge organically from the teens' situations and surroundings added personality to the characters, avoided putting a time stamp on my book, and tapped into a timeless quality of teen speech: word play.

So when it comes to slang, don't borrow. Invent!

DON'T DUMB DOWN

I'm a teacher, and sometimes my students try to elevate their language with a thesaurus. The result is "meteorological phenomenon" instead of "weather." YA writers, conversely, are tempted to oversimplify. But nothing is more condescending than writing as if teens are not smart enough for sophisticated language or, perhaps more important, sophisticated themes. Always remember this: Teens aren't dumb—they're *inexperienced.*

When Kristen-Paige Madonia originally wrote her debut novel *Fingerprints of You*, she imagined it for an adult audience. After selling it as a YA book, she worried about changing it for teens, but her agent warned, "Don't dumb it down."

"Our job is to write the truth—no sugarcoating," Madonia says. "Teens face complex issues, and it's the author's responsibility to provide smart, honest literature, so they have access to stories that empower them and affirm that they aren't alone as they confront the challenges of the teen years."

So how can you avoid dumbing down your fiction? Try smarting it up! To challenge young readers with your material is to help them grow.

First, don't run from big words (or bad language) when they're consistent with a character and not over the top, and don't be afraid to acknowledge the darkness when it comes to plot or theme. Our young people don't live in a perfect world; they live in the real world where bad things do sometimes happen. Jay Asher's bestselling *Thirteen Reasons*

Why, for example, deals with teen suicide, and Patricia McCormick's acclaimed *Cut* features self-mutilation. I'm not suggesting you deliberately use dark themes, but don't deliberately avoid them either. This may appear at first glance tangential, but it ties directly into voice—your characters will not have authentic voices unless they're put in honest and real situations and react accordingly.

Second, let your characters fix their own problems. Too often, aspiring YA writers create a teen-in-distress scenario and then have Mom, Dad, or a favorite teacher come to the rescue. This form of dumbing down is a missed opportunity because it robs teens of the independence they are working so hard to earn. Instead, remove the grown-ups, let your characters handle the tough situations, and remember that they are *trying out* coping tools, not *relying* on them. Their true voices will pop. They won't be able to come out if you stifle them by having an adult do the heavy lifting.

DON'T LOOK BACK

Because YA writers are inspired by their own history, they sometimes write with the benefit of hindsight. The voice, then, is calmer and wiser as the narrator looks back at himself, maybe even judging his foolish past.

The trouble with looking back is that you risk patronizing your readers. You also lower the stakes for your character because if he is telling a story that happened five or ten years ago, and everything has worked out, then his dire situation obviously wasn't so bad after all.

Perhaps the best way to avoid a retrospective tone is to dump the map. In other words, forget the experiences you've collected over the years; throw aside that been-there-done-that attitude. Seeing like a teen means seeing for the first time so that the ordinary is extraordinary again.

Work to capture the overwhelming awe, confusion or joy teens feel. If you can't remember that sense of newness, live without your map for a while. Learn a new dance, for example. Go somewhere you know you'll feel out of place. Wear an outfit that is the complete opposite of your normal style. Do these activities make you feel self-conscious? Good! That's how teens often feel.

Before the new experience becomes a distant memory, write down your emotions, impressions and surprises, rediscovering what it feels like to be a novice, to be awkward, to be a teen.

Wendy Mass, author of the YA novel *A Mango-Shaped Space*, has this to say: "Every writer has a voice in their head that stops at a certain age. For me, it's between twelve and sixteen."

How old is *your* voice? If it's one (or four) decades older than fifteen, don't fret. Some people get face-lifts to look younger. So why not get a "voice-lift"? Play with language, "smart up" your story, dump the map, and remember that sounding like a teen is not related to your age but to your state of mind. Your young readers will thank you for being real.

DIANA LÓPEZ is the author of several middle grade novels, including *Confetti Girl, Ask My Mood Ring How I Feel*, and *Nothing Up My Sleeve*. She teaches creative writing at the University of Houston-Victoria.

CHAPTER 24

TOO MANY VOICES

BY G. MIKI HAYDEN

In the Confidence of Strangers by Patricia G. Kurz has many finely crafted and admirable facets. The minutiae of family life are well detailed and believable; the characters interact in unexpected and intriguing ways; and the setting is a quite explicit one. The main flaw in the writing is simply the author's failure to choose a point of view for each scene and to use the character's motive to illuminate what's going on. While minor point-of-view touches are provided from time to time, these never develop into a full-fledged character voice.

EXCERPT: *IN THE CONFIDENCE OF STRANGERS* BY PATRICIA G. KURZ

Four-year-old Libby Ocean stood among pale blue fescue, white hollyhocks and morning glories, silent and still, straining to see her mother through an inverted plastic colander

"Where's dinner?" she heard her father ask.

"It's about to be on your daughter's head if I can't get the strainer from her and if she doesn't get out of my flowers." From spring to November, Stella Ocean willed a sunless northern garden to grow on her kitchen patio. The brick enclosure dammed back two surrounding acres of prairie wild flowers, trees and shrubs, hiding the frenzied urban fugitives from her panoramic view.

She took the sieve from her daughter's head.

"I am *invisible*," Libby whispered, as only a child can.

"Like a sucker," her mother hissed as she prodded several tomatoes from their vines, placed them in the colander and trudged back to the kitchen sink. Under running water, she probed each one for invisible imperfections.

"Come in and wash up, angel," her father called, holding the door open for his wife, coaxing Libby out of hiding. She flicked specks of dried soil from each bedroom slipper. Then, with outstretched arms, she flew back to earth from her mother's bed of flowers.

"But I was *invisible*, Daddy," Libby said, tugging at his arm. "Grandma said I should be *invisible*."

Stella turned around to see Libby climb up on the chair at the end of the table. "That's your father's chair. Get down."

"It's okay, Stella. Libby can sit there tonight," Donald Ocean said.

"Let her sit there once, and she'll never give it back," said Deborah, their oldest daughter.

Stella said nothing. Libby looked at them from the head of the table where she had already installed her booster seat. She snapped her bib in place and held her child-sized silverware in her hands, ready to eat.

"Where is Libby Ocean?" Stella said, shielding her eyes while she scanned an imaginary horizon.

"Here I am, Mommy," Libby said, waving the implements in the air.

"Where is Libby Ocean, Deborah? I can't find her," Stella went on.

"Here I am, Mommy," Libby repeated, arms still high in play.

"Does anybody know where I might find Libby Ocean? I don't know where she is." The four sisters ignored their mother.

"Here I am, Mommy. Here. Look. I am right here." Libby's shoulders melted.

"I guess she's gone. She vanished," Stella taunted, looking this way and that in her imaginary vista.

"I'm right here, Mommy. I'm not *invisible* anymore. Here I am." Excitement no longer colored Libby's voice. "I was just playing, Mommy."

Stella turned to her pouting child. "Don't play in my flowers or with my things, missy. And trust me, you're not invisible. I see you every minute of every day."

"Jeez, Mom, let it go," fifteen-year-old Victoria Clare mumbled into her empty plate.

"Let it go? She tramps through my garden, gets dirt all over her, takes my things from the kitchen, and then wants me to pretend she's not here."

"She's four, Stella," her husband said.

"I'll be five next week," Libby said, holding up three fingers. Her voice sparkled with baby sweetness, someplace between a gurgle and a chime.

"No, Libby, next year. In five months," Victoria said, moving Libby's fingers to show her five.

Without food for distraction, the girls stared at their parents in the voiceless room.

Stella filled plates at the stove, and Donald carried them to his daughters. When he served Libby, he cut hers into small spoon-size strands.

"Salad?" Victoria asked.

"No. I didn't make one," Stella answered.

"Toss me one of those tomatoes, Dad," Victoria said.

"Not these." Stella grabbed Donald's hand. "There are some from the store in the refrigerator if you want. These are the first ones this year, and I want to keep them."

"Mommy eats tomatoes," Libby said, wrapping her arms over her head.

"Yes she does, baby," her father cooed from where he sat in Libby's chair between Deborah and Victoria.

"Dad, let me wear your sweater, please," Victoria said.

Donald reached behind himself to retrieve his sweatshirt.

"You cold, honey?" Donald asked his daughter.

"Always, Dad. I can't keep warm sometimes," Victoria answered. She put her dad's sweater over her back.

"None of you were ever like this," Stella said, pointing at Libby while squeezing past Victoria to place an arrangement of roses at the center of the table.

"Let's eat," Donald Ocean said, proud of the healthy family portrait his family created. All four daughters were together for the first time that summer.

After dinner, Libby stood beside Victoria on a stepstool. Her gurgling laughter rang throughout the house as they blew into the soapy water and painted suds on each other's arms and faces.

Not long after dinner, the older girls said goodbye, and Victoria left with her friends. Libby went to her room, and her parents went to theirs. Her father's good-night knock at the door startled the child who ran to open it.

"Good night, sweetie," he said, lifting her.

"G'night Daddy." She snuggled into his neck. "When's Vickie coming back?" she asked.

"After you're asleep. Go say good night to Mommy."

Libby disappeared beneath the cloud of her own white comforter.

"I love you, Daddy. You say it for me. I'm *so* tired," Libby said, bolstering her fib with a noisy yawn. Libby heard him say I love you before he left her room.

After a few moments, she knelt on the empty bed by the window to wait for her sister but fell asleep with her head on the sill.

CRITIQUE

Choose a Point of View

Without a specific character perspective, all readers have to enlighten them is physical description (though, to be sure, these externals can go some distance in helping to understand a character's emotions). A close point of view, however, whether first person or third, will supply the inner meaning to a story. Such intimate points of view bring insight and warmth to any fictional piece, as well as a more direct feeling of empathy for the character.

In contrast to the author's strong ability to convey setting detail and family dynamics, she's gone astray by seeing and telling all but revealing not quite enough of what's going on in the characters' thoughts:

> "Come in and wash up, angel," her father called, holding the door open for his wife, coaxing Libby out of hiding.

Now suppose the author were to actually write this from Donald's viewpoint.

> "Come in and wash up, angel," Donald Ocean called, holding the door open for his wife, coaxing Libby out of hiding.
>
> All Donald wanted at dinner tonight was peace. Stella had been edgy lately in a way that mystified him. Perhaps he himself was to blame, as the head of the household. But then she took out her unhappiness on Libby. And Libby could no more help being Libby than, well, okay, than Stella could help being Stella.

This expansion of meaning is merely a conjecture, because I have no idea what Donald might really think or feel. We'd have to be given his viewpoint to know what's intended. We see that Stella is on edge, of course, and that everyone in the family is well aware of her outspoken temperament and annoyance with the four-year-old (which Stella hardly tries to hide), but all we can do is observe—and we're not clued into the emotional ramifications.

Pinpoint the Conflict

The central conflict of this story—and, yes, every novel needs one—doesn't readily come to the fore. The sooner Kurz directs her audience to the dramatic issue of the piece, in a personal and involving way, the more riveted readers will be to the page.

Throughout this excerpt, Stella's hostility toward the rest of the family is obvious, though whether this is a one-time irritation with her loved ones or an ongoing condition isn't made clear. Reflecting the story through the prism of a real viewpoint will make the emotional atmosphere more transparent.

Given what readers are able to witness here, the disturbance within the family seems to be Stella's refusal to accept Libby as she is. Going deeper into a character's viewpoint can accentuate how this affects each one of them.

For instance, after her father tells Libby to say good night to Mommy, she refuses:

> "You say it for me. I'm *so* tired," Libby said, bolstering her fib with a noisy yawn.

What this really means isn't obvious enough; the statement needs amplification. For instance, something from Donald's view that shows he realizes that Libby isn't immune to her mother's coldness would further help to spell out the conflict.

Representing Children

Another problem with the text is that four-year-old Libby doesn't seem accurately portrayed. While young children's thoughts and points of view are very difficult to reproduce, as writers, we need to do our best to portray them—just as any other character—as realistic as possible.

At the start of this story, Libby speaks minimally and with a lisp. Later on in this chapter (not excerpted here), she makes a long, coherent speech, interrupted only by brief questions from those around her. The author needs to create not only a pattern of speech that's age-appropriate but also one that stays consistent throughout the story.

Too Much Attribution

One thing that's obvious in this piece is that the author uses dialogue tags nearly everywhere, especially early on. Kurz diverges from using the standard *said*, but in some portions of the text, she uses that word far too often. Whatever the citations, however, they become too visible as she employs them. Dialogue tags are a distraction here, and the exchanges should be simplified and handled with greater variation. Situational clues may serve to tell us who's speaking at any given moment.

For instance, in the following exchange:

> "She's four, Stella," her husband said.
> "I'll be five next week," Libby said ...

might become:

> "She's four, Stella," her husband said.
> "I'll be five next week." Libby held up three fingers.

Correcting Minor Flaws

The author tells us four daughters have sat down to dinner, but only three are named and actually speak—Libby, Victoria and Deborah. A great deal is made of meal preparation, but aside from the tomatoes, which are off limits, no other actual food is ever mentioned.

At one point, we're informed that the fours sisters ignored their mother, but actually, Libby is very focused on her mother at that point; she's trying to get her attention. Then, in Libby's bedroom, the character runs to her father but doesn't need any effort to return to her bed— she's simply there.

The problem with such flaws is that they confuse the reader and force him to go back and reread just to make sure he didn't miss any details. This slows down the story and creates a certain amount of distrust for the reader.

Also minor, but taking readers away from the immediate matter of the story, are little questions of word choice: Libby's shoulders "melted," for instance. And when Stella tells Libby she's invisible "like a sucker," what does she mean? I really don't know.

A lack of point of view and a failure to pose the main intention of the story are lethal defects that have to be resolved before the work can be published. I like this story and want to know what happens to this family. The characters are well-drawn and subtle. I also find the tone of the writing quite appealing. I just want to understand even more about them, in a way that strong point of view can reveal.

G. MIKI HAYDEN has published several novels (including the *New York Times*-lauded *Pacific Empire*), countless stories, and two writing instructionals: *Writing the Mystery* and *The Naked Writer*. Miki has taught at Writer's Digest University for many years and loves working with serious students.

PART V

NONFICTION-SPECIFIC VOICE

CHAPTER 25

GIVE NONFICTION AN AUDIBLE VOICE

BY ROGER MORRIS

Writers often read their works-in-progress out loud. I hear mine in my head.

It's not that unsummoned voices are telling me to commit antisocial acts; rather, the voices are familiar ones that I've conjured to help me with my writing. Whose voice it is depends on the tone I want for a particular article or a key passage, such as the lead for an article. That's when I become a ventriloquist and start "throwing" different voices.

Let me explain.

It all started several years ago. As a young freelancer in Washington, DC, I was struggling to make the transition from writing in newspaper style, with its shorter, more formulaic prose, to magazine style, with its lengthier, more free-form structure. While I could easily knock out magazine articles that were little more than expanded news stories, I had trouble setting the scene for more involved pieces.

One Sunday evening I was working on an article about the little-known Mattaponi Indians, who live on a reservation in Virginia. I wanted to begin the piece by giving the reader a word picture of what I saw and felt on my first visit to the reservation. But one draft felt too stilted, while another came off as too casual, perhaps even flippant.

Earlier that day I'd watched an NFL feature film (these were just coming into vogue back then, as the league gained popularity), and the grave, baritone voice of the narrator was still resonating in my mind.

So when I sat down at my keyboard again, I began imagining that authoritative voice reading my copy, and suddenly words and sentences started falling into place. Then I had the voice reread the piece, and as it provided such feedback as, "No, that word sounds wrong," and, "No, that sentence comes across as too short and choppy," it soon became easy to spot places where my voice had strayed. Gradually, with each revision, the voice in my head became more natural, more suited to its reading of the words on the page, until I finally had the long, descriptive lead that I needed to entice the reader into the article.

The voice I had summoned was that of the late Philadelphia newscaster John Facenda, whose combined tone and cadence has many times been called "The Voice of God"—sober without being somber; precise and confident, yet never pretentious or falsely serious. This particular voice had perfectly captured the tone I wanted to set for my piece on the Mattaponi Indian tribe.

Many aspiring writers are convinced that they have to develop their own voices and their own styles, but those of us who write for multiple print and online publications more often need to be adaptable and channel multiple voices like a ventriloquist. Here's how to use my technique to do just that.

MATCHING VOICE TO TONE AND TOPIC

The voices you conjure for each piece you write should change according to the following:

1. The style of the target publication and the audience it attracts. The tone of an article for a testosterone-charged magazine like *Details* will be different from that used in *AARP The Magazine*—i.e., sardonic versus sedate.
2. The subject matter and its seriousness or lightness. An article about a natural disaster will obviously have a grimmer tone than a piece about what happens on first dates.
3. The length you have to "speak." If you're writing a 250-word food short for the online *The Daily Meal*, you may use a few edgy words,

but you'll have no space in which to throw your voices. A 2,000-word article for *Beverage Media*, on the other hand, gives you more room to play.

4. The style of what you've written before (if you're a regular contributor). For example, I regularly write for the British trade publication *The Drinks Business*, and I always look back at prior pieces before writing the next one. I want each to be presented a little differently and to sound a little different to show some versatility. I never want an editor to consider assigning me a plum story but then decide, "Nah, this isn't Morris's style."

Much of nonfiction writing is straightforward exposition of information, facts, and quotes from interview sources. It seldom needs embellishment. But trying to convince a reader of something—to build a credible case—requires a convincing voice. Likewise, using an anecdote to illustrate a point requires a conversational voice.

So the purpose of conjuring a voice is not to ensure that the reader recognizes and identifies it in your piece; rather, it is to use the voice you have chosen to make a difficult passage read better.

THROWING YOUR WRITING VOICE LIKE A VENTRILOQUIST

To best illustrate this technique, let's look at a few examples of the conjuring process in action.

With his "Voice of God," Facenda is still my go-to reader when I want to paint a dramatic picture. For a recent article for *Wine Enthusiast* about a day in the life of a Bordeaux wine château, I wanted to immediately immerse the reader in the atmosphere of Château Lagrange at the beginning of that particular day:

> Dawn's approach lifts the darkness across the gravelly plateau that runs along the Left Bank of the Gironde River where it spreads open to meet the Atlantic. Overhead, a tattered blanket of purple clouds scuds across the remaining sliver of the moon, and a burnt-orange rim flares along the horizon to the east. The air is chilled, just above freezing, and somewhere

beyond the sea of shadowy, darkened vines, a solitary cock crows out its welcome to an early February morning.

Of course, it would be totally inappropriate to have Facenda reading the smart-assed, sardonic passage I needed to describe a wine for the online site of a rollicking men's magazine. How about, instead, the voice of Mike McGlone, the actor in a GEICO TV commercials who looks like a PI and asks us such penetrating, sarcastic questions as, "Does a little pig cry 'wee, wee, wee' all the way home?"

> Other Aussie winemakers may like to slap critter labels on their bottles, but Barossa Valley's Grant Burge has loftier thoughts. He names his big reds "Meshach," "Shedrach," "Abednego" and "Holy Trinity." Now, we're not ready to suggest he change the name of his "Benchmark" Shiraz to "Sweet Jesus," but it does have a lot of rounded mulberry flavors and a long finish. And your prayers for a reasonable price have been answered.

What about when you need to tell the reader a little story—whether it's your personal experience or a tale told to you by a source that you want to paraphrase? Reread that brief story I wrote at the beginning of this piece about struggling with the Indian reservation article. I heard George Clooney telling that one.

Why Clooney? If you saw the movie *Up in the Air*, perhaps you remember the scene when he's in a bar trying to impress Vera Farmiga with his air-travel experiences. Clooney has a sincere, calm, easygoing tone of voice and the manner to go with it—traces of a slight grin, downcast eyes examining his drink, then slowly glancing up, looking at Farmiga eye to eye to punctuate a point. It makes you want to listen to every word.

And Clooney uses this device at least a couple of times in every movie. So, I want Clooney telling my own stories, and if it doesn't sound like Clooney, then it's back to rewriting.

Robb Report, an upscale publication that appeals to our desire for the finer things in life, requires a very different voice. When I write for this magazine, I need an educated—preferably British—voice. So I call on Pierce Brosnan, with his clipped, upper-class enunciation and lots of "bespoke" words. For example, let Brosnan tell you about a rare Bowmore "white cask" scotch:

> Nosing the glass, there are at first candied-fruit, tutti-frutti smells, and then hints of rancio that one gets in older Cognacs. It is incredibly smooth on the palate, with exotic fruits joining in, a little crème brûlée lingering from the Bourbon toast, and just a whisper of peat. It exemplifies an ethereal elegance in contrast to the Black's fuller, more jovial fruitiness and is quite possibly the most elegant Scotch I have ever tasted.

For key descriptive parts of a piece for a women's magazine on the three Antinori sisters from the Italian winemaking dynasty, I called on Meryl Streep with the dreamy, faraway narration she used in the film *Out of Africa:*

> The scene could be from a romantic film set in the 19th-century Italian countryside. It is a cloudless day in June, and we are riding in a horse-drawn wagon down an unpaved country road in Maremma, that almost mystical and sparsely populated plain along the Tuscan Coast. Behind us is the Tyrrhenian Sea, and ahead of us is an ancient castle perched atop low mountains whose slopes sport bright green patches of vineyards—some quite famous—carved out of the darker forest. "It's a kind of Eden—something sort of magical," says Allegra, 38 years old and the middle Antinori sister.

On at least one occasion, I've had President Obama build an argument I was making. You know his style from his speeches—calmly laying out, piece by piece, in short declarative phrases, key points and examples throughout the presentation of his case.

Of course, the situational needs that arise in my writing won't necessarily be the situational needs that come up in your nonfiction. Nor will the voices that sound "true" to the content for me sound true to you. Even when playing ventriloquist, you need to find your own voices.

A summation from a truly distinctive voice seems to be in order. I'll call on an actor I've seen and heard "laying it all on the line" on the big screen for years now—Jack Nicholson:

Look, we all know that we have these little talks—monologues, whatever—with ourselves in our heads all the time. We fire back what we should have said or what we would have said to our bosses or our wives if we had only thought a little quicker or had a few more guts.

Here's the thing: Why not put these voices to good use? I mean (here that trademark, wicked smile crosses Nicholson's face), what's the use in having these voices in our heads if they don't do us some good?

So get over to that laptop or pick up your little pad of paper and start writing down what these voices are saying to you. Use a little imagination here!

I mean, am I right or am I right?

SUMMONING THE PERFECT VOICE

Think about which familiar voices—on TV, in movies, or even among your own friends and family—you would use if you needed to test out your prose in these situations:

- You're writing in first person, and you want to show how wearied, tired, and bummed out you are, or were, about something. Whose voice always seems to be laboring under some great weight—someone who has constant weariness with life?
- You're describing an action scene in which everything is happening rapid-fire. Is there a voice, perhaps that of a sports announcer, who is always giving quick, blow-by-blow commentary?
- You want to set a scene that is eerily calm before all hell breaks loose. Who comes to mind that talks in a gleefully evil yet soothing tone?
- You want to describe a scene of great joy and release. Is there someone you know—perhaps your minister or a motivational speaker you've heard—whose wonderment at the glory of life would be perfect?

....

ROGER MORRIS is a Delaware-based writer who contributes articles on wine, food, travel and culture to a variety of American and European publications including *Robb Report*, *Wine Enthusiast*, *Beverage Media*, *World of Fine Wine*, and *Meininger's*.

CHAPTER 26

FIRST-PERSON FINESSE

BY MARNIE HAYUTIN

It's been a perfectly lovely evening. The food was delicious; the conversation lively. You're just reaching for another glass of wine when suddenly, without warning, your host whips out (gasp!) his vacation photos. Halfway through your vicarious descent into the Grand Canyon, your pulse slows to the mule's sure-footed plod, and you imagine being airlifted to safety by an urgent call from the babysitter.

Remember that feeling as you approach your keyboard. That's exactly how a reader feels in the middle of a poorly executed first-person article.

Despite the journalism-school admonition that "the story is not about you," writers often can't resist the urge to put themselves right in the middle of it. In the hands of a skilled nonfiction writer, the first-person voice is a valuable tool to set a scene or describe a person. In the hands of an amateur, we're back at the Grand Canyon.

Don't leave your readers begging for an escape route. Follow these guidelines for effective first-person writing.

THE PERSONAL ESSAY

Even when the story is about you, it's still not about you. A good personal essay offers insights that readers can use in their own lives. It's not your moment to reveal every mundane detail of yours. Save that for your journal.

Right from the beginning, you need to make a connection with your reader—you may even address her directly using *you*—and assure her that the article will make a point. A writer using the pseudonym of Paula Michaels understood this well in a personal essay published in the August 2001 issue of *Parenting*. She led by acknowledging the reader's predisposition not to read her story.

> This is a scary story, a cautionary tale.
>
> It's the kind of story that, a year ago, I would have turned away from because, after all, what did a story about a sick baby have to do with me?

The point is clear from the first two paragraphs: Parents will learn something from reading this woman's story. She continues with background information that's directly relevant to the point:

> When Zach was born, he was perfect. His Apgars were 9-9. He was 7 pounds, 4 ounces and 21 inches long. He had fine blond hair and those murky blue infant eyes that look like the bottom of the ocean. He breast-fed easily, and he grew. He did all the things he was supposed to do, at all the right times. He smiled at 7 weeks. Rolled over at 12.
>
> When we visited Zach's pediatrician for his once-a-month well-baby visit, her favorite word, when asked any question, was normal. She'd say it in a singsong voice. It became a joke between my husband and me. Normal, normal, normal, David and I would sing as we left her office.
>
> I can pinpoint the day we stopped singing normal so happily: It was a weekend afternoon in early fall. We were sitting at the kitchen table, interviewing a babysitter, and I had Zach, then 6 months old, in my arms. Suddenly he flung his arms up, and his eyes rolled back slightly.

Notice that Michaels doesn't share personal musings about becoming a mother or stories about the baby's cute behavior that only his grandmother would find interesting. She sets up Zach's history as a "normal" baby so that other parents of "normal" babies understand how quickly everything can change.

Zach's pediatrician continued to insist he was normal despite Michaels' gut instinct that something was terribly wrong. But her determination got Zach an appointment with a neurologist who diagnosed and treated his rare seizure disorder before he'd suffered any brain damage. The message to readers: Trust your instincts.

Staying focused on the reader can be tricky, however, and writers can inadvertently slide into self-absorbed essay writing. Watch for these common first-person pitfalls:

- **TOO MANY DETAILS.** You can call this the "First, there were dinosaurs" approach. Make every effort to tell the story as succinctly as possible. Readers don't need a step-by-step account of your thought processes; often the bottom line will suffice. Michaels probably discussed her worries with family, friends and a lady in line at the grocery store, but she didn't write about it—ultimately, she told us just what was necessary to move the story forward.
- **TOO MANY I'S.** Take stock of how many times you use the *I* sentence construction, as in I felt … I watched … I wondered. Too many *I*'s are a good indication that you're too internally focused.
- **TOO PERSONAL.** Leave out thoughts or anecdotes that only close friends or family are likely to get a kick out of. Unless your husband's outstanding work-performance evaluation or your teen's SAT scores directly relate to the point of the story, don't include them. (Bonus tip: Nobody appreciates them in your holiday letter, either.)

THE PROFILE

The first-person voice can be a useful writing device in profiles—but only if the technique is used to provide insight into the subject's personality or character. If you put yourself in the story just to tell us that you conducted the interview at Starbucks, you've missed the mark.

In the May 2002 issue of *GQ*, writer Elizabeth Gilbert uses first person to help describe Jim MacLaren, an unlucky hero who becomes a quadriplegic after suffering not one, but two harrowing traffic accidents. (The article, titled "Lucky Jim," was a finalist in the American Society of Magazine Editors' 2003 National Magazine Awards.) Gilbert puts herself in the story because her interactions with MacLaren paint a vivid picture of him.

I first spoke with Jim MacLaren on the telephone one morning in the spring. I told him I wanted to write about him.

"For *GQ*?" he asked, and laughed. "OK, but I don't really look the part these days. Armani doesn't exactly make Velcro flies on their pants, you know?"

Gilbert goes on to describe meeting MacLaren on the campus of the Pacifica Institute, the Santa Barbara university where he was working on a doctorate in mythology and psychology.

He was in a wheelchair, but he didn't look anything close to helpless. He was a big and handsome man, broad through the chest. He was wearing shorts, and there was a peglike prosthesis attached to the stump of his left leg. His other leg was muscular and tan. A catheter bag half filled with urine hung from the side of his wheelchair, and a thin hose snaked up from it and disappeared under his shorts. He was lighting a cigarette with fingers that were frozen into painful-looking talons, bent and twisted like little Joshua trees. I rolled down my window.

"Jim MacLaren, I presume?"

He smiled. "How'd you recognize me?"

"You smoke?" I said.

"Don't start," he warned.

Gilbert could have just told us that MacLaren is a strong man with a good sense of humor who isn't going to be pushed around, literally or figuratively. It was much more effective, however, for her to show us his strength and humor by letting her conversations with MacLaren speak for themselves.

Gilbert doesn't, however, use the first-person voice to tell us anything about herself, as this student journalist mistakenly does:

After transferring to Northern Kentucky University this summer to play baseball, I had the privilege to meet [John Smith]. He coached the team I played for.

Gilbert also avoids extraneous details, unlike this student journalist:

John and I met at local fast-food restaurant, where he arrived wearing a red T-shirt and a pair of jeans.

Most important, Gilbert weaves the first-person voice through the entire article. A common mistake of inexperienced journalists is to jar the reader with one unexpected first-person interjection, then return to narrative voice as if nothing happened.

In a story about a family who lovingly restored an old house, a Cincinnati writer inserted one first-person sentence about a quarter of the way through the piece. After an anecdotal lead and nut graph about how the homeowners acquired the house, the writer tosses in this sentence:

> Bridget and her mom, Carol, are just as [eager] to tell me the stories behind the house as they are to give me a tour.

Because the rest of the article is written entirely in narrative voice, the reader is thrown off course with the introduction—and unexplained departure—of a new "character" into the story. If you're important enough to be in the scene at any point, you'd better stay there for the whole show.

THE SOFT NEWS STORY

If you were there when an earthquake rocked San Francisco's Candlestick Park during the World Series, or when hundreds of fans lined up at a local bookstore to be the first to own the newest Harry Potter book, the story may be best told through your eyes. A news event can be described quite eloquently from the perspective of an unobtrusive writer (emphasis on *unobtrusive*).

Amanda Ripley was in Paris in August 2003 when temperatures soared above the normal 75 degrees to a smoldering 104 degrees. Her account of the hottest weather on record for Paris, published in a *Time* magazine article titled "Do Parisians Perspire?" creates a vivid snapshot for readers of what she calls "a time when the French briefly lost their cool." Here are a few excerpts:

> I went to the movies, naively, only to find the theater humid and stale. On a Friday at 11 p.m., I found myself in a supermarket on the Champs Elysees. It was packed. We all browsed in slow motion, feigning interest in frozen chicken.

> There were no fans left—anywhere … Unable to let go of the fan idea, my husband and I contemplated buying a hair dryer with a cool setting and rigging it into a fan. We opted for two bottles of glass cleaner instead; we filled them with cold water and madly doused each other. At night this strategy yielded a good 20 seconds of cool, during which we hoped to God to fall asleep …
>
> A week after the heat wave began, the government set up a hotline offering advice on how to cope. I tried calling but it was closed for the evening, like any good French bureaucracy. Senior officials, all of whom had vacated Paris for August, tried to downplay the drama. But by Thursday, the number of French people killed from heat-related causes was estimated at 3,000.

From Ripley's vantage point, the reader can almost feel the Paris heat. Any news story would have carried the statistic of three-thousand heat-related deaths, but the image of Ripley and her husband spritzing themselves with squirt bottles gives the statistic a human face.

But just like Michaels in the *Parenting* article, Ripley refrains from sharing anything about herself that's unrelated to the heat wave. We don't know how long Ripley and her husband have lived in Paris, we don't know what her husband does for a living—Ripley understands that we don't care. She's simply taking us on a journey to Paris during an extraordinary week … and it's much more interesting than that slow mule to the Grand Canyon.

MARNIE HAYUTIN is Director of Marketing for a healthcare technology firm headquartered in Cincinnati, Ohio. She's a former magazine editor and adjunct journalism professor.

CHAPTER 27

HEARING VOICES

BY DAVID A. FRYXELL

Pretty much every publication you'll write for in your freelance career has a "voice." It might be sassy or scholarly, official or offbeat, depending on the magazine. How do you "hear" the voice of the publication you're writing for—and how can you best chime in with the chorus within its pages?

Some titles enforce a rigid "house style," homogenizing all copy until it seems as if a single writer authored it. Others encourage a variety of voices in their pages—but often compensate for this creative freedom with meager pay. Most commercial magazines fit somewhere in between. You can write a bit more breezily (if that's your natural voice) than the magazine's average article—but stay within its comfort zone.

To figure out a publication's voice, read several issues until you feel you can almost channel its tone and style. Scrutinize headlines and subheads, and don't forget the contents page and cover lines, which reveal how the magazine sees itself and sells itself. Try to answer these questions:

- How seriously does it take itself and its subject matter? Although a magazine might run a range of articles, from important to frivolous, you can discern an overall tone. *Entertainment Weekly*, for example, doesn't take itself too seriously, and its editors obviously know Tom Cruise isn't as important as global warming. But *Harper's Magazine* maintains a more serious voice throughout, even though pieces can have a sardonic edge.

- Is it more scholarly or popular? Look at the language the magazine uses—does it read like a textbook or sound more like television? How heavily does it employ contractions? Hunt for pop-culture references; if the publication eschews them, your zippy Radiohead allusion will feel off-key.
- How smart is the publication? That is, how smart does it presume its readers to be? Check the vocabulary, the complexity of sentences, even the punctuation. A magazine that never uses a semi-colon may not appreciate your own convoluted sentences and riffs on Proust.

The chief difference between good writing and better writing may be measured by the number of imperceptible hesitations the reader experiences as he goes along. The author functions as a kind of forest guide. Does our reader trip over unfamiliar words ... stub his toe on an ambiguous antecedent?

—JAMES J. KILPATRICK

- Is it a red or blue state? Never mind politics—this is a cultural divide. Is the magazine addressing suburbanites, or is it more attuned to city dwellers? Whatever the actual demographics, who's the typical reader with whom the editor envisions the magazine having a conversation? *The New Yorker* is obviously a blue-state title; *Reader's Digest* speaks to the red states.
- What is its core appeal? If a magazine's fundamental promise is helping readers look and feel sexier (e.g., *GQ*, *Cosmopolitan*), its voice must reflect that. A magazine that helps readers become published writers—like this one—must speak in a different voice than one promising better abs. Make sure your voice is tuned to that pitch.

THREE EXERCISES IN VOICE AND TONE

Rewrite pieces of published articles to study the affect of changes in voice and tone.

- Find an article or portion of a book that's written for a serious, even academic audience. Rewrite several paragraphs to change the tone so it's appropriate for a city magazine or a magazine such as *People*.
- Take the same original sample you used above and rewrite it as though it were a letter to a friend.
- Take an article from a popular magazine, such as an entertainment magazine or women's magazine, and rewrite several paragraphs, changing all the contractions to full words and replacing any slang or popular expressions.

Once you've identified the voice, you don't have to match it exactly—but don't be a bass in a soprano chorus. After all, you probably have many voices, multiple sides of your personality. Successful writers know how to provide the voice that fits the assignment.

Though our publishers will tell you that they are seeking "original" writers, nothing could be farther from the truth. What they want is more of the same, only thinly disguised. They most certainly do not want another Faulkner ... Melville ... What the public wants, no one knows. Not even the publishers.

—HENRY MILLER

CHAPTER 28

FIND AN ANGLE TO BRING YOUR SUBJECT TO LIFE

BY ADAIR LARA

Have you ever poured your heart into a personal essay only to find the piece has grown like an untended plant? You really have no idea where to begin, where it should end and what goes in the middle. The problem isn't with your subject; the problem is that you don't yet have an *angle*.

You find the counterpart of the angle in every form and genre. In books, it's called the premise (a woman works her way through Julia Child's cookbook in a year). In advertising, it's called the handle (Trix are for kids!). In movies, it's the concept (humans invade the magical habitat of peaceful blue beings on another planet). In an essay, an angle is the controlling idea.

Say you want to write an essay about how you love to cook. You have a subject, but you don't yet have an angle. Subjects invite you to write and write but give you no particular direction in which to take your writing. Angles, on the other hand, tell you *exactly* what to write—and that's what makes them so essential. An angle for a piece on cooking could be that for you, reading recipes is like reading one-act plays, and preparing the dishes is like acting out the scenes. If you ask a group of people to write about the contents of their closet, each person would likely approach the same subject from a different angle. One might say, "My closet is full of clothes bought for another woman." Another's take might be, "My closet does not live in the present. It lives in the past."

Writing Voice

An angle always includes an element of surprise. For her piece in the Modern Love column of *The New York Times*, Cathleen Calbert put the angle in the first line: "I've never liked men. I like guys." Calbert surprises her readers with a twist, a conceit, that grabs their attention long enough for her to say what she wants to say. In other words, when you begin to craft a personal essay, you can't just blurt out what comes to mind. You need an unexpected way of approaching your subject.

Once you have a good angle, the actual writing is a snap, because you know what to put in and what to leave out. In fact, once you have an angle, what often follows is the easiest thing in the world to write: a list. If your angle is that your closet lives in the past, you might start with the fur, then move on to the Lambertson Truex handbag, showing how each represents an earlier version of you.

Let's consider some ways to find angles that will lend focus, originality, and appeal to your personal essays.

START WITH THE OPPOSITE OF WHERE YOUR PIECE WILL END

When I wanted to write about how stupid my cat was, I couldn't just blurt out: "My cat is really stupid. Let me give you some examples." That might be a good subject, but it's no angle. So I began with the opposite of a cat:

> I watched that *National Geographic* show, the one that was a shameless ode to cats—their wisdom, their aloofness, their mystery. I wanted to believe it, but then I looked over at my cat, Mike, rapt in front of the reflection of the TV in the patio door. ...

This angle, which I call the *setup*, provides a strong starting point. If you're writing about a humiliation, you might start by being full of yourself. If you're writing about bravely leaping from the tall rock into the pond, begin with cowering at the edge. This creates natural tension and guarantees that the piece will be about a change in the narrator. As with other types of writing, at the heart of many good personal essays is the story of how someone changed under pressure.

MAKE UNLIKELY COMPARISONS

Elizabeth Rapoport wanted to write an essay about how everybody wants more sleep—but it's easy to see how a straightforward approach to that subject could have been something of a lullaby itself. Enter the angle: "Sleep has become the sex of the '90s." Once she had that twist, the rest came naturally; all she had to do was write about stolen naps as if they were trysts. "I'm not mentally undressing my dishy seatmate on the commuter train," she wrote. "I'm wondering whether he'd take offense if I catnap on his shoulder until we get to Hartsdale."

When I wanted to write that being the parent of teens requires different thinking than being the parent of little kids, I stumbled upon an angle with the potential to amuse readers while still providing some hard truths:

> While children are dogs, loyal and affectionate, teenagers are cats. When you tell them to come inside, they look amazed, as if wondering who died and made you emperor.

Such unlikely comparisons keep your audience tuned in because they want to see just how similar these otherwise dissimilar ideas are. Reward them with humor and unexpected truths.

BRING IN OPPOSING VIEWPOINTS

Conflict and change lie at the heart of many of the best personal essays, and one way to highlight that conflict is to include an opposing point of view. For instance, you might want to write about a quirk of yours—something you always do, never do, love to do, or hate to do. Maybe you wear high heels everywhere, or you'd drive two hours just for a fresh mango. But if it's quirky rather than, say, forbidden, the piece has no tension. You can create conflict, however, by bringing in someone who objects to that quirk. I like, for example, to do what I call *piddling*—taking time to putter around and check my mail, refold T-shirts, collect pennies from my dresser and drop them in the Alhambra jar marked "College Fund" and, in general, piddle around with my stuff.

By itself, this isn't all that interesting. But my husband, Bill, is the weekend warrior who doesn't understand the need to piddle, who wants to go for a bike ride in the park or buy dowels for the fabric we bought or take cartons of books to the used bookstore. Now there's conflict—opposing viewpoints on worthwhile ways to spend our shared weekend afternoons. Conflict doesn't have to be heated or serious to make a piece entertaining or authentic—it simply has to be present.

HIGHLIGHT DIVISIONS OR CATEGORIES

Creating unexpected groupings by dividing people into unusual categories can yield an angle that both lends humor and invites readers in as they think about which group they belong to.

In our earlier example, Calbert used this angle when she divided the male population into "men" and "guys." In another, Steven Lewis writes in the Last Word column of *Ladies' Home Journal*:

> The world can be divided into those who will let a telephone ring off the hook when they are even mildly indisposed and those who would cheerfully trample small children and flower beds rather than let it hit the third ring.

When you use categories as your angle, you have the option of being either an observer or a participant, in which you add an additional twist by including yourself in one of the categories. I took this approach in a piece dividing the world into scolders, who frequently correct others who are breaking the rules, and scoldees (like me) who frequently need correction.

CONTRAST YOUR TONE AND SUBJECT

If an angle is always a kind of surprise (whether it's an approach, a comparison, or an idea), then it follows that a surprising tone can be an angle in itself. We expect a new mother to talk sentimentally about giving her baby the care he needs. Instead, my student Bernadette Glenn took a tone that highlighted her contrarian point of view:

> I had to face the misery of filling the day with a boisterous, self-centered little bully who had no control over his own bowels, never mind his emotions. I had imagined a small period of rest every day, but he was outgrowing naps, and he drooled on the newspaper and punched me if it looked like I was not paying attention to him.

This approach makes us perk up, not only because we're surprised that a mother would talk about her baby this way, but because we're engaged by her irreverence. One way to practice this angle is to write about something you hate as if you love it, or vice versa.

Another of my students, Marsh Rose, used a similar approach to write a piece about having a falling-apart rental and an indifferent landlord. We would expect a tone of complaint (and of course we don't want to hear it, do we?), but instead of that predictably angry voice, she adopted a tone of yearning akin to one you might use for an adored but elusive lover. This enabled her to get her point across while delighting the reader along the way:

> Dear Zoë,
> I would like to introduce myself to you. In fact, I often sit in this dim living room—cross-legged on the floor furnace, praying for warmth—and imagine what that might be like ... to introduce myself to you. I see myself racing into the street, flinging myself at your noisy green Camaro as you drive by with your gaze averted, and shouting out. "Landlady!" I would cry, "Landlady!"

BE TOPICAL

The best way to get into print quickly is to hitchhike on the news of the day. Every editor wants to run pieces that are current. The governor of South Carolina is on the Appalachian Trail, and you walked it once yourself. Swine flu is coming back? Here's the chance to send editors that essay on your near-death experience from a mysterious illness or your formative years on a pig farm.

When Joe McGinniss' book on Senator Edward Kennedy caught flak for putting thoughts in the senator's head, an enterprising writer for *American Way* magazine wrote a piece in which he invented the thoughts of other famous figures, such as this imagined interior monologue of George Washington crossing the Delaware: "I can't believe this. I'm their leader. I should definitely have a seat." Add a topical angle to your piece, and you might be amazed at how quickly it makes its way through the submission pile and into print.

DISCOVERING YOUR ANGLE

Still don't have an angle? Don't worry. There are many ways to get your angle to reveal itself:

- **JUST KEEP WRITING.** Very often, I'll start with something on my mind that I feel like writing about and just keep going, draft after draft, hoping the angle will announce itself. It frequently will, in a sentence that surprises you, even jolts you, when you step back and read it again.
- **LISTEN TO YOURSELF.** Often the angle will come out of something you hear yourself saying. My former writing partner, Ginny, wrote a piece about not being able to relax on the weekends, a trait that tended to annoy her partners. She not only ran 10K races, painted the garage floor, and balanced her checkbooks on Saturdays, but she also drew up elaborate weekend to-do schedules for her dubious partners. When she found herself saying in exasperation, "Who says that rest comes from having nothing to do?" she'd found an angle for a piece about why she found her frantic weekends so relaxing.
- **DON'T BE AFRAID TO ASK.** You can try to coax out your angle by writing a final paragraph in which you say, "I don't know what I'm trying to say here. Am I trying to say this? Or that?" When you force yourself to wonder aloud what you're driving at, you just might discover you already know the answer—or at least your typing fingers do.

CHAPTER 29

THE VOICE OF YOUR MEMOIR

BY PAULA BALZER

> I was approaching the dark side of my twenties, but I shook like a rattle, still felt like a teenager with fire ants in my Calvins. The big move to Minneapolis had provoked some psychological agita, and I felt like I had been handed a final opportunity to raise some serious heck-ola without facing grown-up consequences. I say "final" because I had always been a pretty well-behaved human female. Evidence: I'd never ridden on a motorcycle, not even a weak Japanese one. I'd never gotten knocked up or vacuum-aspirated. I'd received every available Catholic sacrament with the exception of matrimony and last rites. I'd completed college in eight tidy semesters (one nervous breakdown per). I'd never thrown a glad of Delirium Tremens in anyone's face. I'd never even five-fingered a lipstick at the Ben Franklin. I was a drag, baby. My mid-twenties crisis weighted my gut like a cosmic double cheeseburger. I guess that's one reason I ended up half naked at the Skyway Lounge.
>
> —*Candy Girl* by Diablo Cody

When I received a manuscript called *Candy Girl* by a former stripper named Diablo Cody, I wasn't too interested based on the subject matter alone. Stripping had been covered before (no pun intended), and I didn't think the author was likely to add much to an already crowded market. But then there was *the voice*. After just one paragraph, I was a) completely convinced that stripping was the solution to all of her problems, b) laughing uncontrollably, and c) definitely interested in being along for the entire ride, or at least 250-plus pages. This is what "voice" is all about.

WHAT IS VOICE?

"Voice" is what gives personality and originality to a work; it's almost like your book's fingerprint—only the author can give a book it's own voice and style. It's that special something that makes one particular book on stripping hilarious and uplifting while another might be just plain depressing. Voice can make a book about almost any topic fascinating, from teaching to cattle ranching, and it can make the most wretched of circumstances uplifting. Your voice is also a uniting element. It's the glue that ties everything together. The structure you choose to build your memoir on, your setting, your story, all of these elements are tied together by the voice you use. It's what introduces all of these elements to the reader. Think of your memoir's voice as your book's personality. We won't know if your memoir is quirky, funny, semitragic, and ultimately uplifting unless your voice lets us know it is. Frank McCourt's childhood in *Angela's Ashes* and Haven Kimmel's childhood in *A Girl Named Zippy* have a completely different feel, even if on some level they are both tragic in their own right. This is because each of these authors has a completely different voice, and they use it to relay their stories in different manners.

REALITY CHECK: What this chapter is not about is trying to be something you're not. We can't all be the next Diablo Cody or Augusten Burroughs, but ultimately, the world would be a pretty dull place if we all wrote just like they did. While you might feel tempted to emulate your favorite writers, *don't do it*. Developing an authentic voice is going to help you create a readable memoir, while a poor copy of something that already exists is going to land your manuscript in the trash.

But does everyone have a voice? The answer, luckily, is *yes*—everyone has a voice. But no, not all voices are created equal. That's okay. This chapter is about figuring out what your voice sounds like and working effectively with what you've got. Every voice has its own strengths, and we're going to figure out what those are and work together to maximize them in your memoir.

What Exactly Makes a Voice Good?

"She's got a great voice," is something you hear in book publishing I would bet as much as you do on the set of American Idol. Agents and editors are always on the lookout for a great new "voice"—and there is nothing more exciting than looking at the first page of a manuscript and having that special, one-of-a-kind voice pop right off of the page. But what exactly *is* a voice? And what makes a good one? It's definitely not the easiest thing to describe, but an author's voice consists of the patterns, habits, and language she uses, and how, when put together, they create a style that is that particular author's alone. I always tell my authors that if they're writing at their best, and they sent me their manuscript without putting their name on it (which by the way, I would *never* recommend doing unless you wanted your agent to be incredibly annoyed with you), that I should be able to tell whether it's the work of writer X or writer Z, if they are using their carefully crafted and well-honed voices. So what elements make up a good voice? A good voice should aim to do the following:

- add style and energy to the writing
- present prose in a manner that is unique, interesting, and readable
- enhance the story being told, not distract from the events taking place
- engage and excite the reader
- relay the events taking place with appropriate emotion

Using your voice means having the confidence and courage to let your writing style shine. This takes loads of practice, diligence, and in some cases, I would argue, "un-learning" some of the very things you spent years learning about throughout your education.

QUICK TIP: Don't be afraid of weird quirky details, as it's often the quirky details that are the most memorable and that add life and color to your story. For instance, in *Running With Scissors*, Augusten Burroughs could have easily thought, "Hey, wow, it's really weird that I used to be so into having shiny pennies that I would BOIL THEM," and decided to leave that detail out of his story. Ultimately, that tidbit turned out to be funny and a great insight into what Burroughs's personality was like as a child. Had he been worried that such a detail would be dismissed as boring, he would have missed a great opportunity to show off both his voice and his personality when he was a kid.

Learning to Break the Rules Correctly

Lest every English teacher on the face of the planet come after me, please note that grammar and punctuation are incredibly important and the English language should be used properly and with respect. So let me start out by saying that my "breaking the rules correctly" method is by no means a substitute for not knowing the rules in the first place. I assure you that any agent or editor will *immediately* know the difference between a writer who is artfully playing with language and someone who just plain doesn't have a clue what they're doing. Furthermore, there are so many wonderful books and online tools that there is no excuse for not having a decent understanding of grammar and punctuation. Ditto spelling. I will confess right now that I am positively wretched with spelling, and I'm not exactly terrific with punctuation either. It's tricky stuff sometimes! But I am never too far from my dictionary, and I have my favorite online tools that I refer to whenever I'm in doubt. I highly recommend you do the same.

So what do I mean by "breaking the rules correctly" anyway? Oxymoron anyone? I have found that sometimes writers feel a need to be correct, and this need to conform to the picture-perfect sentence structure we learned about in grade school can really be an obstacle when it comes to finding your voice. If a writer spends too much energy focusing on creating the perfect sounding sentence, the writing is often completely devoid of any kind of life or energy that makes the prose worth reading. What you end up with, while *correct*, is often flat and dull. What are some signs that you might need to let loose and break a few rules?

- constantly self-editing as you write
- using too many or too few words, i.e., feeling you need to have a specific number of adjectives or verbs to properly describe something
- wanting to write the way you sound in your head, but worrying that the way you sound in your head is "wrong"
- not being able to translate the voice you envision onto paper

Feeling a need to write correctly is common, and believe me, this need springs from good instincts! There are some exercises later in this chapter to help break down some of these barriers and to help you sort out when it is absolutely necessary to follow the rules, and when it might be okay to toss a few out the window. With practice and patience, you'll be safely and comfortably following your own set of rules in no time at all. For now, if finding your voice has been an issue, and you know you've been spending time agonizing over the structure of each and every sentence you write, know that these exercises might be particularly helpful to you, and you just may have discovered one of the major reasons why you've had trouble using your authentic voice. Hang in there, you'll get it.

A QUICK WORD ABOUT POV

Before we get to work on that fabulous voice of yours, there are a few things I should mention. It's a common mistake to confuse "voice" with "point of view." For our purposes, when I'm referring to voice, please know that I'm not talking about which point of view your story is being told from. I'm talking about they *way* you're telling your story or how you use your own unique writing talents to put your personal stamp on your work. That being said, point of view is important, and it certainly plays a role in getting your story across. If you're anything like me, you haven't had a reason to think about point of view since ninth-grade English class, which feels like ages ago. Point of view basically refers to the position from which your memoir will be told. To refresh your memory, following is an example of each type of point of view:

First Person

> Most mornings I got out of bed and went to the refrigerator to see how my mother was feeling. You could tell instantly just by opening the refrigerator. One day in 1960 I found a whole suckling pig staring at me. I jumped back and slammed the door, hard.
>
> —*Tender at the Bone* by Ruth Reichl

First Person Plural

We ached to impress our grandfather—or, at least, not to humiliate ourselves. On our turn, if there was no obvious play, we'd glance uncertainly about the table, hoping for a hint from him as to which shot we should attempt.

—*The Big House* by George Howe Colt

Second Person

You're reading a fairy tale in your evening Italian class when you come across this phrase. You think you know what it means, since the sea princess says it after her one true love abandons her, but you ask the teacher anyway.

—*An Italian Affair* by Laura Fraser

Third Person

My mother enjoyed claiming direct descent from Genghis Khan. Having asserted that one eighth of her blood was Tartar and only seven eighths of it 'ordinary Russian,' with a panache that no one else could have pulled off she proceeded to drop a few names in the chronology of our lineage: Kublai Khan, Tamerlane, and then the great Mogul monarch Babur, from whose favorite Kirghiz concubine my great-grandmother was descended, and voilà!, our ancestry was established.

You couldn't have argued the point with her, for in her quest for dramatic effect Tatiana du Plessix Liberman would have set all of human history on its head. Besides, you mightn't have dared to risk a showdown: in her prime, she was five feet nine and a half inches tall and 140 pounds in weight, and the majesty of her presence, the very nearsighted, chestnut-hued, indeed Asiatic eyes that fixed you with a brutally critical gaze through blue-tinted bifocals, had the psychic impact of a can of Mace.

—*Them: A Memoir of Parents* by Francine du Plessix Grey

Obviously, since you're dealing with memoir, you're most likely going to be dealing with a first-person narrative. But, every once in awhile, some very clever writer does figure out a way to make the second person work for a memoir. One particularly effective example of this is Laura

Fraser's *An Italian Affair*, which I mentioned in the second-person example. This memoir follows the author to Italy after a painful breakup. Notice how her use of the second person creates an extra powerful, gut-wrenching effect. I admit that the first time I read *An Italian Affair*, I was in tears before I finished the prologue:

> *Mi hai spaccato il cuore.*
>
> You're reading a fairy tale in your evening Italian class when you come across this phrase. You think you know what it means, since the sea princess says it after her one true love abandons her, but you ask the teacher anyway.
>
> "You have broken my heart," he says, and he makes a slashing motion diagonally across his dark blue sweater. "You have cloven it in two."
>
> *Mi hai spaccato il cuore.*
>
> The phrase plays over and over in your mind, and the words in front of you blur. You can see your husband's face with his dark, wild eyebrows, and you whisper the phrase to him, *Mi hai spaccato il cuore.* You say it to plead with him, to make him stay, and then you say it with heat, a wronged Sicilian fishwife with a dagger in her hand. But he doesn't understand, he doesn't speak Italian; you shared so many things in your marriage, but Italy was all yours.

Fraser's use of the second person makes the reader feel that she is, in fact, experiencing this loss right alongside the author, or worse, in place of! Believe me, it isn't easy to sustain the second person throughout an entire book—and it's pretty astonishing that she manages to pull it off—but that's what finding your voice is all about, knowing what works right for you, what you're capable of, what works right for your story, and knowing how to implement it. When you find your voice and become comfortable using it, you are giving your memoir a great gift.

COMMON VOICE STUMBLING BLOCKS

Just the Facts Ma'am

Have you ever been seated next to someone at a dinner party who was especially difficult to make conversation with? No matter what you did, you just couldn't get a feel for this person? Their likes or dislikes? Where they came from, what they did for a living, if they preferred dogs over cats, etc.? You ask them, "Hey, how do you know *insert name of hostess here?*" and all you get back is "College." Not a hint of personality couched within some additional juicy information, like, "Oh, we met in college when we were both on parole for diamond smuggling." All attempts to create conversation are met with *yes* or *no* answers, and while this guy may very well be a world-famous NASCAR driver or a leading expert in stem cell research, unless he's capable of communicating the information, you're going to give up and start talking to the person on the other side of you.

I can't tell you how many promising (and by promising, I mean the author has a very interesting story to tell) memoirs I've received, where I actually think, "Wow, if this is as good as it sounds, it could be *huge!*"—only to be hugely *disappointed* by the utter lack of voice. Instead of finding an interesting way to relay their story, many authors fall prey to the "just the facts ma'am" syndrome, where they focus so much energy on telling their story and getting all the facts on the page that they completely forget about the importance of voice—which is where all the storytelling comes in. Worried you might be falling into the "just the facts" trap?

Ask yourself the following questions:

- Am I more focused on getting my story straight, i.e., what happened when, than I am about describing how things felt and looked? Am I more focused on facts than an overall picture?
- Is my manuscript devoid of emotional reactions to the events I am describing?
- Am I feeling hesitant or nervous about letting my personality show in my memoir?

All Voice and No Substance ...
We've all met those writers who could write a beautiful paragraph about a broken pencil or a single strand of grass. Then there are the writers

who can write something that is laugh-out-loud funny about a dead goldfish. Yes, that's what's known as raw talent. While it does exist, it is rare. Please believe me, even those super-gifted people who can write mind-blowing prose about their new toothbrush still have to create marketable and readable works, and that means there has to be an actual narrative buried within their genius musings about nothing. In the age of blogging and with the popularity of essays by writers such as David Sedaris and Laurie Notaro, it can be easy to think you can let your voice do all the work and let your story take the backseat. While I will admit to being a huge believer that a special voice can breathe new life into a tired subject, don't fool yourself into thinking a strong voice can make up for a weak story.

If you answer yes to the following questions, you may be relying on that pithy little voice of yours for too much.

- When asked what your memoir is about, you end up listing several completely disjointed and totally unrelated themes that you can't tie together.
- You've decided you'll "work on your voice first" and worry about your narrative later.
- You've "found your voice" but have been forced to start over using several different stories a few times.
- After several attempts, you admit you "just don't know."

While it's important (and of course fun) to have an interesting or quirky voice, I dare say it's time to borrow a phrase from various MFA programs across the country and spend a moment talking about "authenticity." When I refer to authenticity, to some extent, I'm referring to whether or not you want to sound like a pretentious jerk. And do you? If you write perfectly lovely prose, there is no need to try to mess with it to the point where it sounds so edgy that your wonderful memoir about spending a year herding sheep in rural Italy comes across like it was written by a member of the Hell's Angel's. And on the flip side, if you, in fact, *are* a member of the Hell's Angel's, go ahead and sound like one! A large part of "finding your voice" is finding the voice that suits you. Not only does it need to be readable, understandable, and interesting, but it needs to relate well to the person who is *actually writing it*. That's just something to keep in mind. Let's look at some other examples of voice in recent memoirs. Be sure to keep the following ideas about voice in mind:

- How does the author's voice fit in with the story? Or does it provide an interesting contradiction?
- Technically, how does the author's voice come across? Long and flowing, short and to the point? Humorous? Poetic?
- How does the author use her voice to highlight particular portions of her story?
- Are there parts of my memoir that I could emphasize more using my voice?

Blackbird *by Jennifer Lauck*

In her memoir *Blackbird: A Childhood Lost and Found*, Jennifer Lauck recounts her childhood beginning from the perspective of a five-year-old girl who is in the position of having to do things a child should never have to do for a parent. I remember a very ordinary scene in the beginning of the book that was incredibly painful to read, mainly because it was told in the voice of a child. Had this story been told in Lauck's adult voice, it would have been sad, of course, but frankly it wouldn't have packed the same emotional punch, and I can't actually imagine that her book would have been as successful. Lauck is remembering her morning ritual with her chronically ill mother, who was usually bedridden when she wasn't in the hospital. Lauck was told to wait quietly until she heard her mother use the bathroom, and five-year-old Jenny always obeyed. She then prepared toast, just the way her mom liked it, made coffee, and served her mom in bed on a tray, hoping that today would be a "good day" and that her mom might be well enough to get out of the bed and sit on the sofa and read fashion magazines. As Lauck's mother's health worsens, her tasks come to include cleaning her catheter, washing soiled sheets, and doling out her countless medications. The memoir not only details her mother's death, but also her father's, and finds Jennifer and her brother going from suburbia to the slums very quickly. Lauck's childhood voice is full of innocence, hope, love, and to some extent, of course, naiveté. It's a painful memoir to read at times, but the strength this young voice always manages to hold is truly amazing.

Traveling Mercies: Some Thoughts on Faith *by Anne Lamott*

Anne Lamott is, of course, the best-selling author of *Operating Instructions: A Journal of My Son's First Year* and *Bird by Bird: Some Instructions On Writing and Life* (which is super helpful for writers and a must-read). In *Traveling Mercies*, Lamott gets into her spiritual side, which is often hinted at in her other works. If you've read Lamott before, you know that her background has included some wild living, including bulimia, alcohol abuse—and when she was at her lowest, she became pregnant with her son and became a single mother. So, I couldn't help but wonder how her *"Hey, here's how I became a Christian"* book was going to come off. In typical Lamott style, it's full of quirkiness that she pulls off with ease. Check out this explanation Lamott gives as to why she has her now trademark dreadlocks:

> When I first started coming to this church, I wore my hair like I'd worn it for years, shoulder length and ringletty—or at any rate, ringletty if there was an absence of wind, rain or humidity. In the absence of weather, with a lot of mousse on hand, I could get it to fall just right so that it would not be too frizzy and upsetting—although "fall" is close. "Shellacked into the illusion of 'falling'" is even closer. Weather was the enemy. I would leave the house with bangs down to my eyebrows, moussed and frozen into place like the plastic sushi in the windows of Japanese restaurants, and after five minutes in the rain or humidity, I'd look like Ronald McDonald.
>
> Can you imagine the hopelessness of trying to love a spiritual life when you're secretly looking up at the skies for illumination or direction but to gauge, miserably, the odds of rain? Can you imagine how discouraging it was for me to live in fear of weather, of drizzle of downpour? Because Christianity is *about* water: "Everyone that thirsteth, come ye to the waters." It's about baptism, for God's sake. It's about full immersion, about falling into something elemental and wet. Most of what we do in worldly life is geared toward our staying dry, looking good, not going

under. But in baptism, in lakes and rain and tanks and fonts, you agree to do something that's a little sloppy because at the same time it's also bold, and absurd. It's about surrender, giving into all those things we can't control; it's a willingness to let go of balance and decorum and get drenched.

There is so much going on in just those two paragraphs, and it's all about the voice. Firstly, it's funny. Lamott is great with the self-deprecating humor, and the description of her shellacked hair and her desperate fear of rain is hilarious—but then the story takes another turn. While she stays on the theme of her hair, which we now know goes from Ronald McDonald-level frizz-fest to dreads, the tone becomes much more serious. Lamott is able to use her voice to take the journey in a completely different direction, yet she manages to stay on the path. Her voice switches gears effortlessly from humor to a description of the joy of baptism—the joy of her faith. And it's clear within the weight of her voice that this is extraordinarily important to her, yet her tone remains fairly light—it never gets close to being preachy. It's quite a remarkable mix of emotions that her voice allows her to express in such a short passage. But then again, Lamott has been writing for years, and you don't become a best-selling novelist for nothing.

Candy Girl *by Diablo Cody*

In *Candy Girl* by Diablo Cody, a transplant from Chicago to the Twin Cities finds herself working at an ad agency smack dab in the middle of a Midwestern winter. If you've ever experienced a Midwestern winter (I grew up in Wisconsin where it can be so cold, dark, and gray that sometimes the days just seem to blend one into the other), you know they can be rough. This manuscript landed on my desk, and the first sentence I read was "Nobody comes to Minnesota to take their clothes off, at least as far as I know." It was followed by one of the most lively, but also most accurate descriptions of a Midwestern winter that I had ever read.

Here in the woebegone upper country, Jack Frost is a liberal, rangy sadist with ice crystals in his soul patch. Winter is the stuff of legend: stillborn, snow-choked, still as the ice floes on the ten thousand-odd lakes. The old mill cities are populated by generations of Scandinavian and German Lutherans, rugged soul hewn of blonde wood, good sense and Christ-love. The prevailing gestalt is one of wry survivalist humor and thermal underwear with pins still in the folds. Even the food is properly covered: Everyone's favorite supper is a gluey carbohydrate-rich concoction known simply as "hotdish" and served in community Pyrex. Minnesota is like a church basement with a leaky popcorn ceiling and a bingo caller who's afraid to amp things up past a whisper.

Never mind that I knew the book was ultimately about stripping and the opening paragraph is initially focused elsewhere. If the author could make me shiver with a passage about a Minnesota winter on a sweltering summer day in New York City (August in New York is about as bad as winter in the Midwest, just in a different way), I knew that I had found something special. It was also an indication to me that the author was not out to tell a self-indulgent tale of her wilder days—but able to tell a more thoughtful, colorful, and completely new story about what it's like to be a stripper. It was clear to me that she could see the important details and would be able to relay a story to the reader that would be fascinating and could potentially be a huge seller.

Mennonite In a Little Black Dress: A Memoir of Going Home *by Rhoda Janzen*

This memoir definitely falls into the "truth *is* stranger than fiction" category. If this woman were writing fiction, her agent or editor would probably have had to tell her to tone down the drama a little bit. Here's the basic premise: Shortly after her fortieth birthday, as if that weren't traumatic enough, her husband of fifteen years left her *for another man*. Later that week she was seriously injured in a car accident, leaving her no choice but to move back in with her Mennonite parents. But life was tricky for Janzen even before her husband met another man on Gay.com. She suffered complications during a surgery that required her to wear a "pee bag," and we learn that this husband wasn't exactly award-winning and those fifteen years were full of major ups and downs. But thankfully, going home to the Mennonites isn't about admitting defeat but starting anew.

Janzen's voice comes from not just her skill as a writer but from her ability to translate the quirkiness of her family into passages that are funny but also sweet. A typical conversation with Janzen's mother on the topic of dating one of your own cousins or a pothead you went out with a couple of times looks something like this:

> One of the best things about my mother is that she will follow you any-where, conversationally speaking. She will answer any question at all, the stranger the better. Naturally, I cannot resist asking her things that no normal person would accept.
>
> "Mom," I said, serious as a pulpit, "would you rather marry a pleasant pothead or your first cousin on a tractor? Both are associate professors," I hastened to add.
>
> "You marry your pothead if you like," she said generously, "as long as you wait a while. Let's say two years. But as for me and my house, we will serve the Lord."
>
> "Hey!" I said, indignant. "How do you know the pothead doesn't serve the Lord? As a matter of fact, this pothead does serve the Lord! He's more religious than I am." (I felt safe in asserting this because I had once heard the pothead softly singing "Amazing Grace.")
>
> "I think that the Lord appreciates a man on a tractor more than a man smoking marijuana in his pajamas," Mom said earnestly. "I know I do."

These scenes are laugh-out-loud funny, but because it is so clear that Janzen respects her family and shares a loving relationship with them despite their differences, you don't feel like you're laughing at them—that's not easy to pull off. She's able to use her voice to translate the scenes into something relatable, interesting, and funny.

IS YOUR VOICE STARING YOU RIGHT IN THE FACE?

Most writers have a voice they use that best shows off their writing style, whether it be in business, e-mails to a particular friend or a sister, post-cards while traveling, journaling, or even Facebook status updates or Tweets. But when it comes to "writing," there is an annoying, pesky, in-ternal critic that tells you "it's not good enough, it's too easy!"—and the voice goes AWOL. Writer Sloane Crosley, whose book of essays *I Was*

Told There'd Be Cake became a *New York Times* bestseller, got her first essay published after sending a group e-mail to a bunch of friends. She had managed to lock herself out of both her old apartment and the new one she was moving into, and had to call on the services of the same locksmith twice in one day. Naturally, it helps to have friends who are editors at the *The Voice* as Crosley did, but a) you've got to start somewhere, b) you never know where you're going to make connections, and c) this chapter is about finding your voice—and she clearly found hers in that e-mail!

Exercise 1: Where Are You Most Comfortable Using Your Voice?

In one particular instance, I had a very funny client who had written a straight and very businesslike proposal that just wasn't what I had envisioned. His e-mails were always hilarious, as was his take on the subject. What happened? We decided he would try rewriting the proposal using his "e-mail voice." It worked! Sometimes it's just about finding the mode in which you are most comfortable.

I use this exercise frequently, and many of my clients who are published by major publishers have found this exercise incredibly helpful. Try paying attention every time you write for a couple of weeks. Letters, e-mails, postcards, Facebook posts, letters, cards, anything. Notice what feels right. What flows? Do you find yourself writing especially interesting and colorful accounts of your weekend to certain people? Is your journal work better at a certain place or at a certain time? You will eventually notice a pattern forming. Is there a voice that emerges in one particular format? How can you translate this voice into your memoir?

Exercise 2: Commit the Crowd Pleaser to Paper

Is there a story you tell that always gets a laugh? Something that happened to you that's just too funny and it cracks people up every time you share it? Did something happen to you at some point in your life, and every time you tell the tale you have people on the edge of their seats? Have you been telling this story for years and getting the same positive result? Try committing this story to paper and see if you can get the same result. Don't worry if this story is about something hilarious that happened at the seventh-grade dance and your memoir is about your travels in Africa. This exercise is about finding your voice, and if you're struggling to find it, it's always worth looking in places where you're getting positive reactions. As you commit your story to paper, think about what it is about your story that gets the positive reaction from people. Yes, it's partially about the story of course, but we all know that delivery is key. As you're writing your story, think about your delivery and what it is about how you tell the story that makes it work. How can you translate this to the page? Are there aspects of this "storytelling" that can translate to your writing voice?

Exercise 3: Go Back in Time

While not everyone needs to tell the tale of their childhood from the perspective of a child, it can certainly be helpful to try to look at your story in a different light and perhaps take a stab at writing it from a different angle. Remember, I'm not necessarily suggesting you scrap everything you have and start over, but if you need to loosen up and work on your voice, this may be a worthy exercise. Select a passage that's been giving you difficulty, and try to put yourself back into that place. Remember who you were then. What were things like? What were you feeling? What kind of person were you? What would the person you were then have sounded like? Try rewriting the passage from the perspective of the person you were then. See how it comes out. While this may or may not result in a new voice, it may help you loosen up or become more comfortable using your voice.

Exercise 4: Banish Your Evil Inner Critic

In her inspiring and beautifully written memoir, *This Is Not the Story You Think It Is: A Season of Unlikely Happiness*, Laura Munson deals with some heavy stuff, including a messed-up husband who dared utter the words "I don't think I love you anymore." Knowing there was a damn good chance he didn't mean it, the author stuck to her original plan, which was to "take responsibility for her own happiness." And who was one of the biggest obstacles in all of this? Her evil imaginary twin "Shelia." This is how Munson describes Shelia's arrival:

> Apparently the planets of Hell that live inside me were aligned just so the night before, and tah-dah—regardless of therapy, she's managed to ride in on her broomstick like Samantha's brunette doppelganger, Serena on *Bewitched*.

I dare say we all have known "a Shelia." That person that tells you "You're no good. What you're doing is ridiculous-silly-awful-and-will-never-amount-to-anything." I love that Munson took control of her inner demon by naming her and therefore making it easier to tell her off! Okay, that might sound kind of crazy, but the next time you hear yourself saying, "I suck," think about it.

This exercise is especially helpful for those of us who are plagued by the evil inner critic who shouts out, "Hey! You can't start a sentence with the word *and*! Have you lost your mind? I don't care if you were in the middle of writing one of the best passages you've ever written. And while I'm at it, if you don't even know that, maybe you shouldn't be writing at all, and you should just give up because you suck!" Has this ever happened to you? Okay, maybe my inner critic is slightly more dramatic (and mean) than yours, but most writers have one, and they can be a real pain in the ass. As I said earlier in the chapter, they can often get in the way of finding your voice, as they like to remind us about pesky things like the rules of grammar and punctuation, which can be really annoying when we've finally figured out how to write about a passage we've been stuck on for two months! So, I'm here to say that you should banish your inner critics. Do not allow them into your writing space. They are not welcome.

Step 1

The first thing you need to do is begin practicing freestyle writing. Conjure up your inner café society poet, grab your computer or notebook, and just let yourself write about whatever you want without giving a single care to what Margaret or James thinks. Write about absolutely whatever you want for a minimum of fifteen minutes. Do not worry about the quality of your writing; you're just practicing getting the words flowing. If the idea of writing about whatever you want freaks you out (I know it does me. I like direction!) consider the following:

- Write about where you are right now.
- Write about your favorite room in your home.
- Write about your best childhood friend.
- Write about your greatest fear.
- Write about your biggest regret.
- Write about your favorite food.
- Write about family vacations.

Write for fifteen minutes each day for a week—minimum. Do this for additional weeks if you're still stressing out over what you're writing. The idea is to just get the words flowing. Once you're feeling more comfortable you're ready to move on to the next step.

Step 2

You're ready to try this with your actual memoir. Decide which section of your manuscript you want to work on and make a commitment to yourself that you will not criticize or reread what you're writing while you write, and you will not self-edit. Make a commitment to write a certain number of pages during a specific period of time (you set the pages and time frame). Be reasonable: Don't set crazy goals but do challenge yourself. Work this way until you feel the words flying out and your inner critic is quiet. Will your prose be perfect the first round? No! Maybe not even after you revise! But I guarantee you that it will never be perfect if you don't give yourself a chance to actually get it on the paper in the first place.

RECOMMENDED READING: MEMOIRS WITH GREAT VOICE

- *Mennonite in a Little Black Dress* by Rhoda Janzen
- *Candy Girl* by Diablo Cody
- *Running With Scissors* by Augusten Burroughs
- *A Girl Named Zippy* by Haven Kimmel
- *An Italian Affair* by Laura Fraser
- *Blackbird* by Jennifer Lauck
- *Kitchen Confidential* by Anthony Bourdain
- *Julie and Julia* by Julie Powell
- *Alligators, Old Mink & New Money* by Alison and Melissa Houtte
- *How I Learned to Snap* by Kirk Read
- *A Brief History of Anxiety: Yours and Mine* by Patricia Pearson
- *Traveling Mercies* by Anne Lamott
- *Drinking: A Love Story* by Caroline Knapp
- *Slackjaw* by Jim Knipfel
- *This Is Not the Story You Think It Is: A Season of Unlikley Happiness* by Laura Munson

PAULA BALZER has been a literary agent for over 10 years. Her authors include *New York Times* best-selling author Alexandra Robbins (*Pledged, Quarterlife Crisis, Secrets of the Tomb*); Oscar-award winning writer of *Juno*, Diablo Candy (*Candy Girl*); *American Idol* judge, Randy Jackson (*What's Up Dawg?*); and Bobby Henderson (*Gospel of the Flying Spaghetti Monster*).

CHAPTER 30

A PERSONAL PRESENCE

BY DINTY W. MOORE

Without that strong personal presence, the essay doesn't quite exist; it becomes an article, a piece, or some other indefinable verbal construction.

—JOSEPH EPSTEIN

I remember well the self-doubts of my early writing career, when I felt completely unsure that I could ever write anything that was worthy of notice or publication.

One particular evening a few decades back, firm in my memory even now, I turned toward my wife, Renita, and moaned, "Oh, I'm just so average. Your typical guy with the typical tedious problems. Who wants to hear my story?"

My wife closed the book she had been reading for a moment, and asked, "What do you mean?"

I whined some more, going on about an author who had just landed a big book deal. Ethnic memoirs were all the rage at that point in time and this writer had been raised by parents who once lived in Japanese internment camps. Then I complained a bit about another writer: Her father had been a diplomat, so she grew up all over the world, and at one point even survived a dangerous escape during a foreign *coup d'etat*.

"Me?" I whimpered. "My life is just about identical to every other Catholic white kid raised in the 1960s."

At this point, Renita, bless her generous heart, nodded, smiled, and said, "Well, then you should write about that."

And she was right.

I was undervaluing my own singular nature and experience: Each person, each life, is distinctive, even if you didn't grow up in a family of acrobats or spend ten years sleeping alongside lions on the African veldt. It is not what happens to us in our lives that makes us into writers; it is what we make out of what happens to us. It is our distinctive point of view.

This is true especially for the personal essay, since all that the essay really demands of the writer is to have an interesting mind, and, as Epstein reminds us in the quote that begins this chapter, a "strong personal presence."

WRITING EXERCISE: PLAIN VANILLA YOU

What makes you dull and uninteresting?

That may seem like exactly the wrong place to begin an essay, but consider that 99.4 percent of all readers also worry at some point, or all of the time, that they are dull and uninteresting, not worthy of notice, unimpressive. This sense of personal mediocrity is probably far worse in our current era, where celebrity news is tweeted at us every waking second.

So you never killed someone or escaped from a Thai prison, never married and then quickly divorced a movie star or turned up half-naked in a jittery video on YouTube.

So what? Good for you!

If you feel dull and unspectacular, the reader is already on your side.

Think a moment, as well, of how many of the truly extraordinary people with flashy lives that incite our deepest jealousy end up in scandal or rehab? I've had some scandal in my life, but you know what? Almost nobody knows about it, because almost no one cares.

Maybe just being a regular sort of guy or gal has its advantages.

Explore your feelings about your own personal dullness and normalcy a while, on the page.

ON PERSONA

The concept of persona is crucially important for essayists to understand. Though the personal essay is a form of nonfiction, and thus the self you bring to your essay should be an honest representation of who you are, we are in fact made of many selves: our happy self, our sad self, our indignant self, our skeptical self, our optimistic self, our worried self, our demanding self, our rascally self, and on and on and on. But in truth, if we attempt to bring all of these selves to every essay that we write, we run the risk of seeming so uncertain, so indecisive, that we merely confuse the reader.

Consistent and engaging personality on the page is often a case of choosing which "self" is speaking in a particular essay and dialing up the energy on that emotion or point of view. Henry David Thoreau likely had days when Walden Pond did *not* fill him with wonder and inspiration, but he knew enough to not share those tedious moments. They were beside the point. Or put it another way, dithering is best left to first drafts, and then carefully edited away.

The goal is not to deceive the reader, to pretend to be someone that you are not, but rather to partially isolate a part of who you are, the "you" that you are today, as you meditate on a particular subject, and sit down to write.

You heard the whiny and insecure me in the anecdote that opened this chapter, now listen to the firm and decisive me: Persona matters!

Here are a few examples of how other writers have tackled the question, "Who am I today?"

Be Honest, But Clear

The slogan of the excellent literary journal *Creative Nonfiction* is "You just can't make this stuff up." The slogan is effective, I believe, because of its double meaning. One meaning is that the truth is often stranger than fiction. The second meaning reminds the writer that in nonfiction, you are not just making stuff up.

So don't fake it. Don't act all pious on the page if you are not in fact a devout person. Don't generate false outrage over something you don't care that much about. Don't be a hypocrite.

But you can highlight a *particular* trait, if it is in fact true to your nature, and shine a bright light upon it for a few pages, letting it take center stage.

Look at Robin Hemley's introduction to his essay, "No Pleasure But Meanness."

> I have a mean bone in my body. In fact, I think I have more than one mean bone. For instance, I hate people who smile all the time. It feels good to say that word, "hate," doesn't it? Would you like to try it? Say: "I hate people who ask rhetorical questions in essays that can't possibly be answered."

Hemley is being witty here, poking fun at himself and at his overuse of the rhetorical question. He is also signaling the reader that this essay will focus on that part of him that can be called "mean," or critical.

I happen to know the author of this essay, and he is a very likeable, extremely funny man. Yet he no doubt has his mean moments, times when the things that annoy him no doubt lead to testiness or sharp anger. We all have that side to us, I believe. Perhaps inspired by William Hazlitt's "On the Pleasure of Hating," Hemley is taking a moment in his own essay to explore that aspect of himself, closely and specifically.

The essay continues with the author lodging numerous complaints—against folks who smile too much in photographs, against the checkout clerk at Walmart, against his kindergarten teacher—and though Hemley continues to leaven his bread of anger with humor and occasional winks to the reader, he does reveal a part of who he is honestly, clearly, and with interest.

Another good example might be Joan Didion, one of the finest essayists of all time in my opinion. She begins her essay, "In the Islands," with these two sentences:

> I tell you this not as aimless revelation but because I want you to know, as you read me, precisely who I am and where I am and what is on my mind. I want you to understand exactly what you are getting: you are getting a

woman who for some time now has felt radically separated from most of the ideas that seem to interest other people.

Well, you simply can't get much clearer, or more honest, than that.

You Are Universal

That slight aspect of your personality or fantasy life, or hidden world, that you think so odd, so peculiar, so weird, that you've kept it a secret your entire life, is most likely far more common than you think. We are all made of similar stuff, we human beings. Even our most closely guarded insecurities are often commonly held, though most individuals keep these parts of themselves so hidden that there is little chance to discover the commonality.

But writers are different. We *do* share. And along the way readers come to an understanding that we are all very much alike.

The French essayist Michel de Montaigne devotes much of his essay, "Of Repentance," to this notion of universality.

Consider these sentences:

> Others form man; I only report him: and represent a particular one, ill fashioned enough, and whom, if I had to model him anew, I should certainly make something else than what he is: but that's past recalling ... If the world find fault that I speak too much of myself, I find fault that they do not so much as think of themselves. But is it reason, that being so particular in my way of living, I should pretend to recommend myself to the public knowledge?

Here Montaigne is addressing a bit of anticipated criticism. In modern parlance, that criticism might go like this: "Just who the heck do you think you are, Mr. Montaigne, to write about yourself all of the time? Shouldn't you confine your writings to the vaunted geniuses and holy persons of past ages, instead of focusing all of the time on your own unproven self?"

He goes on to say (in his now quite-dated syntax):

> I have this, at least, according to discipline, that never any man treated of a subject he better understood and knew, than I what I have undertaken,

and that in this I am the most understanding man alive: secondly, that never any man penetrated farther into his matter, nor better and more distinctly sifted the parts and sequences of it, nor ever more exactly and fully arrived at the end he proposed to himself ... I speak truth, not so much as I would, but as much as I dare; and I dare a little the more, as I grow older; for, methinks, custom allows to age more liberty of prating, and more indiscretion of talking of a man's self.

Montaigne is answering his critics by asserting (in my words now, not his): "Oh yeah, well let me tell you this much, buster. What I know best is my own self, and I know my own self really really well, because I'm willing to study this subject and truly consider it in ways that others have not been willing to do. And if what I find is that I'm not so bloody perfect, well then I'll tell you that. Because I'm too old to waste time and hide behind niceties. I'm looking for the truth."

Montaigne, underneath all of the complex sentences and fancy language, is making a simple assertion. It is his belief that if he captures a true portrait of himself, he will capture something universal, something recognizable to everyone.

Or as he puts it, elsewhere in the same essay: "... every man carries the entire form of human condition."

Choose Wisely

Memoirist Sue William Silverman often receives letters and e-mail from readers, and recently she shared a fascinating reaction to some of the responses to her first two books, *Because I Remember Terror, Father, I Remember You* and *Love Sick*.

Silverman's memoirs are deeply personal and honest about events and behaviors in the author's past, and many of the notes Silverman finds in her mailbox say, in so many words, "I feel as if I know you."

In response to this Silverman writes:

Both memoirs frequently elicit this response ... even though both books are very different. What does Karen know about me? Marie? Karen knows what it was like for me to grow up in an incestuous family. Marie knows what it was like for me to recover from a sexual addiction. To Karen, the real me is one thing; to Marie, the real me is something, someone different. Even so, does this mean that *all* I am—as a writer and as a woman—is an incest survivor/sex addict? Is that it?

Silverman, of course, is far more than just that. She is a successful author, a respected teacher, a public speaker, a private person who has had countless challenges and experiences. Everything she has put into her memoirs is true, yes, but then again, neither of her books captures the entire person that she has been and that she is today.

Sometimes she herself wonders who this "Sue William Silverman" on the page really is, Silverman tells us, and she has reached the conclusion that readers are wrong to think that they know her:

> ... they know *something* about me, of course—but only what I choose to show in any given book or essay. It's as if, with each new piece I write, a different "me," or a different aspect of myself, is highlighted.

To make her point, she talks about an essay she is currently drafting, part of her collection-in-progress, *The Pat Boone Fan Club: My Life as a White Anglo-Saxon Jew.*

> When writing about Pat Boone, for example, I had to show how, since my Jewish father had molested me, it made sense that I'd seek out an overtly Christian man as a father figure. But I touched upon this incestuous background as briefly as possible, while, at the same time, implementing a much more ironic voice than that of my memoir. In effect, I removed the dark gray mask I wore while writing the memoir, and, for the essay, slipped on one that had as many sparkles as the red-white-and-blue costume Pat Boone wears in his concerts.

Had Silverman the writer attempted to bring her whole identity—her family past, her sexual addiction—into everything she has ever written, she would likely keep writing the same book or same essay over and over, and no one grows as a writer by merely repeating past work. Silverman is smart enough to know that.

Make sure you remember this as well.

WRITING EXERCISE: THE MYRIAD SELF

Who are you?

    Fill in some of these blanks:

- I am a _____ son/daughter.
- I am a _____ husband/wife.
- I am a _____ parent.
- I am also a _____ parent.
- I am a _____ eater.
- I am a _____ friend.
- I am also a _____ friend.
- I am a _____-friend.
- I am a _____ when confronted with direct criticism.
- I am a _____ when offered warmth and love.
- I am a _____, but most of my friends never suspect this about me.

Now start an essay that takes just one of the personas above and uses it as the "strong personal presence." Choose one more—but just one—and let it be the secondary "you" we meet on the page.

    Let these two true parts of who you are represent you here, but don't attempt to cover the entirety of who you are as a person. It isn't wise, and it likely isn't possible.

A Bit of Sarcasm, Maybe?

Back in high school you were probably asked to read Jonathan Swift's "A Modest Proposal." Actually, the full title is "A Modest Proposal for Preventing the Children of Poor People in Ireland, from Being a Burden on Their Parents or Country, and for Making Them Beneficial to the Publick." You can see why it is often abbreviated.

Writing in 1729, Swift offers a tongue-in-cheek, so-straight-faced-as-to-be-almost-believable "proposal" for how to deal with the countless poor children in Ireland and turn them into "sound and useful members of the common-wealth."

He bemoans the growing numbers of these youngsters to be found on every street and corner, before slyly stating

> ... I have been assured by a very knowing American of my acquaintance in London, that a young healthy child well nursed, is, at a year old, a

> most delicious nourishing and wholesome food, whether stewed, roasted, baked, or boiled; and I make no doubt that it will equally serve in a *fricasie*, or a *ragoust*.

Swift goes on to lay out his plan for separating some of these children "to breed," while "the remaining hundred thousand should be put up for sale to good families," once they have been allowed to "suck plentifully in the last month, so as to render them plump, and fat for a good table."

He even offers some advice on cooking and portions:

> A child will make two dishes at an entertainment for friends, and when the family dines alone, the fore or hind quarter will make a reasonable dish, and seasoned with a little pepper or salt, will be very good boiled on the fourth day, especially in winter.

Yes, Swift is kidding, but not because he wants the reader to laugh. He is skewering his government's lack of action to care for the poor, and mocking the callous attitudes displayed by some in eighteenth-century British society. He is being highly sarcastic to make his point.

That sarcasm, too, is a part of persona. Swift didn't believe that children should be cooked and quartered, nor did he usually talk or write this way, but on the particular day that he decided to write his "Modest Proposal," he chose to highlight and embrace his entirely sarcastic self.

MY ASSAY: WHEREIN THE AUTHOR ATTEMPTS TO FOLLOW HIS OWN ADVICE

I know full well that one of the reasons Boca Raton was so empty—the houses all shuttered, the front porches devoid of rocking chairs and chatting neighbors—was the fact that it is stinking hot in south Florida, even in early April. If I lived in Florida full-time, perhaps even I would fall into the same reclusive patterns. Air-conditioning is a wonderful invention and has no doubt saved lives.

But this is *my* essay, and the person speaking is the part of me that can be critical of others, and the part of me that truly loves walking, and the part of me that truly values my interactions with neighbors;

and this is an area of the essay I perhaps need to flesh out, so the reader understands from where I come, and why I feel so strongly.

So I'm working up a section that begins like this:

> I live in a small college town in Appalachian Ohio, and often walk to work. It takes me forty-five minutes, which can be tiring at times, but the more I do it the quicker the time goes by. For a while, I worried that I could get more work done if I didn't spend 90 minutes walking to and from campus. But eventually I realized I did get more work done on the days that I walked, because I was sharper, clearer, had used some of the foot-time to sort the detritus from my brain and identify the daily to-do list that actually mattered. What I really like about walking to work is that I see people.

To make my point convincing, I think I'll have to get specific—what people, and why does bumping into neighbors and strangers feel so good to me? Can I re-create for the reader the experiences I have walking across my little town?

If I can capture that, the reader may be swayed. If not, I run the risk of just sounding cranky.

Yes, cranky is probably part of my persona as well, but not one that I want to dominate *this* essay.

THE VOICES INSIDE

Do you remember the story that I used to open this chapter, the one where I turn to my wife and bemoan my normal, uninteresting life? I've come to recognize that voice inside of myself, the part of me that wants to undercut my own belief in my own talent or potential. I don't know why that voice exists, but it does, seemingly in all of us who try to write. It is the voice that tells nonwriters that they are not pretty enough, not loveable enough, or not smart enough to succeed in life. It is the voice that tells us that our work is dull, too derivative, corny, trite, ham-handed, or somehow below the line that makes writing worthy or of value.

Well, since we are focusing on persona in this chapter, let me take a minute to say that this is *one* part of your persona that you needn't honor or bring to the table when you sit down to write. Most writers—beginning and accomplished—are just too hard on themselves. Here's my best advice: Be hard on your sentences, be hard on your paragraphs, be ceaseless and unrelenting in your revisions, but stop questioning your ability to be a writer. If you put pen to paper, or put electronic words on the page, you *are* a writer. Let go of that worry and focus on how good a writer you can become.

One sure way to become as good a writer as you can become is to allow your *self* into the writing, to make room for that "strong personal presence."

Of course, it can sometimes be hard not to.

Listen to this advice from the poet, dramatist, and philosopher Johann Wolfgang von Goethe: "Every author in some way portrays himself in his works, even if it be against his will."

DINTY W. MOORE's essays and stories have appeared in numerous publications including *The Southern Review, The Georgia Review, Harpers,* and *Utne Reader.* His books include *Between Panic & Desire, The Accidental Buddhist, Toothpick Men, The Emperor's Virtual Clothes, The Truth of the Matter: Art and Craft in Creative Nonfiction,* and *Crafting the Personal Essay.*

A Personal Presence

PERMISSIONS

"All About That Voice." © 2015 by Adair Lara. Originally appeared in *Writer's Digest*, March/April 2015. Used with permission of the author.

"Awaken Your Authenticity." Excerpted from *A Writer's Guide to Persistence* © 2015 by Jordan Rosenfeld, used with permission from Writer's Digest Books.

"Breaking the Fourth Wall." Excerpted from *The Irresistible Novel* © 2015 by Jeff Gerke, used with permission from Writer's Digest Books.

"Creating a Narratorial Voice." Excerpted from *DIY MFA* © 2016 by Gabriela Pereira, used with permission from Writer's Digest Books.

"Creating Your Own Voice." Excerpted from *Writing Your Way* © 2012 by Don Fry, used with permission from Writer's Digest Books.

"The Difficulty of First-Person POV." © 2004 by James Scott Bell. Originally appeared in *Writer's Digest*, June 2004. Used with permission of the author.

"Find an Angle to Bring Your Subject to Life." © 2010 by Adair Lara. Originally appeared in *Writer's Digest*, October 2010. Used with permission of the author.

"Finding Your Voice." Excerpted from *Story Engineering* © 2011 by Larry Brooks, used with permission from Writer's Digest Books.

"First-Person Finesse." © 2005 by Marnie Hayutin. Originally appeared in *Writer's Digest*, June 2005. Used with permission of the author.

INDEX

narrative nonfiction, 36, 38, 40

romance, 134, 136, 153, 186, 188–190

science fiction, 187–191

thrillers, 29, 46–47, 85, 136, 185–186, 200–202

and voice, 175–184

geography, influence of, 24

Gerke, Jeff, 222

Gettysburg Address (Lincoln), 58–60

Gilbert, Elizabeth, 243–245

Girl Named Zippy, A (Kimmel), 257

Glass Castle, The (Walls), 138

Glenn, Bernadette, 253–254

Goethe, Johann Wolfgang von, 285

Gone With the Wind (Mitchell), 87

"Goodbye to All That" (Didion), 66–67

grammar, 72–73

grammar checkers, 111–113

Great Expectations (Dickens), 83

Great Gatsby (Fitzgerald), 153–154

Grey, Francine du Plessix, 261

Grisham, John, 27, 46

Guernsey Literary and Potato Peel Pie Society (Shaffer and Barrows), 87

Haddon, Mark, 34–35, 155

Half Asleep in Frog Pajamas (Robbins), 156

Half Magic (Eager), 179

Hall, Linda, 115

Hamid, Mohsin, 33–34

happy surprises, 122

Harden, Blaine, 131

Harper, Stephen, 184

Harrison, Colin, 46–47

Harry Potter series (Rowling), 158

Hawthorne, Nathaniel, 73

Hayden, G. Miki, 233

Hayutin, Marnie Engel, 246

Heller, Joseph, 87

Hemingway, Ernest, 55, 73, 115, 158, 214, 217

Hemley, Robin, 278

Henry VI trilogy (Shakespeare), 87

Hero's Journey, The (Campbell), 199

Herzog (Bellow), 157–158

Heyer, Georgette, 103–104

"Hills Like White Elephants" (Hemingway), 214

historical mysteries, 93

Hobbit, The (Tolkien), 187

Hoffman, Alice, 85

honesty, 90–95

Hooker, Robert, 87

Hope to Die (Block), 172

Hornby, Nick, 29–30

horror, 184, 186, 197–199, 206

Hosseini, Khaled, 87

How to be Good (Hornby), 29–30

humor, 42, 79, 97

Hunger Games (Collins), 150

I Was Told There'd Be Cake (Crosley), 269–270

Ibbotson, Eva, 216

If on a winter's night a traveler (Calvino), 156

imagery, repetition of, 74

imagination, 172

imitation

creative, 85–86

vs. emulation, 118–119

See also emulation

In the Confidence of Strangers (Kurz), 227–229

"In the Islands" (Didion), 278–279

inner critic, 271–272

inner self, 97

inner voices, 284–285

insertions, 74

interviews, 130

invisible narrator, 180, 216–217

Isaacson, Walter, 54

It (King), 83

Italian Affair, An (Fraser), 261–262

Ivins, Molly, 137

James, Henry, 217

Jefferson, Thomas, 53–54, 76

Jonathan Strange & Mr. Norrell (Clarke), 158–160, 167–168

Jones, Chris, 130

Junction, Utah (Lawton), 21

Junod, Tom, 131

Jurassic Park (Crichton), 200–201

Kafka, Franz, 217

"Kandy-Kolored Tangerine-Flake Streamlined Baby, The" (Wolfe), 40

Keillor, Garrison, 61–63

Kempton, Gloria, 207

Kerouac, Jack, 128, 217

Killshot (Leonard), 28

Kilpatrick, James J., 248

Kimmel, Haven, 257

King, Martin Luther, Jr., 64, 75

King, Stephen, 1, 83–84, 148, 198–199

Kingsolver, Barbara, 195–196

Kite Runner, The (Hosseini), 87

Koontz, Dean, 115, 128

Kress, Nancy, 146

Kunitz, Stanley, 120

Kurz, Patricia G., 227–231, 233

Lamb, Wally, 202

Lamott, Anne, 23, 266–267

language

archaic, 59, 72

and point of view, 164